# STUDYING
# ELITES USING
# QUALITATIVE
# METHODS

# OTHER RECENT VOLUMES IN THE
# SAGE FOCUS EDITIONS

# STUDYING ELITES USING QUALITATIVE METHODS

**Rosanna Hertz**
**Jonathan B. Imber**
**editors**

**SAGE** Publications
*International Educational and Professional Publisher*
Thousand Oaks    London    New Delhi

*For information address*:

SAGE Publications, Inc.
2455 Teller Road
Thousand Oaks, California 91320
E-mail: order@sagecom.pub

SAGE Publications Ltd.
6 Bonhill Street
London EC2A 4PU
United Kingdom

SAGE Publications India Pvt. Ltd.
M-32 Market
Greater Kailash I
New Delhi 110 048 India

Printed in the United States of America

**Library of Congress Cataloging-in-Publication Data**

Studying elites using qualitative methods / edited by, Rosanna Hertz,
Jonathan B. Imber.
    p.   cm. — (Sage focus editions; 175)
    Includes bibliographical references.
    ISBN 0-8039-7036-6 (alk. paper). — ISBN 0-8039-7037-4 (pbk.:
alk. paper)
    1. Elite (Social sciences)   2. Power (Social sciences)   3. Social
classes.   4. Prestige.   I. Hertz, Rosanna.   II. Imber, Jonathan B.,
1952-    .
HM141.S837     1995
305.5′2—dc20                                                    95-2836

This book is printed on acid-free paper.

95  96  97  98  99  10  9  8  7  6  5  4  3  2  1

Sage Project Editor: Susan McElroy

# Contents

# Introduction

ROSANNA HERTZ
JONATHAN B. IMBER

In recent years, numerous autobiographical writings by social scientists have appeared, and reflections on the writer's place in social-scientific research have received ever more attention (Berger, 1990; Goetting & Fenstermaker, 1994; Homans, 1984; Page, 1982).[1] Many of these writers have given testimonies to a generation whose influence in the post-Second World War development of social science in the United States has been enormous. Some of these writers have used the occasion to reflect on their own lives, demonstrating the intersection between personal biography and research interests. Still others have written about the transformation of social-science research in terms of its shifting assumptions about the self as objective and neutral to the self as subjective and inclusive, by conveying the more fundamental epistemological issues at stake.

The present collection of essays follows in the tradition of sociological analysis in which the researcher takes pause to reflect on the nature and practice of social research (Hammond, 1964; Shaffir & Stebbins, 1990; Shaffir, Stebbins, & Turowetz, 1980). In contrast to some of the uses of autobiography in recent years, this tradition has always emphasized the production of knowledge over the reproduction of self. The creation of research incorporates the individual imagination in ways that need to be made more explicit for those who wish either to become social scientists or to duplicate the process of research.

In many cases, discussions of methodology are consigned to a methodological appendix but still provide little insight about the research design and process. A few of these appendices go further and illustrate the complicated paths that research actually takes, both serendipitously and strategically (Bosk, 1978; Thomas, 1994). What distinguishes the most interesting scholarly work is the "street sense" that researchers call upon in order to collect the data they need to better inform the understanding of social life. Researchers routinely construct "critical decision points" that establish the direction of the next phase of research. These decision points may not be necessarily recognized as such until further along in the process. How does one know when to shift focus, to examine a situation in more detail, to address an issue more comparatively, or to incorporate other sources of data as a means of triangulation?

The essays in this volume focus on how researchers have successfully gained access to elite settings, how they have come to terms with various dilemmas in conducting and writing about their research, and the decisions made with hindsight about their research. As they reflect upon their experiences, they provide constructive advice and cautionary tales about how they learned to maneuver and to become accepted in a world otherwise closed to most of them. They also express their frustrations in the risks they take as they move beyond armchair scholarship to active empirical research.

Few social researchers study elites because elites are by their very nature difficult to penetrate. Elites establish barriers that set their members apart from the rest of society. In similar ways, the study of those at the bottom of the class structure often poses formidable problems for the researcher. While the poor may be more visible and easier to find, to gain their confidence requires what many researchers would consider a different kind of sympathetic understanding. Yet social scientists have traditionally identified with the disenfranchised, believing that to understand them and expose their plight will also eventually empower them. Whether or not this is the case, it is an article of faith in social-scientific research.

This explains perhaps why research on elites is so rarely undertaken. After all, whose purpose does it serve to "empower" the rich and powerful? One strategy in the study of elites is to expose the reach of power in the hope of clarifying it for those who are subject to it. Another strategy endorses the goals of the welfare state insofar as an understanding of the function and responsibilities of elites can be translated into social policy as it pertains to the government and the workplace. Finally, the study of elites offers an opportunity to link contemporary empirical work with major historical transformations addressed in the theoretical traditions of Marx, Weber, Tocqueville, and others.

Although this collection is devoted to reports on the processes of qualitative research, most of the researchers have used other methodologies and types of data in addition to interviewing and fieldwork observations. The best research on elites has utilized a combination of methodological approaches to deepen the research findings. This multi-method approach has begun to influence social science in new ways. Rather than assuming that qualitative and quantitative research methods are always at odds, the multi-method approach casts constructive doubts on relying on the use of any single source of data or method. Of course, money and time constraints may mean that researchers are limited in their ability to examine social settings from multiple methodological approaches.

We have included studies that focus on qualitative work because students of this kind of methodology tend to be more perceptive about the implications of the research process for the production of findings. But researchers who emphasize more quantitative approaches will benefit from reviewing these implications for the design and execution of their own research. There is more to completing a research project than proposing and testing hypotheses. By listening to the present authors describe their encounters with the research process and the people they are studying, the reader will gain a more sophisticated understanding of the many subtle and often elusive features of conducting successful research.

The collection divides into three broadly defined areas of research, on business elites, professional elites, and community and political elites. Community and political elites have received by far the most attention in sociology and political science (Moyser & Wagstaffe, 1987; Scott, 1990). Such elites have always had the greatest public visibility, and they have a vested interest in creating constituencies, including social-scientific ones. They also have an interest in polls, surveys, and other information that social scientists produce and know, thus creating the need for a certain degree of compatibility between such elites and those who study them.

The study of professional elites has been subsumed under the sociology of work and occupations. The most prestigious occupations have been traditionally defined as professions, including law, medicine, and clergy. The common source of their prestige is the long years of education toward advanced degrees and the specialized apprenticeships that precede becoming a professional. Because social scientists are socialized in similar ways at similar places, they have not been outsiders to the study of these professions, but they have also not, by that virtue, always produced findings that are compatible with the self-definitions of the professions themselves. This has created a tension and skepticism on the part of professionals to open their precincts to scrutiny by other professionals.

Business elites have been traditionally the most difficult settings to gain access to by social scientists. The hierarchies of business organizations are designed to protect those who work there and to deter outsiders from learning more about how they operate. The popular assumption remains that business maintains trade secrets, that professionals protect their own, and that politicians have everything to hide. Social-scientific study of business requires the most special kinds of introductions in order to establish confidence that the research will not undermine the organization's competitive edge and goals. In its most extreme form, individual researchers may be asked to submit background checks. In less extreme circumstances, letters of entrée and personalistic ties are often essential. The autonomy of professional elites has been eroded in recent decades by the creation of corporate entities that define their work and organizational settings. This is why the study of business elites will invariably become more important in the future for understanding the evolving nature of professional elites.

These articles represent a synthesis of the present methodological concerns in the study of elites. Although they may revisit perennial questions for some readers, we believe they will add to the growing debate on how researchers gather data, construct interview strategies, write about their subjects, and come to experience the research process.

## Note

1. That list also includes Fox (1990), Horowitz (1990), Lowenthal (see Jay, 1987), and Quinney (1991). Others have included specifically autobiographical reflections in larger or edited works, including Bendix (1993) and Shils (1988).

## References

Bendix, R. (Ed.). (1993). *Unsettled affinities.* New Brunswick, NJ: Transaction.

Berger, B. M. (Ed.). (1990). *Authors of their own lives: Intellectual autobiographies by twenty American sociologists.* Berkeley: University of California Press.

Bosk, C. (1978). *Forgive and remember: Managing medical failure.* Chicago: University of Chicago Press.

Fox, A. (1990). *A very late development: An autobiography.* Coventry: Industrial Relations Research Unit, University of Warwick.

Goetting, A., & Fenstermaker, S. (Eds.). (1994). *Individual voices, collective visions: Fifty years of women in society.* Philadelphia: Temple University Press.

Hammond, P. E. (Ed.). (1964). *Sociologists at work: The craft of social research.* New York: Basic Books.

Homans, G. C. (1984). *Coming to my senses: The autobiography of a sociologist.* New Brunswick, NJ: Transaction.

Horowitz, I. L. (1990). *Daydreams and nightmares: Reflections of a Harlem childhood.* Jackson: University Press of Mississippi.

Jay, M. (Ed.). (1987). *An unmastered past: The autobiographical reflections of Leo Lowenthal.* Berkeley: University of California Press.

Moyser, G., & Wagstaffe, M. (Eds.). (1987). *Research methods for elite studies.* London: Allen & Unwin.

Page, C. H. (1982). *Fifty years in the sociological enterprise: A lucky journey.* Amherst: University of Massachusetts Press.

Quinney, R. (1991). *Journey to a far place: Autobiographical reflections.* Philadelphia: Temple University Press.

Scott, J. (Ed.). (1990). *The sociology of elites* (3 vols.). Hants, UK: Edward Elgar.

Shaffir, W. B., & Stebbins, R. A. (1990). *Experiencing fieldwork: An inside view of qualitative research.* Newbury Park, CA: Sage.

Shaffir, W. B., Stebbins, R. A., & Turowetz, A. (Eds.). (1980). *Fieldwork experience: Qualitative approaches to social research.* New York: St. Martin's Press.

Shils, E. (1988). Totalitarians and antinomians. In J. H. Bunzel (Ed.), *Political passages: Journeys of change through two decades, 1968-1988* (pp. 1-31). New York: Free Press.

Thomas, R. J. (1994). *What machines can't do: Politics and technology in the industrial enterprise.* Berkeley: University of California Press.

# PART I

# *Business Elites*

Studying executives in corporations, Robert Thomas details some practical suggestions to counter the frustrations of getting past the myriad organizational gatekeepers. He insists on a clear agenda before going to the trouble of interviewing these "important people" whose accessibility is constrained not simply by elite status but also by rigorous time schedules. Thomas argues that the researcher needs to disentangle the executive from his or her office in order to get beyond formal corporate scripts and prepared public-relations responses. He turns status inconsistencies between researcher and subject into an advantage by phrasing questions in personal terms and by giving the subject an opportunity to play the teacher.

Michael Useem explains what he has learned (and how he has gone about learning it) in a variety of studies he has conducted. He is encouraging about the serendipitous means by which a researcher may gain access to high-level executives. On the other hand, he indicates some of the inevitable barriers that confront research of this type, including the inability to gain access to the meetings of the highest reaches of corporate power. Nevertheless, his article can be read as a practical guide for overcoming organizational gatekeepers. He also describes the virtues of collecting multiple sources of data, quantitative and qualitative.

Peter Yeager and Kathy Kram reiterate the skepticism expressed toward outsiders, even those with ties to business schools. They elaborate a research design that allows for transformation of the research problem as the research proceeds. Originally the frame was broadened to gain access, but they argue that it ultimately improved the analytic value of the research. Their assessment of the ways in which elite managers define and respond to ethical conflict increased the "likelihood that business leaders would find the study both of practical interest and less intimidating." This suggests that by carefully thinking about the research process, researchers can present even the most sensitive topics in business settings in constructive ways that result in improved access without having to employ covert methods.

The implications of new technologies for the study of elites is represented in John Workman's detailed piece on how he used E-mail and on-line systems for communicating with people in the organization he was studying. These systems enabled him first to learn about people in the organization. Although such systems are not a replacement for traditional participant observation, they do provide a new way to find out what is going on in complex organizations as well as a "rich electronic paper trail that provided context . . . and that could be used to construct the history of specific projects."

Paul Hirsch's piece is a response to our request to him to weave together methodological insights of some of the authors in this collection with his own tales from doing corporate fieldwork. He expounds upon the concepts of "street smarts" and "critical decision points" that we present in our introduction to this volume. He offers newcomers to research a valuable insight: One should study what one knows best. He offers experienced researchers an important maxim: Know your audience. As he states it, "The ease of gathering good data is the mutual realization that the intellectual worlds of the interviewer and elite respondent barely intersect." The fieldworker must be expert in at least two languages, the language of social science and the language spoken by one's respondents. The authority and success of the fieldworker are based on the ability to translate in both directions. Finally, the new business elites may be more accessible for social-scientific study, as Hirsch predicts, because the organizational structures are undergoing rapid transformation, blurring the boundaries in organizational hierarchies, exactly the sort of change best studied by qualitative methods.

*1*

# Interviewing Important People in Big Companies

## ROBERT J. THOMAS

Like many people, I enjoyed the satire in *Roger and Me*, the semidocu-
mentary film about General Motors and its CEO. By contrasting the
imposing physical and economic presence of the company with the
inaccessibility of its leader, Michael Moore, the writer/director, plucked
a populist chord: Important people in big companies have tremendous
power but little apparent accountability to the ordinary worker and
citizen. In the absence of the real Roger Smith, Moore created Roger
the celluloid image: someone who was, by turns, the villain of a matinee
drama and a bumbling clown, whose words (through careful editing)
appeared both callous and ridiculous.

Yet what if Moore had cornered Roger Smith? What would he (and
we) have learned? Would we really expect a version of Dickens's *A
Christmas Carol*—where the CEO of one of the world's largest corporations is struck dumb by guilt and recrimination? Chances are, if Roger
had agreed to an on-camera interview, Moore would not have had a film.
He would have had a confrontation that tested Smith's ability to manage
the situation but provided little insight about Roger, the executive elite
of General Motors, or the nature of important people in big companies.

NOTE: Reprinted from a special issue, "Fieldwork in Elite Settings," edited by Rosanna Hertz
and Jonathan B. Imber for the *Journal of Contemporary Ethnography*, Vol. 22, No. 1, 1993,
pp. 80-96. Copyright 1993 by Sage Publications, Inc.

The questions unanswered by *Roger and Me* have been addressed by sociologists. Indeed, some of the best-known sociological analyses gained notoriety precisely because they sought to reveal what elites think and do (e.g., Dalton, 1959; Domhoff, 1967; Hirsch, 1986; Jackall, 1988; Kanter, 1977; Mills, 1956; Useem, 1979; Veblen, 1923; Whyte, 1956). Yet there is a real paucity of literature available on how sociologists study elites, especially corporate elites. What, if any, special problems do we encounter in the effort to do research on important people in big companies? If our goal is to interview the corporate "Rogers" and, perhaps more important, to get beyond caricature or public relations imagery, how do we go about getting access to people and data?

In this article, I offer some reflections on the barriers to getting access and data and make some suggestions as to how those barriers can be circumvented or at least lowered. I focus specific attention on methods for studying corporate elites—specifically the men and women in the executive ranks—but I will also try to indicate where I think those methods can be applied beyond "mahogany row."

### Visible But Not Accessible

Unlike other segments of the social and economic elite, top corporate executives tend to be relatively easy to identify and even to locate. Most of the major companies in the United States are shareholder owned and are required by law to name their top officers. A trip to the public library is all that is required to get a reasonably complete list of the people "in charge" in a given company or industry. A toll-free call to directory assistance and a conversation with the corporate switchboard operator is all it takes to learn where to find a company's CEO.

Unfortunately, visibility is not the same as accessibility—and it is here that the problems begin to mount. Gaining access can be a tough proposition, even when the point of getting in is innocuous, well-intentioned, or attractive to key people in the organization itself.[1] One reason is that business elites are quite good at insulating themselves from unwanted disturbance. When they do venture out of the corporate suite it is to address important issues and constituencies, such as stockholders, other business leaders, financial analysts, government officials, customer organizations, and community groups (especially charities). The value of time is used to explain amenities like chauffeured limousines (so they can work while they ride), private jets (so they can avoid airport delays), and tightly controlled schedules (so they are not interrupted unnecessarily). As a top executive once told me, "I'm not paid $2 million a year to answer the phone."

Moreover, most businesses, no matter how small, have gatekeepers who keep an eye on the comings and goings of strangers. Large corporations, especially ones with trade secrets to hide, have gates, guards, and security devices. Penetrating the social life of a neighborhood can be difficult, but it usually does not take as focused a form as it does in a large company.[2] You cannot just walk into an office suite and expect to strike up a conversation or hang out and observe the scene—the courtesies a letter carrier or a drugstore clerk might extend to a stranger in the neighborhood are generally not extended by executive secretaries to intruders who obviously "don't belong." Even welcome visitors encounter inner lines of defense: public relations departments, "official spokespeople," and whole levels of management trained in how to represent the company to the outside world.

Unless you have some sort of leverage with which to get their attention, chances are you will get it for only half the time you think you need.[3] Journalists I know are pleased to get an hour with an executive, but journalists have a source of leverage most sociologists do not. A staff writer for the *Wall Street Journal* or *Fortune* magazine can at least imply that he won't say nice things—or he won't say anything at all (which can be worse)—if he does not get access to the executive he wishes to interview.[4] Even then, if you do get the 30 minutes, you may find that an emergency or someone more important bumps you off the schedule. If you get in the door, you will be in foreign territory: Few executives allow themselves to be interviewed on someone else's turf. After you get in, you may find that the executive does not intend to answer your questions or has a script of her own that she'd like to repeat. All of this can happen (and has happened to me) after you've spent several months and hundreds of dollars to get to the executive's office in the first place.[5]

There are few economies of scale in this enterprise. The problems are quite often the same whether you focus on executives in one organization or intend to gather data from a cross section. My experience has largely been in the latter approach: trying to secure access to a broader group of executives in a fairly large number of organizations. The process has been an incredibly difficult one for me—often accompanied by considerable frustration, expense, and lost time. In one case, it took me nearly 2 years of phone calls, screening meetings with executive assistants, and networking to interview two executives in a major manufacturing company.

These problems can be reason enough to avoid direct contact with business elites—but there are ways to circumvent, or at least lower, some of these barriers. Four central tasks warrant closer attention: getting ready, getting access, getting data, and getting more data.[6]

## Getting Ready

The difficulties associated with getting access and data ought to serve as a caution to the aspiring student of business elites: You have to have a reason for going to all the trouble. These may be "important people," but first and foremost, they must be important to you, the researcher. The point may seem obvious, but adequate preparation is an essential ingredient in this kind of research. Part of that preparation involves asking difficult questions of yourself; it means being certain that you cannot be satisfied by collecting data through other means. For example, if your goal is to get an official statement or answer to a particular question, it may not be worth your time and energy to try and talk with those at the top.

If it is not essential to interview or observe directly, there are alternative ways to collect data about corporate elites. For example, questions can be submitted in letter form and, although they will most likely be dealt with by subordinates, they will be vetted through the corporate hierarchy and rendered fit for public consumption. Alternatively, secondary sources may be more appropriate (see Zelditch, 1962). Most university libraries subscribe to extensive data bases (e.g., Lexis, Nexis, etc.) that can provide up-to-date information on the identity, backgrounds, and salaries of most major business executives.[7] Business and professional periodicals, trade association reports, investor newsletters, business school cases, and Who's Who, to name a few, can be easily tapped. Equally important, most business school faculty (even the sociologists among them) have considerable contact with business elites by way of research, consulting, site visits, and executive education programs. Consultants or industry analysts represent another potential source of data and even entrée to business elites.

Even if secondary sources are insufficient, they should still be consulted in the interest of exploiting the little time you are likely to be allotted in the event that you do get access. That is, it is important to know as much as you can before going into the interview.[8] Certainly in this respect the amount of publicly available information about companies and their top executives makes the process of preparing to interview corporate elites easier than it might be in other settings. Equally important, potential interviewees (or their staff) may test your qualifications to do the interview before granting you access, such as asking you to submit sample questions for their perusal; under those circumstances, it can be advantageous to indicate in the wording of your questions some level of prior knowledge.[9]

Finally, there is the issue of self—yours and that of the people you intend to interview. As in other forms of qualitative research, studies of elites raise questions about the researcher's identity, self-concept, and status (see Adler & Adler, 1990; Punch, 1986; Warren, 1988). Given that the opportunities for data collection are limited and not easily repeated, it is important for the researcher to feel at ease with who he or she is in relation to the interview subject and the interview setting (see Davis, 1973; Gurney, 1990; Kleinman, 1990; Shaffir, 1990). At minimum, it helps to have clothes appropriate to the situation and to be comfortable enough in them, as well as in that kind of environment, to not be distracted from your principal goal.[10]

Of course, limits to access also tend to make the opportunity precious or special—even to make the researcher feel like a supplicant granted audience with a dignitary. I must admit to having felt "honored" to be granted time with a well-known executive and to be tempted to be less assertive than I might have been with someone less newsworthy. And, as I go on to note in the next section, it is easy to be drawn in by the articulateness and, in some cases, by the charm of top executives without realizing it. There are few formal devices I know of to counteract these particular halo effects; I can only offer my solution: to recall in my mind people whom I came to respect as a result of what I learned from them, not as a result of their press clippings, their formal titles, or their oratorical skills.[11] Given the pervasiveness of the economic definitions of success and the profusion of indicators that corporate elites are indeed successful (e.g., plush offices, expensive clothes, chauffeured limousines, etc.), it might be best to try and acquaint yourself with the habits, styles of dress, and rituals of interaction that one is likely to encounter among business elites—if only to maintain a measure of detachment.[12]

The other side of self is the persona of the people you intend to interview. Unlike members of other social or professional elites, top corporate executives are often expected to speak on behalf of a formal organization—even to speak as if they were the organization. Because researchers can get "official" views through other means, a critical part of the preparation is deciding which persona you want to interview. If for example, we wanted to better understand what Roger Smith as Roger Smith thought about or did, it would have been essential to construct questions and an interview context that made clear that it was the individual, not the office, we were interviewing. Questions can be addressed to the different personas embedded in the individual—for example, Smith as an individual, Smith as CEO, and CEO as a representative of the organization—but it is essential to make clear which persona you are addressing and when you are switching persona.

### Getting Access

If you do not happen to have a relative or a family friend who is a member of the business elite, it is still possible to avoid the frustration of "cold calling."[13] Most important, it helps to combine a recognizable affiliation with some sort of personal contact. My status as a faculty member in a management school (most recently, with a grant from the National Science Foundation, too) has helped solve the problem of how to represent myself to business executives whom I do not know and who do not know of me. However, while pursuing an earlier line of research (Thomas, 1989), I learned that it was not necessary to actually be on the faculty of a business school to use it as a point of entry into the network of corporate executives; it was possible to tap into that network by tapping into the business school itself.[14] For example, in an average week, at least two executives visit the business school of most any university. Some may be lecturing in classes, but quite often they are giving public lectures or even participating in executive education programs. By attending these lectures and mentioning your interest in an individual or a topic to faculty colleagues, it is possible to get introductions, if not to actually get time with a visiting executive.[15]

Personal contact is obviously more difficult; however, it is possible to "work your way to the top" by getting to know people who already have contact or for whom contact would serve certain interests. For example, MBA students and managers on sabbatical to universities quite often have contacts they would be willing to share; some can even sponsor you in your quest to gain access.[16] Managers below the executive ranks are not only more accessible but if they have an interest in a topic you are pursuing (or a common interest can be negotiated) they also may very well be willing to do the networking for you.

Still, recognizable affiliations and personal contacts can only be qualifiers. They are not likely to open doors unless accompanied by a compelling reason as to why someone should see you. In that regard, it is essential to have a problem or a question lead the way—something that suggests that the person with whom you want to speak is uniquely qualified in some way. Otherwise, you will find yourself limited to talking with someone on that executive's staff.[17]

I generally phrase the problem in terms that personalize it: For example, in my last project (Thomas, 1994), I told would-be interviewees that I wanted "to get a better understanding of how it is that you and your company think about new technology. How does technology development and change fit into your business strategy? How do you go about evaluating alternative solutions to problems?" By framing the questions that way, I introduced three important hooks. First, I was interested in what they thought and did; that is, rather than give them reason to shunt me off to someone else, I tried to indicate that their insights were the ones I was after. Second, I wanted to learn from them; I offered the flattery of a role reversal, one that would give the executive the opportunity (as well as the responsibility) to teach the Ph.D.[18] Third, I was interested in how they and their organization dealt with real problems, not vague ones; in this respect, it is important to recognize that a problem that is real to you may not be especially real or compelling to someone else.[19]

Finally, you should be prepared to meet interviewees at a time and in a place convenient to them. This is more than just a matter of courtesy; executives jealously guard their time (even if only for outward appearances). You may have it in mind to meet them at a neutral spot (e.g., to avoid distractions or to exercise some control over the interview itself), but that may raise problems that you will only be obliquely aware of (e.g., physical security for the CEO). Of course, as I noted earlier, it may cost too much to be too accommodating. Careful advance planning can provide a solution: Executives tend to be far more generous with their schedules when you suggest a date a month or so away; travel reservations booked far enough ahead tend to cost less, too. When my funds are tight (i.e., most of the time), I often suggest that the interview take place the next time the interviewee is in my city or in my part of the country. To be even more accommodating, I have agreed to do interviews on the phone or via video conference, as well as in company limousines, taxicabs, airport waiting lounges, restaurants, and bars.[20]

## Getting Data

Assuming that you have been granted an interview, it is essential to make the most of the event. Excellent guides to doing interviews are readily available, and I will try to avoid repeating their recommendations here.[21] Rather, I intend to focus on issues I have found to be distinctive to the study of corporate elites.

First, it is important to be clear about which persona you want to interview: the individual, the position, or the organization. As I noted earlier, the first two are likely to be of greatest interest to the researcher. However, it is important to recognize that in the absence of clarity, the third is likely to be chosen as the default option by the interviewee. The last person to have interviewed the executive is likely to have been a journalist, that is, someone attuned to recent events in the organization's history, even in the individual's history. For the sociologist or anthropologist with a different (perhaps broader or less immediate) set of concerns, it is important to "recalibrate" the interviewee, that is, set the stage for a different kind of question prior to or at the outset of the interview itself.[22]

Second, it helps to clarify the ground rules for the interview. You should not assume that they are understood. Most executives are familiar with journalistic conventions in interview situations and unfamiliar with social science conventions. The reverse tends to be true of social scientists. To avoid the awkward—and occasionally distressful—situation in which an interviewee tells you in passing at the end that everything he said was "for background only" or the situation in which she obviously (and painfully) chooses words carefully in order to avoid having something untoward attributed to her, it makes sense to clarify how you intend to use your notes, tapes, and so forth at the outset. This need not be an occasion for hand-wringing or mincing of words: Less than 1% of the executives I have interviewed have ever refused to be tape recorded, and most are quite willing to be quoted directly; most also appreciate having the ground rules clarified in advance.[23]

Third, there is the issue of control—specifically, who is in charge of the interview. Although there is ongoing debate as to the merits of semistructured versus unstructured interviewing,[24] I tend to favor the former as part of a strategy for tipping the balance of power in my direction. I do so in part for reasons of efficiency: I would rather have the opportunity to decide when to intervene to cut off a line of response than to have the interviewee free to chart his or her own agenda. I also do so because talk is the stock in trade of corporate executives. That is, they are paid to think and talk and, more pointedly, to talk to a wide variety of audiences. Their public or organizational persona is formed through training in public speaking, in dealing with the press, and even in how to be interviewed. Some have speechwriters, and in virtually every case when they are asked to speak publicly, their speeches are cleared by, for example, the legal, financial, public relations, and/or CEO's office. Thus it is quite common to watch an executive mentally "rewinding the tape" in search of an appropriate phrase or monologue that appears to accord to a particular question. This may be unavoidable (even unintentional), but the effect is the same: He will launch into a speech if the question allows or if the question does not challenge the appropriateness of a speech.[25] If someone is intent on giving a speech, it may be impossible to stop them; under those circumstances I counsel, first, patience and, at the first opportunity, a rephrasing of the question to invite a response from the persona I am most interested in. For example, when an opening arises I will intervene with "Uh huh, but I'm curious . . . how did *you* feel about it?" If that fails, I shift to an entirely different line of questioning to break the flow.

Fourth, the interview can and ought to be supplemented by other forms of data collection. Specifically, I make it a point to ask people in advance and at the time of the interview to provide me with any supporting data they can. This has been a surprisingly successful strategy and one that makes a great deal of sense; however, it is one that few researchers I know routinely pursue. Some tell me that they are happy enough to get access and don't want to push their luck in asking for too much. Others worry about what to do in situations in which the data they are given are proprietary and therefore limited in use value for social science purposes. My view is that anything I receive is better than nothing; I may grind my teeth at not being able to report some data, but I would much rather know what I cannot say than to not know and then be forced to speculate.[26] Requests for data may not always be honored, but the request itself tends not to be dishonored, especially among executives who consider themselves to be "fact driven."

Finally, the formal close of an interview need not signal the end of the interaction. At minimum, it helps to make a practice of asking for the opportunity to follow up with questions of clarification after you have had a chance to review your notes. Although this is not a suggestion applicable only to corporate elites, it is different in the sense that executives are accustomed to interacting with people by way of paper. On a number of occasions I have been advised that letters and memos have a longer half-life than telephone or hallway conversations. In this respect, a letter of thanks can also be an opportunity to remind the person of things she promised or offered to do during the interview (e.g., sending reports, making additional contacts for you, etc.).

## Getting More Data

As I hinted in the preceding section, there are a variety of means for enhancing and enlarging the amount you can learn from an interview with important people in big companies. Here I offer some additional suggestions that may be a bit less structured.

- Corporate executives, as Domhoff (1967) has shown so creatively, are deeply enmeshed in social, political, economic, religious, and even family networks made up of other corporate executives. It makes sense, therefore, to use every interview as an opportunity to employ those networks to your advantage. Ask for the names of people whom your interviewees think you ought to interview and who they think would like to be interviewed about your topic.

- Interviews need not be limited to the amount of time negotiated if you are careful in the way you set them up. For example, I try whenever possible (or appropriate) to schedule interviews for the time immediately preceding lunch. That way I increase the chances of extending the interview into lunch or, alternatively, use the lunch to be introduced to others in the organization. Lunchtime conversation tends to be less formal and therefore more free flowing; if the interviewee had been unwilling to come out from behind her organizational persona, lunch can be a vehicle for lowering inhibitions.

- Because control over the interview may be of vital concern, it is wise to quickly take in the surroundings when being ushered into an executive's office. If you can do so without being impolite, it may be more effective to locate a nonobvious place to conduct the interview, such as at a sofa and adjacent armchair or at a conference table, rather than sit in chairs on opposite sides of his or her desk.

- Do not hesitate to send an abbreviated transcript of your interview or a summary constructed from your notes as a way to both get clarification and prompt additional data. This can be laborious, but it has the advantage of keeping lines of communication open.

## Conclusion

Movies like *Roger and Me* are entertaining and, in many ways, quite instructive, but they often forfeit much of their depth and their persuasive potential by not giving speaking roles to the people whose behavior they seek to explain. *Roger and Me* would, of course, have been a much different movie had Roger been on screen for more than a few fleeting minutes—and quite a different enterprise if director Moore had had it in mind to wrestle with the multiple personas embedded in Roger and other important people in big companies.

In this respect, sociologists interested in studying and explaining the behavior of corporate elites have a major chore on their hands. To avoid caricature, they must cultivate an awareness of multiple personas that make up the reality of important people in big companies. To provide insight as well as to build a firm foundation for sociological analysis, they must separate out the person from the role and the role from the formal context within which it is acted out. Such awareness, however, is often difficult to achieve and sustain for ideological as well as methodological reasons. The setting, the person, and the organization can overwhelm the researcher—both positively (in the sense of impressing him or her and encouraging a form of identification with the people being interviewed) and negatively (repelling him or her and encouraging a level of detachment that can lead to equally partial or one-sided analyses). In both cases, researchers can find themselves focusing on one persona to the exclusion and detriment of the others.

However, awareness can be enhanced through careful preparation—much of which involves the researcher asking difficult questions of him- or herself—and through recognition of the responsibility that researchers have to multiple audiences: readers, one another, and, yes, the elite itself.

## Notes

1. See, for example, Buchanan, Boddy, and McCalman (1988) and Van Maanen (1990).

2. The rule of thumb I've observed is that the bigger the company, the more elaborate the security system—independent of how important security is. Identification badges can be a source of great insight in and of themselves: For example, at one large aircraft company where I've spent a lot of time, badges had (until quite recently) a color code so that you could identify which division ("budget line") a person belonged to, a budget number so you could see what department their time was charged to, a magnetic strip so it could be scanned by security personnel as well as deployed like a credit card to get access to private areas, the person's "hire in" date so you could tell how long someone had been around, and a small black-and-white photograph taken of the person at the time he or she was hired. The last "identifier" was often the most interesting: Because many of the people I met with had joined the company in the mid- to late 1960s, it was quite a revelation to compare their current "executive" demeanor (clean shaven, short hair) with the long sideburns, mustaches, and collar-length haircuts of the 1960s.

3. Executives do, on average, spend very long hours at work with their time tightly scheduled (Mintzberg, 1973); however, this is not the same as saying that all that time is spent working. In this respect, I would say that Walker's (1985) chronicle of life in the executive suite of the large-scale corporation is not altogether inaccurate.

4. Few executives know what sociologists or anthropologists do in general and much less about what they might do in a particular study. Thus they have little reason to treat you as something other than an unimportant journalist.

5. A coach-class ticket from Boston to Detroit (same-day roundtrip with no Saturday stayover) costs approximately $700. Add in a rental car ($35), parking at the airport ($10), a skimpy meal ($5), depreciation on the suit or dress you bought to interview important people ($10), and the cost of your own time (heavily discounted at $40), and you've spent $800. After one of my own $800 interviews was rescheduled, I mentioned it through clenched teeth to a senior colleague; he tried to console me by noting that the cost of that hour interview was roughly equivalent to the hourly wage of the executive in question.

6. This characterization of tasks is based largely on my own experience supplemented by conversations I have had with colleagues about "how they do it."

7. I am sometimes amazed at just how ignorant we are of data sources—not to mention research reports and articles—developed and written by colleagues in professional schools.

8. You may have to sit through recitation of ideas or information with which you are already acquainted, but, if done carefully, it is possible to short-circuit "speeches" that have been delivered elsewhere. In some cases, of course, that may be impossible: For example, I have visited four different Toyota Corporation installations and had to sit through basically the same presentations about the company, its history, and its philosophy as a prelude to broaching a discussion of questions I wanted answered. In each case, I have prefaced my visit with letters indicating (politely) that I am not a stranger and that I have read extensively about the company. This has not, however, circumvented the ritual.

9. In fact, for reasons that I will go on to describe, it may be to your advantage to offer to submit questions in advance. For example, it increases the odds that your questions will structure the interview, that the interviewee will be better prepared to discuss what you are interested in, and, perhaps most important, that he or she will provide you with additional documentation or recommendations for people to speak with as part of their preparation.

10. It is an open question whether executives would refuse to speak with someone who showed up in clothes incongruent with organizational norms. My rule of thumb has been,

however, to avoid drawing excessive attention to myself in order to focus attention on my questions. Graduate students who have worked with me routinely complain about this, of course. On the other hand, it is possible to err in the other direction, too. For example, I routinely don a conservative (navy) suit; however, in a computer company I found that I stood out like a sore thumb by comparison to the pullover sweaters and slacks that were the norm. Being far from home, I did not have much alternative to my suits, and several times over the course of the next week people chided me for dressing too much like a consultant—a comment that was tantamount to an insult.

11. Most vivid in my mind are a chrome-plating machine operator who stood up to his supervisors in an effort to correct a health danger on the job, a *lechugero* (lettuce worker) who supported a family of eight on subminimum wages, an equipment designer whose unorthodox ideas were shunned for years until finally implemented, and a woman who held down three jobs in order to send her kids to college.

12. Actually, some of the best (and least obtrusive) observation can be done via movies about business. For example, recent works—dramas and comedies alike—such as *Wall Street*, *The Secret of My Success*, and *Other People's Money*, as well as classics like *The Man in the Grey Flannel Suit* and *The Fountainhead*, can provide valuable insights as to the nuances of life on "mahogany row."

13. See Buchanan, Boddy, and McCalman (1988) and Pettigrew (1985).

14. A small tip from Japanese business: have business cards printed up that display your college or university's insignia featured prominently. Your name and departmental affiliation should be much smaller because you want to attract attention to the institution. If you feel it important to avoid being associated with a particular department or discipline, you can always affiliate yourself with a larger entity, such as a College of Arts and Sciences. However, because courtesy appointments in research centers or even business schools are not uncommon, you can always use that instead.

15. Executives visit college campuses to educate students and faculty. It is therefore not unreasonable to present yourself as someone who wants to be educated.

16. On several occasions in lectures to undergraduate audiences, I have mentioned my interest in meeting with or interviewing executives in a given company or industry. Twice now, it yielded introductions from the children of important people.

17. At the risk of being redundant, I must repeat that the questions you wish to have answered might in fact be answerable by someone else.

18. This is a point I have stressed but rarely gotten across to colleagues not accustomed to field research. For example, in training faculty in how to do interviews—and then accompanying them as they did it—it was difficult to persuade them to not give lectures with each question and to avoid the temptation to challenge every answer they were given.

19. Obviously, part of your initial research should involve efforts to find out what are currently deemed real and important problems. Without misrepresenting what is your real interest, it is often relatively easy to frame your interest in terms that might pique their interest.

20. To date, my most memorable interview was conducted in the old Playboy Club in Chicago. I have not had the experience of some colleagues who have had meetings in corporate jets, hot tubs, and saunas.

21. See, for example, McCracken (1988), Schein (1987), Seidman (1991), Spradley (1979), and Thomas (1983).

22. For example, I often use a letter to confirm the interview time and place and submit along with it a brief statement of my research interests—usually one that reiterates what

I've said or written previously—along with a sampling of questions that "give the flavor of" what I am likely to ask. I usually repeat the same statement at the outset of the interview as a way to jog the person's memory as to who I am and why I'm there.

23. I make it a practice to tape record and fully transcribe all interviews. I explain this honestly: I have great difficulty listening, writing, and thinking all at the same time. Thus I tape record in order to be attentive and to make sure I understand what people are telling me then and later. I also routinely offer to keep confidential the identities of the people I interview. I do the latter in large part because it is unimportant to me that specific organizations or individuals be identified.

24. Schein (1987), for example, makes a cogent case for the unstructured interview as part of a clinical approach to fieldwork.

25. I recall vividly one situation when I politely interrupted just such a speech by noting that I'd heard the executive make that argument 2 weeks earlier on a cable TV business program. He looked at me first in shock and then in embarrassment—although he did not say exactly why he was embarrassed. He immediately responded, however, that "Oh, I forgot. This is *your* interview, isn't it?"

26. Proprietary agreements—or confidentiality statements—usually do not enter into the picture when the interview is "one time only." However, the ability of corporations and their representatives to sue in the event of a breach of agreement sets up important differences in this kind of research by comparison to other work.

## References

Adler, P. A., & Adler, P. (1990). Stability and flexibility: Maintaining relations within organized and unorganized groups. In W. Shaffir & R. Stebbins (Eds.), *Experiencing fieldwork* (pp. 173-183). Newbury Park, CA: Sage.

Buchanan, D., Boddy, D., & McCalman, J. (1988). Getting in, getting on, getting out and getting back. In A. Bryman (Ed.), *Doing research in organizations* (pp. 53-67). London: Routledge.

Dalton, M. (1959). *Men who manage.* New York: Wiley.

Davis, F. (1973). The Martian and the convert. *Urban Life and Culture, 2*(3), 333-343.

Domhoff, G. W. (1967). *Who rules America?* Englewood Cliffs, NJ: Prentice-Hall.

Gurney, J. N. (1990). Female researchers in male-dominated settings. In W. Shaffir & R. Stebbins (Eds.), *Experiencing fieldwork* (pp. 53-61). Newbury Park, CA: Sage.

Hirsch, P. M. (1986). From ambushes to golden parachutes: Corporate takeovers as an instance of cultural framing and institutional integration. *American Journal of Sociology, 91,* 800-837.

Jackall, R. (1988). *Moral mazes.* New York: Oxford University Press.

Kanter, R. (1977). *Men and women of the corporation.* New York: Basic Books.

Kleinman, S. (1990). Field-workers' feelings: What we feel, who we are, how we analyze. In W. Shaffir & R. Stebbins (Eds.), *Experiencing fieldwork* (pp. 185-195). Newbury Park, CA: Sage.

McCracken, G. (1988). *The long interview.* Newbury Park, CA: Sage.

Mills, C. W. (1956). *The power elite.* New York: Oxford University Press.

Mintzberg, H. (1973). *The nature of managerial work.* New York: Harper & Row.

Pettigrew, A. (1985). On studying organizational cultures. In J. Van Maanen (Ed.), *Qualitative methodology* (pp. 82-104). Beverly Hills, CA: Sage.

Punch, M. (1986). *The politics and ethics of fieldwork*. Newbury Park, CA: Sage.

Schein, E. (1987). *The clinical perspective in fieldwork*. Newbury Park, CA: Sage.

Seidman, I. E. (1991). *Interviewing as qualitative research*. New York: Teachers College Press.

Shaffir, W. B. (1990). Managing a convincing self-presentation: Some personal reflections on entering the field. In W. Shaffir & R. Stebbins (Eds.), *Experiencing fieldwork* (pp. 72-82). Newbury Park, CA: Sage.

Spradley, J. (1979). *Ethnographic interview*. New York: Holt, Rinehart & Winston.

Thomas, R. (1983). *Doing an interview*. Working paper, Center for Research on Social Organization, University of MIchigan, Ann Arbor. Copies available on request to author.

Thomas, R. (1989). Participation and control: A shopfloor perspective on employee participation. In S. B. Bacharach (Ed.), *Research in the sociology of organizations* (Vol. 7., pp. 117-144). Greenwich, CT: JAI.

Thomas, R. (1994). *What machines can't do: Politics and technology in the industrial enterprise*. Berkeley: University of California Press.

Useem, M. (1979). The social organization of the American business elite and participation of corporation directors in the governance of American institutions. *American Sociological Review, 44*, 553-572.

Van Maanen, J. (1990). Playing back the tape: Early days in the field. In W. Shaffir & R. Stebbins (Eds.), *Experiencing fieldwork* (pp. 31-42). Newbury Park, CA: Sage.

Veblen, T. (1923). *Theory of the leisure class*. New York: McGraw-Hill.

Walker, G L. (1985). *The chronicles of Doodah*. Boston: Houghton Mifflin.

Warren, C. (1988). *Gender issues in field research*. Newbury Park, CA: Sage.

Whyte, W. H. (1956). *The organization man*. New York: Scribner.

Zelditch, M. (1962). Some methodological problems of field studies. *American Journal of Sociology, 67*, 566-576.

# 2

# *Reaching Corporate Executives*

## MICHAEL USEEM

Of those who wield great influence over the fortunes of millions, few are better described or more dissected in the public record than senior managers of publicly traded corporations. Private enterprise has long been the dominant institution in American life. Those who preside over its operations are natural objects of curiosity among the millions whose fates they shape.

Corporations make it easy for their leaders to be in the public eye. Most companies voluntarily disclose the identities, positions, and directorships of their officers, a roster that can range from a handful to dozens. Standard and Poor's annual *Register of Directors and Executives* and other directories routinely compile all that is disclosed by thousands of companies. Many executives themselves also voluntarily reveal their educational credentials, career milestones, and directorships to Marquis for its *Who's Who in America* and *Who's Who in Finance and Industry*, *Business Week* for its annual "Corporate Elite" volume, and a host of regional and specialty publications. Upon the request of journalists or researchers, most corporate public-affairs offices also furnish biographical sketches of their top managers.

Publicly traded companies are required by law to disclose still other information about their senior people. Under U.S. securities regulations, the company's annual proxy statement must identify the age, occupation, and company shares of all candidates for the board of directors, with several company executives almost always among them. All forms of compensation—salaries, stock options, stock appreciation rights and the like—must also be reported for the five highest-paid officers. Though not formally required, many companies also include photographs of their officers and directors in the annual report, adding visual image to small print.

Complementing the disclosed record is extensive news coverage of top management. *The Wall Street Journal, Fortune, Forbes,* hundreds of industry publications from *PC Week* to *Transportation Digest,* and business sections of major newspapers devote extensive coverage to the captains of industry. Celebrated figures such as Chrysler's Lee Iacocca, General Electric's Jack Welch, and Disney's Michael Eisner sometimes garner as much coverage as American politicians or British royalty. Many of the less celebrated receive no attention, and the press record is uneven. Still, for events from executive appointments to executive dismissals, from takeover battles to bankruptcy proceedings, top managers are regularly featured in the nation's media.

Corporations also leave a well documented record of their own performance. The U.S. Securities and Exchange Commission (SEC) requires quarterly and annual reporting of financial and accounting data, an information base readily available to researchers in electronic form through a service known as Compustat and soon through the SEC itself. Here we have earnings figures and R&D investments going back over many years. Institutional investors must also periodically report their company holdings, and in compiled form these data are available for analysis through Disclosure and other commercial sources. From this information base we learn the identities of virtually all of a company's largest shareholders. Mutual-fund managers are required as well to report their holdings, and that information in compiled form is also available for further study through Morningstar and other proprietary operations. These sources can tell us which companies Fidelity's Magellan Fund and more than 4,000 other mutual funds presently and historically prefer. Still other organizations aggregate and repackage these and related data sets for distribution. *Hoover's Handbook of American Companies* and *Standard and Poor's 500 Guide* can be found in most major bookstores. Stock analysts' reports on most major companies, routinely prepared for paying and would-be clients, can be unearthed with a little more digging.

As rich as such sources are, they are insufficient. Beyond a company's executive roster and financial performance, few systematic data are to be routinely found on the nation's major businesses. A company's culture is almost nowhere so recorded. A firm's adoption of self-managed work teams, strategic business units, and technology training programs are rarely reported. We could discover precious little about an enterprise's restructuring or re-engineering by relying entirely on public resources.

Compared to research on many organizations, the study of business is privileged by a rich array of readily accessible information. Community agencies, local hospitals, and art museums place but a fraction of the equivalent data in the public record. But compared to what is needed to answer some of the most vexing questions about the world of business, we often have little choice but to enter that world directly.

I have done so a number of times, and I will share that experience with the intention of encouraging others to pursue research questions that require such access as well. The wealth and authority of corporate executives can be daunting terrains for the first-time visitor. Their status barriers may seem virtually impregnable, especially when contrasted with the thinly guarded and well-trodden paths to the poor and powerless. Yet few of the ramparts, I have found, are unbreachable.

The techniques for doing so are by no means unique. They are adaptations of relatively standard strategies for the study of almost any ground. They include mail surveys, telephone interviews, personal discussions, and direct observation. On occasion a combination of all has proven both necessary and feasible. None is necessarily superior to the others, and the choice of one depends on the nature of the problem, the information required, and the resources available. All can usually be made to work. I will describe the five approaches that I have most often found to work at a price that is acceptable.

## Companies by Mail

The use of the U.S. postal system to reach well-placed company informants, the first of my several approaches, is a time-honored method, and it can prove a reliable source for certain forms of company information. Despite the limitations of an impersonal technique, the mails can nonetheless provide a cost effective vehicle for extracting substantial company information from substantial numbers of companies.

By way of example, a colleague and I became interested in the organizational and leadership determinants of corporate giving. Why do some companies contribute more than others to philanthropic endeavors? Why do some favor public education while others favor human services or culture and the arts? A mail survey proved a practical instrument in this case because most companies designate a single manager to be responsible for company contributions. Sometimes it is the chief executive, especially at smaller companies. Often it is a full-time giving manager, particularly at larger firms. Wherever the authority was invested, one person almost invariably held primary responsibility for overseeing the company program. This individual carried much of the information we sought in his or her memory or knew where it could be found in the files.

Our procedure was accordingly straightforward. We first telephoned a set of sampled companies to identify the person with primary responsibility for company giving. We then dispatched a pre-tested written survey to those so named. With a telephone follow-up to reluctant respondents, we acquired the information that we needed from 62 firms, half of those initially approached. This study proved relatively inexpensive in both time and money, but it also produced relatively little data on several related areas of interest, such as the process by which companies formulated their giving policies or evaluated their prospective recipients (Useem & Kutner, 1986).

## Managers by Survey

Equally valuable can be a second approach, the direct interview survey of company managers. Like people in almost any organization, if you can reach their office, most are ready to share a rich lore on the worlds they inhabit. Reaching their office is the problem.

One personal example of an attack on the office barrier comes from a study of the human-resource policies of large companies. Akin to the research questions in the study of corporate giving, I had become interested in why some firms invest far more than others in the education and training of their employees. Moreover, some corporations actively encouraged employees to volunteer for work with the public schools and offered personal leaves for teaching. Others provided no incentives. The variability among large firms in these areas was striking, and much of it was surely embedded, I speculated, in the organization and leadership of the companies.

A survey of corporate managers proved a good source of data for examining such questions. As part of a broader study of company human-resources policies, the Conference Board, a non-profit business-information organization, had contracted with Louis Harris & Associates to approach a national sample of 623 firms drawn from among the Conference Board's company membership. Of the sampled firms, Harris found that 20 had gone out of business or otherwise proved ineligible. Another 37 did not respond after four requests, and 160 refused to participate. The final 406 cooperating companies thus constituted two-thirds of those initially pursued, a reasonably representative cross section of the several thousand large firms composing the Conference Board's membership.

As in the previous study, we sought information from the company managers most knowledgeable about the firm's policies in this area. The survey organization successfully located them and gained access to most. The managers it contacted carried primary responsibility for the human-resources function, and they brought nearly two decades of work experience in the human-resources arena. Professional interviewers were able to interview them in their offices for an hour on average and persuaded most to complete a supplementary questionnaire as well. The interviewers compiled detailed information on company practices ranging from training and benefits to diversity and downsizing. A personal interview survey of this magnitude would ordinarily be well beyond the means of most individual researchers, but a private foundation, the Commonwealth Fund, had stepped forward with the necessary financing.

The use of a single key informant to appraise organizational practices, albeit a highly informed one, raised worries about the reliability of the data. The responding managers, by virtue of their elevated positions and some two decades of company experience, were certainly well positioned to appraise their firm's general practices. But they were also far less well informed than local plant or office managers about specific practices in those locations. Moreover, with some 15,000 employees on average, headquarters managers could surely offer little appreciation for the world of workers deep in the trenches. Still, they were likely to be as well informed as any manager about overall company policies (Johnson & Linden, 1992; Mirvis, 1993; Useem, 1993b).

The use of several inside but diversely placed observers rather than just one would have enhanced the quality and breadth of our record for each firm. But given our resource constraints, that would have dictated cutting the number of companies by half if even only a second observer were included, and by greater fractions if more. We opted in this instance, as have other researchers from time to time, for greater breadth across companies rather than more depth within (see, for instance, Friedman & Singh, 1989; Lawler, Mohrman, & Ledford, 1992). This choice was a product of both the specific research questions and pragmatic constraints. In other instances described below I have opted for a trade-off the other way around, but here the argument for breadth prevailed.

## Managers by Telephone

Survey firms, marketing companies, and the U.S. Census often rely upon telephone approaches for relatively inexpensive access to large numbers of dispersed people. Those interested in the corporate landscape can find the telephone a convenient and cost-effective instrument. This third approach provides an inexpensive strategy for reaching the geographically diverse.

Though I have rarely drawn upon this lane of the information highway, the telephone has proven invaluable on occasion. As a case in point, a colleague and I were seeking to characterize how institutional investors viewed the increasingly conflictual relations between them and the large corporations in which they had placed their wealth. Among our more specific concerns were the extent to which large owners were initiating direct contact with corporate executives and directors, and other investors, to press faltering companies for reform.

Institutional investors were a relatively late addition to the premier circles of American business. Before the 1980s, they had been little known to those beyond the denizens of Wall Street, but during the late 1980s and early 1990s, the institutions amassed a majority of the outstanding shares of large companies. They thereby acquired the power if not necessarily the unquestioned legitimacy to exercise great influence over the course of American business. Among their leading members were pension funds such as TIAA-CREF and California Public Employees' Retirement System; money-management and investment companies such as Fidelity and Vanguard; and endowments of nonprofit organizations such as the Ford Foundation and Pew Charitable Trusts.

The evolving views of institutional investors were at the root of much of the movement for governance reform and corporate restructuring during the early 1990s. Yet those views had rarely found public expression. This study thus sought to characterize them through direct interviews with a cross section of large institutions. To do so, we drew a sample of the 40 largest pension funds, 40 largest investment managers, and 20 largest foundations. For each institution, we identified a top executive and dispatched a letter describing the purpose of our study and requesting cooperation. Our first choice for a top person was the institution's most senior equities manager, followed by the chief investment officer if no equities specialist could be identified. We sought face-to-face interviews with these individuals if they were located within several hundred miles of our offices in Philadelphia.

Many of the institutions were scattered across the country, from Ohio and Illinois to California and Washington. The telephone thus proved the only feasible means in this instance for reaching far and wide while remaining within our budget constraints. We were able to complete either personal or telephone interviews with executives at nearly half of the nationally sampled institutional investors that we had initially approached. Compared with face-to-face discussions, such interviews were less revealing of each investor's mind-set. They did help reveal, however, the thinking of a larger set of minds (Useem, Bowman, Irvine, & Myatt, 1993).

### Executives by Interview

A fourth research strategy is to conduct personal interviews with company executives. Time and resources permitting, I have often favored this technique for the insights it offers into the culture, organization, and activity of the executives and their firm. For certain topics, in my experience, there are few better procedures for acquiring detailed information from an array of managers and companies. The executives can be asked about their own careers and business roles. They can also be approached for information about their own firms. I have conducted both kinds of studies. The focus on executives themselves is illustrated in this section. A focus on the executives' companies is chronicled in the following section.

To better understand how company executives represent their firms to the outside world, and to better map the informal relations and understanding that they develop among themselves across many firms, I chose to interview senior managers of large companies in Boston, New York, and London. I had sampled 326 names from a larger data set that I had created from an array of public sources on American and British corporations and executives. Though I might have approached several of the sampled names through intermediaries, drawing on the strength of weak ties, for most I had no practical alternative to what might be termed a "cold" call. I simply sent a letter requesting assistance with the study, and then placed a telephone follow-up to the executive's office shortly thereafter. By time I reached the executive's secretary, the latter had almost invariably been informed of the boss's wishes. If the boss had not declined, the secretary was usually instructed to insert me into a crowded schedule as soon as feasible.

Some executives declined to receive me at all. Others were unavailable during my windows for interviewing in New York and London. One British executive, for instance, had taken a prolonged leave from his office for the "shooting season," another for a Himalayan expedition. Still, I was able to reach and interview three-fifths of those initially contacted on both sides of the Atlantic. What emerged from the completed interviews was a picture that I had not fully anticipated. Those at the higher levels of companies in both countries, I learned, formed a kind of self-selected circle whose views and agenda transcended the concerns of any single firm. On matters of public policy they tended to voice the broader concerns of the business community as a whole, not just the specific concerns of their own firm (Useem, 1984).

## Companies by Interview

A fifth approach is to interview company executives less for their own careers and experiences and more for the assessments of their own organizations. Their personal biographies and perceptions of course play into the latter, but the guiding agenda here has been to construct an account of the organization of the executive suite and its relationship to other groups both within and outside the corporation. For this there are no better placed nor better informed than the executives themselves.

The several executives occupying the firm's apex often oversee different sides of the business and take different roles with its external constituencies. The chief executive, chief operating officer, chief financial officer, and general counsel each know much of the same inside terrain, but usually not all of the same. Similarly, they share in their work with outside constituencies but here too they specialize some. Those occupying the next layer down, such as group vice presidents and divisional heads, are themselves well familiar with certain aspects of the business but far less so with others. Each of these senior managers carries an appreciation for partially distinct facets of the business. Contact with all was therefore desirable for constructing as full a picture as possible.

With this approach in mind, I have completed two relatively recent studies of company organization. In one instance I was primarily concerned with the impact of corporate restructuring on top management. In the second I was mainly interested in the relations that had emerged between large firms and their major institutional investors. I will offer a more extended account of the first study to illustrate some of the practical problems and experiences that come with the approach, and then briefly describe the second project to illustrate a specific problem that I have not yet been able to solve.

### Learning About Restructuring

As no single source could round out enough of the corporate-restructuring picture, I built the account by combining several kinds of information. The sources included interviews with an array of informed observers, attendance at seminars for company officials, and the results of company surveys and other research studies. But to examine the organizational consequences at close range, I had concluded that I would have to establish direct contact with top management of companies that had undertaken restructuring (the following account draws on Useem, 1993a, pp. 247-254).

For this I focused on the experiences of seven large corporations. During the late 1980s and early 1990s they each had undertaken significant steps of organizational restructuring. In no instance had ownership changed hands, but in every case they had undergone wrenching transformations. I concentrated on this comparatively small set of companies in order to characterize more fully the changes. By design, the seven companies' major product areas represented seven distinct sectors of the economy (chemicals, electrical products, financial services, machinery, pharmaceuticals, retail, and transportation).

The seven firms ranked in the upper rungs of any size ladder. The smallest company employed more than 10,000 people and two firms more than 100,000; together, the firms met the payrolls of nearly half a million. On the traditional *Fortune* rankings, the four manufacturing companies numbered among the Fortune 200, and the three service companies were among the top 10 of their respective rankings. All seven stood among the nation's largest 300 corporations in market value.

Gaining access to the senior tiers of the seven companies was essential, and high-level entrée had opened the first doors. In six of the seven cases, the president of a sponsoring organization, the National Planning Association, wrote and then telephoned a senior manager of each of the corporations whose cooperation I sought for the study. Based in Washington, the National Planning Association is concerned with current policy issues affecting companies and employment, and its membership is drawn from large corporations, national unions, and university faculties. Its president asked executives representing their companies to arrange for me to have access to a range of senior managers within their companies.

The executives generally agreed, and I was soon passing through headquarters security on the way to an early morning appointment with the executive serving as liaison for the study. This was typically followed by back-to-back, tape-recorded interviews with five to fifteen of his senior colleagues throughout the day or days that followed. I completed interviews with those responsible for operations, finance, human resources, industrial relations, strategic planning, public affairs, communications, legal affairs, acquisitions and divestitures, and investor relations. Interviews were also conducted with executives carrying general responsibilities, including chief operating officers and presidents of major business units. The study's information was thus drawn from top staff members, heads of operating units, and general managers, cross sections of the senior ranks common to most large companies. Many of those interviewed also consented to requests for extensive follow-up discussions and reviews of company documents and files.

In one instance, however, initial access to the firm proved exceptionally arduous. An executive had agreed to serve as liaison for his company, and I sought to make an appointment to see him. For several months he was almost continuously out of the office on special assignment. During one period, he was leaving the country at the start of every workweek, returning to the United States only for weekend sojourns. His secretary politely reported that he would try to get back to me, but it became evident that most non-essential business for him was on hold. After several months of no response, an intermediary well known to the executive placed several calls to his office, even faxing a query when the executive failed to return the calls. Discrete questions to the executive's associates confirmed that the unresponsiveness simply reflected time constraints rather than any reversal of commitment to the study. Finally, in an act of creative desperation, his secretary suggested an early-morning call to an unlisted car telephone while her boss commuted to the office. Shorn of all organizational buffers, I reached the executive on his way to work, and within days he had opened his organization to the project.

In a number of instances, companies provided relatively free access to their files on specific issues related to this study. One senior public affairs manager, for example, was scheduled to participate in a charity tennis tournament, an event viewed as a natural extension of his work life because the governor and other political and corporate notables were among the contestants. He pre-arranged for me to use his office for the day, making available a filing cabinet of correspondence, memoranda, plans, and other documents related to the company's successful effort to secure anti-takeover legislation in the state. In another case, the company's chief administrative officer walked me to a cabinet containing internal memos and other documents outlining the firm's plans for defeating a shareholder proxy resolution that would have weakened management and strengthened investors in the event of an unwanted takeover bid. In a third instance, I was seated in the room of an absent executive and provided the company's performance-related compensation plan for senior management. In still another case, I was able to review the strategic plans of a number of the corporation's operating business units.

Among several additional steps used to sharpen the study's findings was a presentation of my preliminary findings to headquarters staff of one of the participating corporations. A four-hour seminar with seven managers, four of whom had been interviewed for the study, provided helpful affirmation and refinement of the study's thrust, especially in two areas. One concerned an explanation for why the firm had focused relatively early on shareholder value. Having played important roles in its early development, the managers knew the events well. As group discussions often do, the collective insight from pooled experience added invaluable nuance to the account. The second area concerned the next phases of the company's decade-long process of restructuring. Several of the participants stressed the need to extend the logic of organizational alignment already set in motion. The group identified several areas especially ripe for targeting, including the company's industrial relations and management of non-exempt employees, neither of which had been mentioned during the one-on-one interviews.

Other sources provided additional context on organizational restructuring. These included interviews that I conducted in 1988 with a number of managers with three other corporations as part of a study of turbulence in managerial and professional employment (Doeringer et al., 1991). Those corporations comprised a manufacturing and service company; a maker of office equipment; and a large manufacturer of information systems. The revenues of each exceeded $10 billion. Like the other seven firms, none had undergone a change in ownership but all had launched extensive internal redesigns.

To assist interpretation of the information coming from the seven main companies, I also arranged interviews with twenty-five individuals who were directly familiar with the issues of corporate restructuring. These individuals included two senior partners of a firm specializing in financing and managing leveraged buyouts of other companies, an individual who had served as the chief financial officer of a large transportation company that had unsuccessfully resisted purchase by a well-known takeover specialist, the former chief executive of a company that had successfully resisted acquisition when he and his family had repurchased a large bloc of outstanding shares, and the former chief executive of a company that had undergone extensive restructuring in response to Wall Street pressures.

Information was selectively gathered through still other avenues. I visited the Washington offices of several of the major associations concerned with shareholder relations and corporate governance (e.g., the Investor Responsibility Research Center). I conducted interviews with representatives of other organizations and groups involved in these issues (e.g., Institutional Shareholder Services). I also attended meetings of several groups, including those of the Investor Relations Association and the National Investor Relations Institute. Business there was not always strictly business. A meeting held in 1990 at New York's Waldorf Astoria, attended by hundreds of investor relations specialists and fund managers, received fresh insight on the ways of Wall Street from one its fictional experts, author Tom Wolfe of *The Bonfire of the Vanities.*

Finally, moving through company corridors and around executive offices sometimes results in unscheduled but fruitful opportunities. As I traveled between appointments on the executive floor of one of the corporations, for example, I encountered a manager whom I had interviewed earlier in the day. She was accompanied by an instantly recognizable colleague to whom I was introduced. It was the company's chief executive, and I found an unexpected moment to learn more about the view from the top. In another instance, I obtained access to company files on company strategy for defeating a shareholder proposal. As I perused the files in an open reception area surrounded by the offices of the firm's top management, two senior officers wandered by for lengthy informal conversations, an unanticipated extension of my earlier discussions with them.

Even the most mundane moments sometimes proved revealing. I had completed an interview with the president at one of the companies and was about to start an interview with the vice president for marketing. While we were securing coffee from an executive kitchenette, the president walked in for a cup as well, changing the coffee-maker's filter in the process. He had earlier described a radical reduction in his central office staff, resulting in an extremely lean headquarters. Following several minutes of banter, he left the room quipping, "you can say that the real secret of our success is that I make the coffee."

In building my accounts I sought to draw upon information from at least several sources. In one incident of crisis management, for instance, I witnessed an edge of the crisis directly, obtained company documents on it, and subsequently interviewed several managers about it. All three sources proved useful in reconstructing the event. More generally, key points were checked with the commentary of at least several managers and documents when possible. New issues that emerged spontaneously in early interviews were often explicitly raised in later interviews.

Although each manager's experience and each company's practice contained unique elements, my objective of course was to extract the generic patterns. In selecting materials for reporting, I preferred experiences and practices that found parallels or equivalents in at least several corporations and were confirmed by a number of managers and documentary sources for each. Construction of the restructuring portrait was thus built on integrated and cross-checked information from many documents, observations, and interviews. Other studies were also drawn upon for corroborating evidence or to suggest where the observed patterns had found more widespread application. The goal was to identify the most salient, widespread, and enduring forms of organizational restructuring.

This entry into the world of managers carried recognized hazards. One stemmed from a traditional problem of asking managers what they and their organization do. A billiards expert, argued Milton Friedman, may be superb at the game but would be a poor source on Newtonian mechanics. The poolroom player must have intuitive mastery of the laws of physics, yet mastery does not depend on articulating the laws. To understand the laws, so the argument goes, one must observe the ball movement, not ask the ball mover. Extended to the managerial setting, this hazard might be termed, "they know not why they do." By virtue of company size, time constraints, and hidden pressures, a manager may knowledgeably act but imperfectly understand why (see, for instance, Blinder, 1991; Gordon, 1991; Shiller, 1991).

A second hazard was related to the ever present danger of "going native," of uncritically accepting a paradigm that one had arrived to appraise. Relying not on cold statistics but warm contact, the itinerant interviewer may insidiously be drawn into the subject of inquiry. Max Weber's call for *verstehen*, for understanding the world of those under the microscope, carried the attendant risk that the observer might come to understand it too well.

Both dangers appeared as I entered the seven executive suites. The first hazard was perhaps most starkly seen in the opposed interpretations that managers sometimes rendered of the same event. The conflicts were never as discrepant as when first-marriage husbands and wives some-times report different numbers of children to Census interviewers. But managers did differ on fundamentals from time to time, implying bounded rationality for at least one and sometimes all of the insiders.

The second danger was also present from the moment of arrival. Management offices were richly furnished and sometimes given to magnificent views. On occasion, interviews would conclude with an invitation to the executive dining room or a private club. Even a one-time visitor was often received with exquisite courtesy and privi-leged treatment. On arriving with coat and briefcase for an early morn-ing interview, I would sometimes find both waiting at the outer office of the last manager on the day's schedule, along with a company car for return to the airport.

Protecting against both dangers, however, went with the territory. I recognized of course that managerial perceptions were often limited and sometimes biased. This necessitated a cross-checking of information with multiple sources, sifting through the extensive recorded interviews for consistent threads, returning for follow-up discussions to resolve inconsistencies, and scheduling additional interviews to flesh out inade-quate descriptions. It also necessitated a skeptical eye. Though there was little incentive for the managers to distort reality, they were presumably as subject as anybody to misinterpreting the events that swirled around them.

Guarding against going native required fewer preventive measures. Anthropologists are sometimes granted titular status in tribal groups, often an honorary kinship position making clear their local acceptance. Though I might have gladly embraced a title of honorary chief research officer to facilitate access, it seemed that no such offers were forthcoming. Nor were there any tests of loyalty, as when William Foote Whyte was asked to join in fraudulent voting practices during his sojourn in Italian-Boston's *Street Corner Society.* Aside from needing to be presentable enough to walk the executive floor without immediate suspicion, I was a well defined outsider without titles, tests, or targeting for assimilation.

A third danger stemmed from the fact that managerial perceptions were in part socially constructed. That is, their interpretations were not only a mapping of the organization in which the managers resided but also a product of the circles in which they traveled. By the late 1980s and early 1990s, for instance, extolling shareholder value had become fashionable, much as diversification had been during the 1960s. Managers who had neither contact with major investors nor direct responsibility for producing such value had nonetheless become highly conversant in its importance. As in any bounded group, business cants came and went, and this was certainly one of the dominant ideologies of the era.

Yet it was also evident that shareholder value carried numerous operational implications. Although some managers were not in a position to so operate, many were, and I could see that they carried shareholder-related criteria into their performance reviews, planning cycles, and organizational redesigns. Moreover, the rising rhetoric of shareholder value was rooted in the rising power of institutional wealth. This rhetoric was thus both socially rooted and socially constructed, necessitating special efforts to identify the organizational roots and operational implications while at the same time recognizing where it was only skin deep.

Although the primary sources of information were the restructuring accounts by the executives of the seven corporations, an array of other sources provided invaluable supplementary information. Yet gathering information from inside the seven companies, and above all from their senior managers, proved indispensable. I became familiar with media reports, stock reports, and self-reports on each of the corporations. Given their size and prominence, all of the companies garnered extensive public coverage. As publicly traded firms, all generated numerous reports for the public, but the story that emerged from discussions with the senior managers proved more complex and interesting than what could ever be gleaned from any public record. The known hazards of direct questioning of managers can never be fully overcome, but certain facets of organizational life might also never be understood otherwise. Indeed, most of the working hypotheses on the basis of publicly available information with which I had entered the companies were soon discarded as the interviews came to reveal a set of largely hidden and unanticipated developments.

### Learning About Corporations and Their Investors

The second study using extensive interviews with company executives focused on the invisible networks that had emerged during the late 1980s and early 1990s among large firms and their major investors. Little evident until the past decade, these networks reshaped and redefined relations between shareholders and their corporations. In the aftermath of an earlier "managerial revolution" that had separated ownership from control, the new networks had fostered a dialogue between those who own and those who control. They had also helped re-establish executive accountability (Useem, forthcoming).

Facets of the company-investor networks sometimes emerged in the public domain, but most remained far from view, well known to participants but also well out of the public eye. For mapping them there could be no alternative to direct access. What proved critical here was brokerage by the study's sponsor, the Institutional Investor Project of Columbia University's Center for Law and Economic Studies. Large corporations, institutional investors, several trade unions, and the New York Stock Exchange sponsored the Institutional Investor Project, and it had assembled a prominent advisory board to guide its work. The chair was a nationally prominent attorney who had served as outside counsel for a number of companies. He was widely known, either personally or by reputation, by chief executives and general counsels at many corporations. The chief executive of one of America's best known makers of food products also served on the advisory board, as did the general counsel of the nation's largest insurance company. They too were widely recognized or personally known within executive suites across the country.

To enter the targeted firms, each of these three advisory-board members approached an executive at firms with whom he was personally acquainted. "I am writing about an issue that I believe is of significance to [your company] and many other large firms," their letters would open: "the evolving relationship between publicly traded companies and their major institutional investors." Elaborating on the importance of the issue and noting the dearth of information upon it, the letter requested the company's participation. More specifically, it asked for an interview with the addressed executive and time with the firm's other senior managers.

The personalized request brought the desired response in almost all cases. The cooperating executive would identify the other executives with whom I should meet. All that remained was to find a mutually convenient set of dates. Given executive travel schedules, that proved no simple matter. But once at headquarters, I found the executives open to a wide-ranging exploration of the issues and willing to arrange for me to see still other executives, relevant documents, and themselves again.

With this sponsorship I was able to gain the participation of twenty major companies. The firms had been selected to represent an array of product sectors, ranging from automobiles and apparel to broadcasting, computers, insurance, and telecommunications. They were all large: market capitalization ranged from $1 billion to $20 billion, annual revenues from $2 billion to nearly $100 billion, and employees from 5,000 to almost 400,000. I completed interviews with a number of senior managers, including chief executives, chief operating officers, general counsels, chief financial officers, pension fund managers, directors of investor relations, and heads of divisions and operating units.

Again, I supplemented the interviews with a host of other sources. They included related studies conducted by both university researchers and industry analysts; company statistical data provided through SEC filings; a company survey sponsored by the National Investor Relations Institute; and archival sources with information on company ownership, proxy records, and related areas.

What proved problematic in this study, however, was gaining access to real-time executive encounters with investor representatives. I had concluded that observing these moments would valuably supplement what I was learning from interviews and elsewhere. It would permit direct observation of executive behavior which I had surmised was not always synonymous with reported behavior.

Accordingly, I asked permission to attend the quarterly meetings that top managements normally schedule with investor analysts just after their quarterly earnings reports are issued. The analysts meeting is usually a large forum with dozens present, and though technically a private event, it normally acquires a public ambiance because anything said there can be reported by the participants. The several companies that I asked readily provided me access to the meetings, and I believe that virtually all companies would have done so if requested.

I also asked to attend the meetings that top managements frequently hold with individual investors. These are sometimes held in company headquarters, at other times in investor offices. They tend to be far more informal and frank, and some of what is exchanged is considered off the record. The several companies where I sought an invitation said that they would extend one, but they eventually balked at actually doing so.

Finally, I had sought to push the boundaries one step further. Corporate boards often address issues of the company's relations with its shareholders, and I believed that those discussions would reveal valuable insights into the role of directors in mediating the links between managers and investors. Because of a governing board's financial and legal obligations, however, executives and directors were naturally sensitive about what transpired inside the boardroom and even more so over what might be transmitted outside it. I felt nonetheless that it would be worth inquiring about.

One firm seemed especially suitable for the request. The individual who had arranged entrée to the company also served on its board of directors. I consulted with him and he suggested that it might be feasible. At the end of an interview with the chief executive, also attended by the chief operating officer and general counsel, I gingerly asked if I might attend a board meeting. I had earlier stated that all information collected in the study was being treated as confidential and that neither individuals nor companies would be named or identifiable in any reports on the study. Despite reaffirmation of the guarantee and a plea for openness in the name of academic scholarship and improved governance, the three executives exchanged glances and the chief executive quickly declined. The boardroom, he affirmed, was too sacrosanct to permit such an intrusion.

Reasons for company reluctance to bring me directly into such settings, I concluded, were the presence of participants of equal standing and the dangers of entering uncharted territory. A chief executive could ask subordinates to meet with me without great concern about their willingness to do so. They accepted requests of this kind all the time as a normal part of business. For the chief executive to ask the company's directors or investors to meet with me, however, was another matter. Here he or she would need to explain a highly irregular request to those not under the CEO's authority, assure them that I would treat the event as totally confidential, and persuade them of its merits. To arrange my presence would thus require using personal capital for an event of limited value to the company at best.

I nonetheless remain convinced that such high places can and should be visited by outside researchers. Britain's Andrew Pettigrew, director of the Center for Corporate Strategy and Change at the Warwick Business School, has gained access in the UK, proving that the natural barriers can be surmounted. Some analysts of board behavior, such as Britain's Jonathan Charkham, have served as outside directors, thereby implicitly enriching their commentary with an insider's experience as well (Charkham, 1994). Gaining access to company boards through personal appointment to them lies beyond the career prospects of most researchers, but an opportunity to appear as the fly on the wall is not, I believe, entirely beyond the realm of possibilities.

## Conclusion

On the basis of these and related research experiences, I can offer several guidelines for thinking about studies of the higher reaches of the corporate pyramids. First, studies of those heights—the executive suite, the governing board, and their relations with others within and outside the organization—can require that top management be reached directly. For some research questions, the public record is simply insufficient. Entering their private worlds is the only way to acquire the necessary information.

Second, each research problem requires a customized research strategy. It may entail telephone interviews, mail surveys, or personal interviews. It might require asking executives to reflect upon their own careers, or it could dictate asking them to reflect upon their own organizations, or perhaps both. There is no best practice here, only alternative practices whose selection depends upon the investigator's research agenda and pocket depth.

Third, for some problems it may be worth combining several approaches. I have tried this once. The guiding research question concerned here the value of liberal learning and a liberal arts education for careers in the private sector. I had early concluded that no single research strategy could acquire sufficient information to build the kind of assessment that I felt was necessary. I had also obtained financial backing from the Corporate Council on the Liberal Arts, an association of a dozen major employers. With its support, I was able to conduct a mail survey of 535 major companies (focusing on their policies and practices in hiring and promoting liberal arts and other college students), a parallel telephone survey of 505 middle and senior managers of large companies (concentrating on their experiences in their own careers as well as in working with other managers of varying educational backgrounds), and a personal interview study of the experience of five major corporations in the hiring and promotion of college graduates. Drawing together these sources, I believe that I was able to construct a more comprehensive story than if I had relied upon any single strategy for acquiring inside data (Useem, 1989).

Fourth, the experience of acquiring information from within the firm usually proves both challenging and stimulating. Virtually all interviews and discussions with company executives, for instance, fostered new research questions. At times it can even prove entertaining. During one of my interview visits as part of the study of American and British executives, for instance, I encountered muffled laughter as I arrived in the executive suite of one of America's leading airlines. Such areas are sometimes known as morgues or graveyards because of their overwhelming silence. Today was evidently quite different, even for those accustomed to subdued quarters. The chairman of the board had just arrived in a grim mood. He had been a passenger on one of his airline's wide-bodied flights across the Atlantic Ocean. Also on board the fully booked flight were some one thousand laboratory mice. Their crate had been damaged in loading, but the European ground crew had taped the fracture and loaded the mice anyway. In the freezing temperatures high over the Atlantic, however, the mice had eaten their way through the tape and then found their way up into the warmer passenger cabin. In the ensuing pandemonium, the chairman was said to have sank deeply into his seat (Useem, 1984, p. 21).

Fifth, company executives can sometimes surprise, making access far easier than expected. Paul Hirsch in a personal communication relates an account of complaining to a gathering of corporate executives visiting his university about their unwillingness to allow researchers to roam over their terrain. Several weeks later he began receiving telephone calls from the offices of other company executives asking when he would be coming to interview them. It seems that one of those hearing the complaint had subsequently contacted a set of executives and asked them to participate in a study not yet fully launched.

Sixth, for many research questions, there can be no alternative to depth investigation. The information required to address the research questions may be too hidden or scattered to permit extraction through any means other than extensive personal digging. It may be too convoluted to permit numeric coding, and it may be too complex to allow adequate characterization through only quantitative methods. A combination of data sources and research strategies can usually overcome these problems, resulting in a richer account than if only a single source or strategy were employed. The absence of depth, qualitative information from the combined approach runs the risk of generating an organizational portrait only partially completed, more a line drawing and less the complete canvass.

Finally, the experience of listening to company executives describing their worlds can help build a useful framework for developing subsequent research questions, whatever the method of approach. My most recent study of company relations with investors, for instance, has proven invaluable for evolving three subsequent studies, one focused on pension funds (the largest single type of institutional investor), another of strategic-business units (a corporate form that has emerged partly in response to investor pressures), and a third on executive compensation (a topic of great concern to both managers and investors). Although one of these studies will again largely rely upon insider interviewing and observation, the other two will draw upon several quantitative data sets. None could have been developed as far and as fast without understanding that corporate staffs occasionally find amusement in executives follies and other facts of corporate life that could only be known if personally witnessed.

# References

Blinder, A. S. (1991). Why are prices sticky? Preliminary results from an interview study. *American Economic Review, 81*(2), 89-96.

Charkham, J. (1994). *Keeping good company: A study of corporate governance in five countries.* New York: Oxford University Press.

Doeringer, P. B., Christensen, K., Flynn, P. M., Hall, D. T., Katz, H. C., Keefe, J. H., Ruhm, C. J., Sum, A. M., & Useem, M. (1991). *Turbulence in the American workplace.* New York: Oxford University Press.

Friedman, S. D., & Singh, H. (1989). CEO succession and stockholder reaction: The influence of organizational context and event content. *Academy of Management Journal, 32,* 718-744.

Gordon, R. J. (1991). Discussion on "Why are prices sticky?" *American Economic Review, 81*(2), 98-100.

*Hoover's handbook of American business.* (Annual editions). Austin: Reference Press.

Johnson, A. S., & Linden, F. (1992). *Availability of a quality workforce.* New York: Conference Board.

Lawler, E. E., III, Mohrman, S. A., & Ledford, G. E., Jr. (1992). *Employee involvement and total quality management: Practices and results in Fortune 1000 companies.* San Francisco: Jossey-Bass.

Mirvis, P. H. (Ed.). (1993). *Building the competitive workforce: Investing in human capital for corporate success.* New York: John Wiley.

Shiller, R. J. (1991). Discussion on "Why are prices sticky?" *American Economic Review, 81*(2), 97-98.

*Standard and Poor's 500 guide.* (Annual editions). New York: McGraw-Hill.

Useem, M. (1984). *The inner circle: Large corporations and the rise of business political activity in the U.S. and U.K.* New York: Oxford University Press.

Useem, M. (1989). *Liberal education and the corporation: The hiring and advancement of college graduates.* Hawthorne, NY: Aldine de Gruyter.

Useem, M. (1993a). *Executive defense: Shareholder power and corporate reorganization.* Cambridge, MA: Harvard University Press.

Useem, M. (1993b). Management commitment and company policies on education and training. *Human Resource Management Journal, 32,* 411-434.

Useem, M. (Forthcoming). *The new investor capitalism.* New York: Basic Books.

Useem, M., Bowman, E. H., Irvine, C., & Myatt, J. (1993). U.S. investors look at corporate governance in the 1990s. *European Management Journal, 11*(June), 175-189.

Useem, M., & Kutner, S. I. (1986). Corporate contributions to culture and the arts: The organization of giving, and the influence of the chief executive officer and other firms on company contributions in Massachusetts. In P. DiMaggio (Ed.), *Nonprofit organizations in the production and distribution of culture* (pp. 93-112). New York: Oxford University Press.

*3*

# Fielding Hot Topics in Cool Settings

## The Study of Corporate Ethics

PETER CLEARY YEAGER
KATHY E. KRAM

## Introduction

Traditionally, the sociology of deviancy—including criminology—has concentrated its research on the offending of nonelite and/or dependent populations and on the bureaucracies created to manage them,

AUTHORS' NOTE: We gratefully acknowledge both the Human Resources Policy Institute at Boston University and the Amsterdam Foundation for providing the funding and encouragement that made this research possible. We are also grateful for the excellent contributions of our research associates in this endeavor: Maria-Paz Avery, Wendy Handler, James Hunt, Kathleen Jordan, Jeanne Leidtka, and Gary Reed. In addition, we are indebted to many colleagues, executives, and other professionals who have graciously contributed valuable ideas and feedback at various stages of the work: Chris Argyris, Lloyd Baird, John Braithwaite, Dave Brown, John Fleming, Fred Foulkes, Ken Goodpaster, Tim Hall, Don Handler, Zeba Hyder, Steve Kerr, Alan Wertheimer, Ralph Kilmann, Harvey Kram, George Labovitz, Mark Leach, Barry Leskin, Steve Levin, Meryl Louis, Murray Melbin, Phil Mirvis, Henry Morgan, Marty Moser, Jim Post, Jim Rosenwald, John Russell, Barbara Toffler, Michael Useem, and Jim Waters. We also benefited from the advice and counsel of several anonymous reviewers. Finally, Yeager owes a debt of gratitude to Harvard University's Program in Ethics and the Professions for providing both the stimulation and the opportunity to more deeply pursue this research.

e.g., prisons and mental hospitals. Sociologists have seldom undertaken inside studies of deviancy in elite organizations, such as corporations and the upper level government agencies that monitor them.[1] Indeed, Perrow (1972, pp. 197-199) noted a general tendency in sociology to study "trivial" organizations in industry and government rather than dominant ones, and sociologists have continued to urge the field to greater research efforts on the latter to improve both organizational and general social theory (cf. Clark, 1988; Kanter, 1980).[2]

Even the growing stream of sociological research on corporate law-breaking has thus far not included close, systematic study of the relevant organizational contexts. Instead, these studies have taken one of three forms: statistical examinations of the financial and structural correlates of offending as determined in the public record (e.g., Clinard & Yeager, 1980; Clinard, Yeager, Brissette, Petrashek, & Harries, 1979; Simpson, 1986, 1987), case studies of specific illegal events as recorded in public records and by investigative journalists (e.g., Geis, 1967; Mokhiber, 1988), and surveys of business executives' and managers' attitudes and behaviors regarding ethics and law (e.g., Clinard, 1983; Zey-Ferrell & Ferrell, 1982; Zey-Ferrell, Weaver, & Ferrell, 1979). Although sociologists have drawn a number of tentative conclusions regarding the roles of organizational cultures and structures in the production of business deviancy, we have neither adequately developed nor tested these arguments through the requisite fieldwork in the very settings they purport to describe.[3]

In key respects, the continuing imbalance in organizational research reflects formidable barriers to access to elite organizations. These barriers reside in the organizations' interests and purposes and, arguably, in some concerns of researchers. The organizational resistance to research by outsiders is rooted in the bureaucratic "instinct" to protect against intrusion into potentially sensitive matters and the unproductive use of valuable managerial time. For their part, academic sociologists may avoid this research for fear that it will compromise their scientific aims. As Whyte (1986, p. 556) has recently noted: "In general, social scientists have refrained from linking research directly with action. We have been afraid that our involvement in action will contaminate the scientific basis of our research. Therefore, we have remained on the sidelines, playing the role of professional experts who could tell people what to do if only we were asked."[4]

The purpose of this article is to describe our own efforts to overcome such obstacles in pursuing sensitive and highly intrusive research in powerful organizations. Our experiences suggest not only that access for such research may be successfully negotiated but also that the careful combination of basic and applied purposes can produce richer data and thereby improve the science.

## A Study of Corporate Ethics: The Research Plan

The motivating purpose of our research design was to develop an integrated understanding of the organizational forces and constraints that shape how corporate managers act in situations that pose ethical dilemmas. In other words, we wished to examine the ways in which the structures and (sub)cultures of *specific organizational contexts* variously shape managerial action on the ethical dimension, including the domain of law.

This interest implied two key sampling design criteria. First, it would be necessary to systematically sample and interview managers in key functional areas (e.g., finance, operations, marketing) and at *all levels of responsibility,* from chief executive officer (CEO) down to first line managers. Only such a strategy would enable the careful assessment of the ethical dimension from multiple, key angles of vision within the same firm. Second, it would be important to compare and contrast results from different corporate settings. A comparative case study approach would allow us to develop hypotheses regarding the various roles of industry and organizational features in shaping managers' behavior. Taken together, these approaches would allow us to determine whether there were systematic differences by managerial position in the perception and handling of dilemmas, and which features of organizational design, environment, and culture appeared to account for such variation.

Early on we decided to choose our research sites from the banking and high technology industries, both because they are key to the nation's future economic health and because they were experiencing substantial uncertainty or "turbulence" in their respective markets during the 1980s, a condition that often highlights ethical tensions in corporate management (cf. Clinard & Yeager, 1980; Staw & Szwajkowski, 1975). In addition, corporations in these two industries—as illustrated in the two companies ultimately examined—often manifest important differences in their organizational structures, cultures, and management practices. This variation would permit the development of hypotheses regarding the effects of organizational forms and belief systems on managers' ethical judgments.

Our research interests also required the use of clinical field methods, in particular the use of intensive, semi-structured interviews.[5] We intended the research to be largely an inductive enterprise reflecting a grounded theory approach (Glaser & Strauss, 1967); we wanted to develop propositions on the basis of managers' own accounts of dilemmatic situations rather than impose any firm theoretical constructions on either the nature of managerial morality or its social contexts.

In order to get at managers' conceptions of the ethical dimension of their work, and of the organizational features potentially shaping it, we designed a lengthy interview process involving each manager in three to four hours of discussion spread over two sittings within a 2- to 3-week period. To build rapport prior to raising sensitive questions regarding the respondent's moral dilemmas and the company's role in them, the first interview began with a series of questions on the individual's work history and perceptions of the company culture and practices (e.g., reward systems, key corporate values). Then the interview moved to in-depth consideration of a difficult decision the manager had recently made or implemented in which the right thing to do was either not clear, not easily implemented, or contradicted by a company directive or policy.[6] Here we were concerned with the features of the situation that made it difficult and with the manager's thinking and behavior (e.g., whom did she consult in making the decision) in resolving it. The second interview began with detailed consideration of a second difficult situation that the manager chose to discuss and then turned to an exploration of the extent to which three "typical" ethical dilemmas (described in scenarios we had prepared to represent various situations in the companies' respective industries) occurred and the concerns they generated. Finally, we asked a series of questions about the individual's personal background and influences that shaped her own values.

In sum, the research design was very intrusive in two ways: it required substantial commitments of management time on the part of both the company leadership and individual managers, and it probed for material that is typically highly sensitive for both individuals and organizations. Moreover, to faithfully capture the complexities and nuances of managers' accounts, we intended to tape record as much of the interview material as we might be allowed. To overcome these barriers to entry, it would clearly be necessary to present the proposed study as one having significant implications for improving management but not posing substantial risks of harm or disruption.

## Fielding the Research

Our efforts to negotiate these barriers stand in contrast to those of the two earlier studies that addressed aspects of managerial ethics *in situ,* Dalton's *Men Who Manage* (1959) and Jackall's *Moral Mazes* (1988). Although Dalton's interests did not focus on ethics *per se* (he was concerned with the relations between formal and informal processes in management), he—like Jackall (for whom ethics was key)—pursued highly intrusive investigations in corporations and found it necessary to configure the research in various ways in order to manage the natural resistance to it.

Neither investigator gained access through the formal permission of the organizations' leaderships. Dalton employed covert methods of field research; he collected much of his data while employed in two of the four firms he studied (1959, pp. 2, 278). After having been refused access by 36 companies before successfully arranging his sites, Jackall (1988, pp. 13-16, 205-206) gained access to his three principal sites largely through chance connections that led to "well-placed" executives vouching for his research to colleagues.

Both of these investigators suggested that corporate leaderships would not permit such research on its own terms. Dalton did not even attempt to propose his research to top management, noting that "I have seen other researchers do this and have watched higher managers set the scene and limit the inquiry to specific areas—outside management proper—as though the problem existed in a vacuum" (1959, p. 275). In a similar vein, Jackall concludes on the basis of his struggle to gain access that "managers can afford to give approbation *only to studies that officially are on a short leash* and that can be publicly defended with the vocabularies of justification normally at hand in the corporation" (1988, pp. 13-14; emphasis added).

Dalton and Jackall also found it necessary to use deception to conduct the research, in quite large measure in Dalton's study and in a much more mild form in Jackall's. For example, Dalton not only conducted much of his research covertly as an employee of two companies, he also had inside confederates provoke specific sorts of conversations among unknowing employees while Dalton—appearing to be involved in unrelated activities in another part of the room—secretly observed and took notes. He basically defends the technique as unobtrusive and harmless (1959, pp. 276-277). For his part, Jackall found it necessary to have his research represented as something rather different from what he actually intended, at least in his two principal sites. Having been turned away from numerous sites because of managers' resistance to a study of their ethics, he finally gained access to his first site after reformulating his proposal in a way that "recast the moral issues of managerial work as issues of public relations." On this basis managers began to vouch internally for his study "on their perception that I already grasped the most salient aspect of managerial morality as managers themselves see it—that is, how their values and ethics appear in the public eye" (1988, p. 15). For his second site, he also gained access to managerial networks on a "voucher" basis, this time "with the active assistance of [an] executive who officially and publicly had framed my access as a narrow technical study" (1988, p. 15).

In partial contrast to these experiences, we found it possible to negotiate access at the highest corporate levels without compromising our plan to study business ethics or misleading executives and managers about the basic nature of the investigation. This was a consequence of having broadened the scope of the research to encompass a study of espoused corporate values (including those of an ethical nature) and the extent to which these are realized in practice (see below). Here we hoped to increase the project's attractiveness to corporate leaderships' purposes, while retaining our own interests in the nature of ethical decision making. But two caveats remain in order here. First, the utility of this technique will likely vary with such factors as companies' changing market, regulatory, and public relations climates, and with their internal corporate cultures, including whether human resource management issues have high priority.

Second, because our "broadening" technique included the reduction of potentially inflammatory ethics language to both describe the research and ask questions of interviewees (in letters of introduction, we spoke of value conflicts and difficult decisions), and because we did not assert our interests in the ethical dimension as our *primary* purpose, we too engaged in an element of deception. Morally, any such deception requires justification, and we believe such justification exists for this project (although we shall not develop it here). In any event, this research technique arguably minimized the deceptive element. If this is so, it comprises a strong collateral benefit in addition to the design's efficiency at generating access to corporate sites.

**Overcoming Organizational Barriers:**
**Framing the Research**

As indicated in the first section, the way in which the research issues are framed is key to the ability to gain formal access to powerful organizational settings. The research must have an identifiable "payoff" for the organization, and it must be presented in terms neither threatening to the organization's purpose nor foreign to its culture. During the design phase of our research, 1984-85, the challenge was precisely how to meet these requirements. Along the way, we found it necessary to make a key adjustment in the way in which we would present the project to potential sites.

Initially, we had planned to present it simply as a study of "Ethical Decision-making in Corporate Life," focusing specifically on the ways that corporations shape managers' handling of ethical dilemmas through both their organizational structures and their "ethical climates." Our hope was that this direct approach would appeal to companies interested in assessing the ethical domain of their cultures, if nothing else so as to develop policies to avoid publicly embarrassing revelations of misdeeds such as major companies like General Dynamics, General Electric, and E. F. Hutton had experienced during the early months of 1985. Indeed, that spring *The New York Times* published a major story suggesting that a "white collar crime wave" was plaguing the country, and a New York Times/CBS News poll found that most Americans believed that such wrongdoing was common in business. It seemed reasonable to suppose that some companies might wish to engage in research that could improve ethical decision making of managers and the firm's public image.

By the summer of 1985, however, we had been warned off this approach. Experts with ongoing consulting and academic research experience in corporations strongly advised us that such labels as "ethical judgments" and "ethical climates" constituted warning flags for most corporations. They told us that corporations are highly unlikely to permit unknown outsiders to undertake an assessment of their corporate ethics, either because of their sense that such academic research would be simply judgmental or because they feared damaging disclosure of sensitive corporate activities and information.

We redesigned both our approach and our interview guide. Instead of focusing on "ethical dilemmas" and "ethical decision making," we refocused the research in terms of companies' interest in managing the value dimensions of their cultures, in particular their value conflicts, and in terms of how such conflicts might impede the reaching of corporate goals (e.g., efficiency, growth, productivity). The final interview guide ranged widely over such matters as managers' understandings of the companies' key values and the extent to which they were realized in practice, the operation of corporate reward systems, and dissatisfactions with the company and/or their individual positions.

The focus on "value conflicts" logically encompasses conflicts of an ethical nature, although it is not limited to these (e.g., managers may also experience conflicts between such *business* values as near-term profitability, on one hand, and research and development expenditures, on the other). Thus the study lent itself simultaneously to the interests of corporate leaderships in assessing various aspects of their corporate cultures—such as whether key business values were understood and implemented down the ranks—and to ours in analyzing the role of organizational factors in shaping managers' perceptions and handling of ethical dilemmas. At various points, the interview process explicitly elicited managers' conceptions and handling of *ethical* conflicts at work. For example, there were a number of questions about the ethical climate of the firm, including whether the company maintained any unethical practices in the respondent's view and whether the manager had ever felt pressured to compromise her values to meet company expectations. Enlarging the scope of the investigation had the effect of "trading" the collection of some data not originally considered essential to our goals (but which became quite useful; see below) for the greater likelihood that business leaders would find the study both of practical interest and less intimidating.

Our written materials of invitation to responsible corporate officials (vice presidents for administration/personnel/human resources and presidents/CEOs) emphasized the pragmatic aspects of the research for corporate purposes. In describing our purposes generally, we wrote of developing an "understanding of how large organizations' structures and practices affect managers' perception of the role of values in their decision-making, and how managers make decisions in situations that pose value conflicts for them." In more applied terms, we proposed that the research offered the opportunity "to develop organizational strategies for more effective management of the value components in decision making, so that decisions down the [managerial] line are consistent with corporate policies, goals and code of ethics." In suggesting the applied value of the research we also emphasized the alignment of the study's purposes with the interests of our funding agency, the Human Resources Policy Institute at Boston University, which is largely composed of corporate executives concerned with current issues in human resources management. We anticipated that this association would lend added legitimacy to our arguments for the practical utility of the research.

It is also important that such research projects be couched in terms familiar to the organizational environments one is approaching. In this regard, our emphasis on *values* allowed us to link our work to the relatively recent business and academic preoccupation with corporate cultures. Stimulated by such developments as increasingly powerful Japanese competition and growing demands by—in particular—white collar employees for greater autonomy and job enrichment, the concept of a corporate culture was legitimated as relevant to business success only in the 1980s. Not long ago, American business executives viewed such ideas as little more than the conceptual fantasies of impractical academics. But the publication of the best selling *In Search of Excellence* (Peters & Waterman, 1982) and other books on the subject (e.g., Davis, 1984; Deal & Kennedy, 1982; Kilmann, Saxton, & Serpa, 1985; Schein, 1985) contributed to widespread acceptance in the corporate world of the argument that organizational culture was not only important to business success but was also *manageable.* Our access to corporate research settings benefited from these newly salient managerial concerns.

### Selling the Research:
### The Overlapping of Interests

We contacted 12 corporations—five banks and seven high technology companies—before securing our two research sites. Typically, our approaches were to senior vice presidents or chief executive officers of the companies. A number of the companies showed initial interest but declined after learning more of the details of the proposed research.

The reasons corporate officials offered for declining participation varied and were often rather vague. For example, after showing initial interest in our mailed proposal, the CEO of a large bank declined upon hearing our more detailed presentation, saying that "it was not the right time" for such a study. When a computer company declined, its representative said it had just completed an internal study and did not wish to undertake another. Another company's representative indicated that although his corporation had been engaged in an "ethics push" until recently, it had now turned its attention to other, market-based concerns. Only one corporate spokesperson openly suggested that the company's rejection was due to the sensitive nature of the research focus: In the glare of major media attention, this major U.S. bank had just been prosecuted for substantial violations of the federal Bank Secrecy Act and could not tolerate any additional outside investigators (as federal regulators were then intensively scrutinizing the company).

Although the often vaguely stated rejections do not lend themselves to easy interpretation, we assume that they were generally due either to the study's intrusiveness (management time, data sensitivity), to companies' relatively low interest in the ethical domain relative to their concern with market success, or—perhaps more likely—to a combination of the two. For example, the bank CEO who found it "not the right time" argued variously that he couldn't lend his managers' time to this research as they were tied up with present efforts to manage a number of recent mergers the company had undergone (e.g., working to integrate all the new relationships and procedures entailed in such mergers) and that corporate policies and the counsel of superiors were generally adequate to manage the few potential value conflicts that might develop in his very large organization. At the level of statement as well as in their apparent contradictory relation to each other, these reasons suggest that both the study's intrusiveness and relatively low priority concern for the ethical domain explain his resistance.

Ultimately, however, we were finally able to "sell" the research to two promising corporate sites by mid-1986, one each in the high technology and banking industries. The high technology company, which we pseudonymously refer to as Jaycor, Inc., is a multinational manufacturer of components, employs several thousand persons, and has annual sales of several hundred million dollars, qualifying it for listing in the *Fortune* 1000 largest U.S. industrials. The bank, referred to as Williams National, is a large regional institution that employs several thousand persons and has assets of several billion dollars.

We were able to gain this access with greater dispatch than we had expected because of the way in which our research frame coincided with the companies' current senses of their self-interests. In each company, top management's policy interests overlapped our research agenda without being identical to it.

In neither corporation was the executive leadership interested in the study of ethics *per se*. Instead, the top managements had the very pragmatic concern with whether key corporate values they were empha- sizing—e.g., quality, innovation, and decentralization in the manufac- turing firm; productivity and entrepreneurship in the bank—were being successfully communicated and internalized at lower ranks. They were concerned about whether there existed any unforeseen gaps between the espoused and implemented values in the culture, or any unintended contradictions between two or more of the espoused values themselves (e.g., quality control and productivity). In general, the leaderships were principally interested in the relation between achieving these values and the financial success of the firm. The concern to manage their respective corporate cultures was heightened by ongoing environmental turbu- lence. In both companies top management was endeavoring to ensure that the corporate culture was well matched to changing market condi- tions: in high technology those resulting from increasing foreign com- petition, in banking those resulting from deregulation combined with growing rates of loan failure. As our study was sufficiently complex to assess such matters, it proved attractive to these corporate leaders.

Thus, in these two cases, the ethical content of the investigation appeared to be of relatively little interest, but neither was it a barrier. In this connection it is noteworthy that we were able to implement our interview guide precisely as we had designed it. We showed the lengthy interview guide only to our "access" liaison person in each company, the vice president for human resources. These executives asked for no modifications in content whatsoever, despite the interview's straight- forward reference to ethical matters in several places. They also agreed not to show it even to their superiors, because we would later interview many of them, including the CEOs. In both cases, the CEO approved the research simply on the basis of the vice president's strong endorse- ment and our own brief presentations to them.

But if we had achieved official entrée to these two sites, we had yet to successfully engage the participation of managers *qua* interviewees. This too necessitated a strategic approach to minimize potential partici- pants' resistance to the research.

### Entering the Field: Relations With Managers

Upon gaining, formal permission to conduct the research in the two organizations,[7] we confronted the dual challenges of generating support for the study within the organizational culture and obtaining individual managers' agreements to participate. In this section, we describe the procedures we used to accomplish these tasks and the additional benefits they brought in terms of enriching the data.

### Liaison Activities

Consistent with the organizational development and action research literature (e.g., Alderfer, 1980; Alderfer & Brown, 1975; Argyris, 1970; Beer, 1980), we developed a number of liaison relationships with internal groups of managers early on in the fieldwork in both sites. We hoped these groups would act as internal advocates for the study and provide guidance on the approach to individual managers when soliciting their participation as interviewees. In addition, the groups served as a useful microcosm of the organization as a whole, offering insights into the cultures and subcultures of the companies.

Our first step at each company was to request the opportunity to form an ongoing liaison group of managers representing the three levels of management we would study (top, middle, and lower). In each organization the vice president of human resources invited managers from the divisions and managerial levels of interest to compose the research liaison groups. In our initial presentations to the two groups we outlined our research objectives and the primary issue areas we would cover in the interviews, but we did not share the interview guide or specific interview questions with group members. These two groups, which contained between six and eight members apiece, proved valuable in three ways.

First, they provided additional internal support and a wider, more "democratic" basis of legitimacy for the project. This was a particularly important function in a situation in which the corporate leadership was endorsing a very intrusive study seeking sensitive information from subordinates. Moreover, as others have noted, the quality of rapport in individual interviews tends to reflect that achieved with members of such liaison groups and others involved in the entry phase of the research (cf. Alderfer, 1980; Argyris, 1970; Beer, 1980). The quality of research entry into a site shapes the quality of the data collected (e.g., willingness to report sensitive information), both by the nature of the legitimacy thus secured and by the additional (related) processes discussed below.

Second, the liaison groups were instrumental in helping to ensure that our presentation would prove acceptable and inviting to potential interviewees. For example, the groups advised us about what we should emphasize in letters and phone calls to managers selected for interviews in order to improve the chances that they would agree to participate, and whom to approach in the separate corporate units (such as regional offices) to arrange local support for the research. The group members also agreed to be identified in our letters of solicitation as willing to answer questions about the research that managers might have. Some managers ultimately interviewed reported that they had, in fact, contacted a liaison group member for more information (and likely, some assurances about our purposes) before consenting to participate.

Third, though we did not ask them to serve as interviewees, liaison group members were quite important data sources in the research. They offered important insights into key components of the corporate cultures and subcultures in their companies, as well as background information on some of the major issues facing their respective organizations. This preliminary "briefing" information gave us something of an "insider's" status while interviewing, enabling us to engage managers on an informed basis about salient corporate values, priorities, and issues.

In addition to these specially constituted liaison groups, we also made several other early presentations to existing groups of managers and executives (e.g., the top executive team, the human resources advisory committee), again largely for purposes of enhancing the internal legitimacy of the investigation prior to the interviewing phase. We promised all of these groups copies of the final feedback report we would prepare for the company and the interviewed managers. We intended that the offer of concrete analyses of dilemmas and conflicts in managers' corporate cultures, and specific recommendations for managerial practice, would increase interest in—and commitment to—the research. At the same time, we solicited their responses to our eventual report, asking for corrections, corroboration, and other information that would improve both analytic understanding of the data and the practical utility of the research.

### Managing Interviews, Interviewing Managers

Having gained formal access to the companies and then developed what might be called organizational rapport, it remained for us to access and develop rapport with the manager interviewees. Our approach to prospective interviewees was made by individual letters (see Appendix

A) and follow-up phone calls. To further enhance the likelihood that invited managers would find the project legitimate and agree to participate, each CEO agreed to send a cover letter (Appendix B) that endorsed the research and encouraged managers to take part; in both cases, we drafted the CEO's letter and then he and/or his human resources vice president edited it (but modestly) to fit his own style and views.[8] The letters did not speak of ethics as such but of interest in "difficult situations" and "value conflicts," where "the right thing to do is not clear, or not easily implemented"; the latter phrase is a reasonably workable definition of ethical dilemmas. In addition, the correspondence made the appropriate assurances of anonymity and confidentiality. We noted among other things that no one in the company would see our list of sampled respondents and that the internal feedback report would not contain any details that might identify an individual as the source of the information (because, for example, of its role-specific nature).

In the end, the combination of access strategies proved effective. Of the combined total of 72 managers and executives originally invited to participate in the interview process, only one declined to participate at all, while another completed only the first interview.

In the interview process itself, we carefully designed our study's pivotal question to encourage managers to discuss sensitive ethical issues without appearing to judge them or otherwise intimidate them. Although we used some ethics language here, we avoided emphasizing the concept of ethics *per se* in this phase of the interview. Instead, we posed the issue in the following way:

> I'd like to hear about situations at work in your present position that have been particularly troubling for you. I'd like to hear about *decisions* that you've made or implemented in your current role as manager that have been difficult for you. For example, decisions where you were trying to decide what is the right thing to do, or where you were faced with a value conflict or ethical dilemma that has been difficult to resolve. [Two such decision situations were sought from each respondent.]

The working assumption, proven in the research, was that this relatively nonthreatening request to consider "difficult" or challenging managerial decisions would uncover some fundamental value conflicts in respondents' work, most with moral content (see Kram et al., 1989).[9]

The broadening of our research frame—originally intended to improve our chances at access—arguably improved the analytic value of the research as well. In particular, the broader focus on *value conflicts* appears to have been useful in detecting differential concerns with the ethical dimension (as such) of management by position. (That is, it avoided any tendency to interpret ethics only in terms of "Golden Rule" morality involving largely the effects of one's actions on identifiable others.) In short, there was some tendency for top executives to see conflicts as tensions between strategic imperatives or concerns and to emphasize the key value of the *organization's welfare* in their decisions. On the other hand, lower level managers more often rendered accounts of decisions in terms of their impacts on *individual welfare.* Such variation represents important organizational processes that shape and constrain managerial views of the ethical domain in business (Kram et al., 1989).

By the conclusion of the interviewing process, we had amassed some 250 hours of interview material, about 3½ hours per manager. As other field researchers have found, once involved in the process, most managers enthusiastically engaged in discussing the vexing nature of their responsibilities. Virtually all agreed without question to have the interviews audiotaped, rarely taking us up on the offer to turn the recorders off at any point they wished. In all, we were permitted to tape roughly 98 percent of the interview material.

### *Conclusions: On Merging Science and Action*

The study of "hot topics in cool settings" requires attention to some matters that are not commonly addressed in traditional social science research paradigms. In particular, those conducting the inquiry will typically need to establish an appropriate balance between the objectives of science and social action. They will also need to build and manage collaborative relations with research participants and will often benefit from taking a cross-disciplinary approach to the investigation. In our fieldwork, these techniques broadened our research focus, both enhancing its legitimacy in corporate settings and enriching the quality of the data collected (cf. Argyris, Putnam, & Smith, 1985; Whyte, 1986).

In merging the objectives of science and action, it is essential that we regularly step back and revisit the scholarly objectives and scientific standards of the investigation. With increasing immersion in the field, one can easily lose sight of the importance of particular design decisions, particularly if these tend to conflict with the practical concerns of participating organizations. On several occasions we found it necessary to review decisions about sample size, sampling procedures, and the nature of the feedback report, when members of the liaison groups made suggestions (linked to corporate purposes) that could undermine the scholarly integrity of the study.

It was not necessary, however, to compromise our standards. By broadening the scope of our study, we were able to accommodate the applied concerns of the companies. In addition, our liaison activities within the organizations not only communicated our interest in management's concerns, thus enhancing the project's legitimacy, but also lent us a credibility—a sort of "good faith" posture—that allowed us to deflect suggestions that threatened our research purposes without appearing to be indifferent to participants' views.[10]

Moreover, these access strategies strengthened our data and both broadened and deepened the insights we were able to develop. In effect, we rediscovered the rich relation of praxis between knowledge and human action. On one hand, we found that in managing access we learned much about the organizations, particularly from our conversations with liaison group members and from responses to our internal feedback reports. On the other, our more nuanced appreciation of the various corporate purposes and pressures not only contributed to our scholarly analyses but also enhanced their appeal for practical reforms in the companies; in turn, when such reforms were than attempted in one of our two sites there were new opportunities to study the organizational dynamics of choice and constraint.

In retrospect this project benefited from the interdisciplinary nature of the research team. Not only did the complexity of the research questions demand both macro and micro levels of analysis, but the fieldwork also required attention to a multitude of issues which one set of disciplinary lenses alone could not adequately address. Bringing the perspectives and tools of both sociology and organizational behavior to the project enabled us to consider a wide range of organizational forces in our inquiry and to manage access, data collection, and analytic issues effectively. From the academic sociologist's standpoint, it was particularly important to have the collaboration of a colleague with long experience with applied problems in corporate settings. This was also key to the apparent legitimacy of our concerns and interests in the eyes of management. Finally, along with the benefits of multiple lenses we encountered the challenge of addressing the concerns and meeting the standards of both disciplines. This challenge has consistently enhanced our analytic work by forcing us to make unarticulated assumptions explicit and intellectual arguments clear to sociologists, management scholars, and practicing managers.

None of this is to imply that ours is the only viable method for generating valuable understandings of elite organizations. Depending on circumstances, a number of approaches will have utility, particularly in combination, even without organizational permission. These include analyses of the public record (e.g., court transcripts, legislative hearings, etc.) and snowball samples of organizational members. The latter technique, for example, has been successfully used to study both business ethics (e.g., Leidtka, 1989) and scandal in a government agency (Szasz, 1986).

But we do suggest that in-depth, organizationally based and informed research can also be conducted in powerful bureaucracies, even on highly sensitive topics. Elite organizations in both business and government are particularly likely to host such investigations when they are experiencing crises, whether acute or chronic, market-based (i.e., in competitive relations) or political in nature (e.g., legitimation crises). In these circumstances, the interests of science and action may not only merge but also afford an especially ripe opportunity for research: It is in the situation of crisis that the structures and processes of social organization most vividly manifest themselves. As even large, powerful organizations now regularly experience strong challenges in both politics and markets, the bureaucratic doors may be increasingly open to creative research proposals, with consequent benefit for both theory and practice.

## Notes

1. There have been a few fieldwork based studies of regulatory agencies charged with the social control of business. See for example, Braithwaite (1985), Grabosky and Braithwaite (1986), Hawkins (1983, 1984), Shover, Clelland, and Lynxwiler (1986), and Yeager (1987, 1990). In addition, Braithwaite (1984) and Fisse and Braithwaite (1983) have interviewed top officials in U.S. companies about various aspects of corporate lawbreaking.

2. Although there has been a large imbalance in organizational research there have been a number of noteworthy studies that have very usefully applied qualitative methods (e.g,, interviewing, observation) in relatively powerful corporate organizations. In addition to the research cited in note 1, see also the studies of Jackall (1988), Kanter (1977), and Useem (1984).

3. Jackall's (1988) recent work has made a nice contribution in this regard. We briefly note some aspects of his methodology in the next section. It is also worth noting that researchers in schools of management have a greater record of success in mounting field work in corporate settings, presumably being more willing than most sociologists to contract with managers and organizations for research work of mutual benefit (i.e., for both scholarly and applied purposes). Such researchers have even enjoyed some success in investigating "hot" topics in organizations, such as race relations (e.g., Alderfer & Tucker, 1980; Thomas, 1990), organizational conflict (e.g., Alderfer & Smith, 1982; Brown, 1981), and more recently business ethics (e.g., Derry, 1987; Toffler, 1986; Waters & Bird, 1987). Although these latter studies also demonstrate the potential for meaningful access to corporate settings for such research, they generally have been conducted with samples of "disconnected" managers from different organizations, or with a quite limited subset of managers (e.g., lower level personnel). Thus they have been less intrusive to companies than the "saturation" sampling used in our study and therefore presumably faced less formidable barriers to implementation.

4. In addition, and perhaps rather more speculatively, there arguably exists a sort of culture gap between academic sociological researchers and corporate elites, rooted in the reformist impulse of many of the former and the conservative, self-protective instincts of many of the latter. The consequence is mutual suspicion of the other's motives and purposes and, we suggest, even psychological discomfort on the part of many sociologists at the prospect of dealing with powerful research subjects.

5. We define clinical methods as those aspects of the research that require the direct involvement of the researchers with the individuals and social systems being studied, inquiry that favors depth over breadth in any single investigation, and the flexibility to change theory or method in response to experiences in the field as the study unfolds (cf. Berg & Smith, 1985; Schein, 1988). Clinical methods include interviewing and participant observation strategies that invite active participation and considerable self-disclosure on the part of those being studied. For these to be carried out meaningfully, researchers must engage in an ongoing process of self-reflection to ensure that personal biases are examined and managed throughout the investigation.

6. We define the ethical dimension of management as the consideration—implicitly or explicitly—of right and wrong in managerial decisions and actions that affect other persons. Thus ethical conflicts or dilemmas occur when managers experience conflicting duties and obligations. They therefore include a wide range of situations in which what *ought* to happen—in relationships with customers, employees, creditors, stockholders, suppliers, distributors, neighbors, and law—is vexing. (See Kram, Yeager, & Reed, 1989.) As Dalton (1959, p. 243) long ago suggested, such managerial dilemmas are not only common but also are part of the very "stuff" of management: "All decisions imply choice and can therefore be regarded as moral acts. But when decisions directly involve others, as in organizations, and are made in an atmosphere of uncertainty, they become acutely moral."

7. We had originally planned to study two firms in each of the two industries, rather than one. However, we reduced the design when we discovered that the development of a site—from negotiating permission to completing the feedback report for the participants—involved roughly a year's work in each.

8. The presidents' letters raise another ethical question for research, in this case the problem of possible coercion of subordinates. The problem is as difficult as it is subtle. On one hand, it seems important to demonstrate to sampled managers that the research is

supported by the corporate leadership and therefore has *prima facie* legitimacy. On the other hand, it is possible that some managers will experience such letters as pressuring their participation, an undesirable result both for research ethics and data validity. In the end, we received little indication that this had occurred.

9. We are grateful to Chris Argyris for originally suggesting this approach to us after our long consideration of the most effective way to get at the sensitive ethical issues in management. In our interviews, managers spoke thoughtfully of ethical dilemmas ranging from whether to fire a long-standing and loyal employee who was now performing poorly, to situations involving the misaccounting of very large sums as profits, corporate espionage, and the compromising of quality standards.

10. For example, our liaison at the bank, the vice president of Human Resources, argued that one of our scenarios of banking dilemmas (pushing customers to buy products not in their best interests) was meaningless because "it never happens." Nonetheless, we insisted on its research merits and found that branch managers commonly agreed they were pressured to engage in such activity; he nonetheless continued to deny this, confirming in a rich way some of our other findings regarding the inadmissibility of ethical dilemmas in work settings. (See Kram et al., 1989.)

## References

Alderfer, C. P. (1980). The methodology of organizational diagnosis. *Professional Psychology, 11*, 459-468.

Alderfer, C. P., & Brown, L. D. (1975). *Learning from changing: Organizational diagnosis and development.* Beverly Hills, CA: Sage.

Alderfer, C. P., & Smith, K. K. (1982). Studying intergroup relations embedded in organizations. *Administrative Science Quarterly, 27*, 35-65.

Alderfer, C. P., & Tucker, R. (1980). Diagnosing race relations in organizations. *Journal of Applied Behavioral Sciences, 20*, 35-65.

Argyris, C. (1970). *Intervention theory and method: A behavioral science view.* Reading, MA: Addison-Wesley.

Argyris, C., Putnam, R., & Smith, D. M. (1985). *Action science.* San Francisco: Jossey-Bass.

Beer, M. (1980). *Organization change and development.* Santa Monica, CA: Goodyear Publishing.

Berg, D. N., & Smith, K. K. (Eds.). (1985). *Exploring clinical methods for social research.* Beverly Hills, CA: Sage.

Braithwaite, J. (1984). *Corporate crime in the pharmaceutical industry.* London: Routledge and Kegan Paul.

Braithwaite, J. (1985). *To punish or persuade: The enforcement of coal mine safety.* Albany: State University of New York Press.

Brown, L. D. (1981). *Managing conflict at organizational interfaces.* Reading, MA: Addison-Wesley.

Clark, J. (1988). Presidential address on the importance of our understanding organizational conflict. *The Sociological Quarterly, 29*(2), 149-161.

Clinard, M. B. (1983). *Corporate ethics and crime: The role of middle management.* Beverly Hills, CA: Sage.

Clinard, M. B., & Yeager, P. C. (1980). *Corporate crime.* New York: The Free Press.

Clinard, M. B., Yeager, P. C. Brissette, J. M., Petrashek, D., & Harries, E. (1979). *Illegal corporate behavior.* Washington, D.C.: National Institute of Justice, U.S. Department of Justice.

Dalton, M. (1959). *Men who manage.* New York: John Wiley.

Davis, S. M. (1984). *Managing corporate cultures.* Cambridge, MA: Ballinger.

Deal, T. E., & Kennedy, A. A. (1982). *Corporate cultures: The rites and rituals of corporate life.* Reading, MA: Addison-Wesley.

Derry, R. (1987). Moral reasoning in work-related conflicts. In W. C. Frederick (Ed.), *Research in corporate social performance and policy* (Vol. 9, pp. 25-49). Greenwich, CT: JAI Press.

Fisse, G., & Braithwaite, J. (1983). *The impact of publicity on corporate offenders.* Albany: State University of New York Press.

Geis, G. (1967). The heavy electrical equipment antitrust cases of 1971. In M. B. Clinard & R. Quinney (Eds.), *Criminal behavior systems* (pp. 139-150). New York: Holt, Rinehart & Winston.

Glaser, B. G., & Strauss, A. L. (1967). *The discovery of grounded theory: Strategies for qualitative research.* Chicago: Aldine.

Grabosky, P., & Braithwaite, J. (1986). *Of manners gentle: Enforcement strategies of Australian business regulatory agencies.* Melbourne: Oxford University Press.

Hawkins, K. (1983). Bargain and bluff: Compliance strategy and deterrence in the enforcement of regulation. *Law and Policy Quarterly, 5,* 35-73.

Hawkins, K. (1984). *Environment and enforcement: Regulation and the social definition of pollution.* New York: Oxford University Press.

Jackall, R. (1988). *Moral mazes: The world of corporate managers.* New York: Oxford University Press.

Kanter, R. M. (1977). *Men and women of the corporation.* New York: Basic Books.

Kanter, R. M. (1980, August). *Power and change in and by organizations: Setting intellectual directions for organizational analysis.* Paper presented at the annual meeting of the American Sociological Association.

Kilmann, R. H., Saxton, M. J., & Serpa, R. (Eds.). (1985). *Gaining control of the corporate culture.* San Francisco: Jossey-Bass.

Kram, K. E., Yeager, P. C., & Reed, G. E. (1989). Decisions and dilemmas: The ethical dimension in the corporate context. In J. E. Post (Ed.), *Research in corporate social performance and policy* (Vol. 11, pp. 21-54). Greenwich, CT: JAI Press.

Leidtka, J. M. (1989). Managerial values and corporate decision-making: An empirical analysis of value congruence in two organizations. In J. E. Post (Ed.), *Research in corporate social performance and policy* (Vol. 11, pp. 55-91). Greenwich, CT: JAI Press.

Mokhiber, R. (1988). *Corporate crime and violence: Big business power and the abuse of the public trust.* San Francisco: Sierra Club Books.

Perrow, C. (1972). *Complex organizations: A critical essay.* Glenview, IL: Scott, Foresman.

Peters, T. J., & Waterman, R. H., Jr. (1982). *In search of excellence: Lessons from America's best-run companies.* New York: Harper & Row.

Post, J. E., & Andrews, P. N. (1982). Case research in corporation and society studies. In L. Preston (Ed.), *Research in corporate social performance and policy* (Vol. 4, pp. 1-33). Greenwich, CT: JAI Press.

Schein, E. H. (1985). *Organizational culture and leadership.* San Francisco: Jossey-Bass.

Schein, E. H. (1988). *The clinical perspective in fieldwork.* Newbury Park, CA: Sage.

Shover, N., Clelland, D. A., & Lynxwiler, J. (1986). *Enforcement or negotiation: Constructing a regulatory bureaucracy.* Albany: State University of New York Press.

Simpson, S. S. (1986). The decomposition of antitrust. *American Sociological Review, 51*(December), 859-875.

Simpson, S. S. (1987). Cycles of illegality: Antitrust violations in corporate America. *Social Forces, 65*(June), 943-963.

Staw, B. M., & Szwajkowski, E. (1975). The scarcity-munificence component of organizational environments and the commission of illegal acts. *Administrative Science Quarterly, 20*(September), 345-354.

Szasz, A. (1986). The process and significance of political scandals: A comparison of Watergate and the "Sewergate" episode at the Environmental Protection Agency. *Social Problems, 33*(February), 202-217.

Thomas, D. A. (1990). The impact of race on managers' experiences of developmental relationships: An intraorganizational study. *Journal of Organizational Behavior, 11*(6), 479-492.

Toffler, B. L. (1986). *Tough choices: Managers talk ethics.* New York: John Wiley.

Useem, M. (1984). *The inner circle.* New York: Oxford University Press.

Waters, J. A., & Bird, F. (1987). The moral dimension of organizational culture. *Journal of Business Ethics, 6*, 15-22.

Whyte, W. F. (1986). The uses of social science research. *American Sociological Review, 51*(August), 555-563.

Yeager, P. C. (1987). Structural bias in regulatory law enforcement: The case of the U.S. Environmental Protection Agency. *Social Problems, 34*(October), 330-344.

Yeager, P. C. (1990). *The limits of law: The public regulation of private pollution.* New York: Cambridge University Press.

Zey-Ferrell, M., & Ferrell, O. C. (1982). Role-set configuration and opportunity as predictors of unethical behavior in organizations. *Human Relations, 35*, 587-604.

Zey-Ferrell, M., Weaver, K. M., & Ferrell, O. C. (1979). Predicting unethical behavior among marketing practitioners. *Human Relations, 32*, 557-569.

# Appendix A:
## Letter of Invitation to
## Managers Selected for Interviews

October 14, 1986

Dear Mr./Ms._____

We are writing this letter to invite you to participate in a new research project concerned with the role of values in managerial decision-making. In particular, our research team would like to understand the factors that influence how managers handle difficult situations at work where the right thing to do is not clear, or not easily implemented. We are very pleased that (the Company) is participating in this project (please see accompanying letter from [Company CEO]), and hope that you will find interest in it as well.

There are several topics that we would like to ask you about: your career history and how you got to your current position; your perception of [the Company's] culture and practices; difficult situations that you have faced which may have posed value conflicts for you; your perceptions of the extent to which a range of value dilemmas are encountered by [the Company's] managers; and other life experiences which have influenced the way you handle difficult decisions at work.

In order to cover all of these topics, one member of our research team would like to meet with you twice during the next six weeks. Each meeting will last between one and one half and two hours, and can be scheduled at a time that is convenient for you. In exchange for your time, it is our hope that you will find the opportunity to review your career history, your perceptions of [the Company's] culture and practices, and difficult decisions that you have faced in your managerial role, an enjoyable and valuable experience.

Our plan is to interview [25 or 46] managers in the Company who span first, middle and senior levels of management and who represent several divisions. Invited participants' names have been randomly selected by level and division from a list of management personnel that was given to us by _____, Vice President of Human Resources Planning and Development. To insure complete anonymity and confidentiality for those who are invited to participate in the study, no one within the company will have access to the list of individuals whom we have contacted.

The information that you provide will be kept entirely confidential and your anonymity will be rigorously maintained. This means that only the [four or six] members of our research team will have access to the interview data which will be securely stored in our faculty offices. Feedback of the study results will consist only of GENERAL THEMES that may have implications for management practices at [the Company]. These themes will be reported to those who participate in the study, and to an advisory group of managers from several divisions and levels that [named executives] convened at our request. This group will act as a sounding board for our interpretations of the findings.

One of us will call you in the next week to answer any questions about the study and to see whether you are able to participate. If you would like additional information beforehand, please feel free to call [the vice president] in Human Resources, or a member of the project's advisory group [identified on enclosed list].

We are excited about the potential for this innovative research effort to make significant contributions to organization theory and management practice, and we look forward to talking with you about it.

Sincerely,


Kathy E. Kram, Ph.D.
Project Co-director

Peter C. Yeager, Ph.D
Project Co-director

[Also signed by other members of the research teams]

# Appendix B:
## Sample Letter of Introduction From CEO


September 26, 1986

Dear Colleague:

I would like to inform you about a research project that is about to begin at [the Company]. Managing Values in Corporate Decision-Making is concerned with the roles of values in managerial decision-making and, in particular, the ways managers handle difficult situations within their areas of responsibility.

The study's purpose is quite relevant at this time since we are actively reviewing [the Company's] principles and practices. As the company grows, it is essential to periodically update our espoused principles and to assess the extent to which they are effectively implemented. I believe this research will enhance our efforts to do this.

This study is being directed by Professors Kathy E. Kram and Peter C. Yeager, who are faculty members at Boston University in the School of Management and the Department of Sociology, respectively. I have had the opportunity to talk with both of them about the study, and I am confident that their work will result in valuable insights into how [the Company's] culture and practices influence the ways managers handle a variety of difficult decision-making situations.

The study of [the Company] is part of a larger program of research involving companies in two different industries. The research is funded by the Human Resources Policy Institute at Boston University, a group of corporate executives and academics that sponsors leading edge research that promises to substantially contribute to organizational theory and management practice. We are fortunate to have the opportunity to participate in the study and to benefit from the insights that will develop. Peter and Kathy have carefully designed the study so that the confidentiality and anonymity of all participants will be rigorously maintained. Thus, only GENERAL THEMES will be reported back to the company, and only they and their research assistants will know who has been asked to participate. Any publications that result from the research will not reveal the identities of individuals or companies that have participated. These measures are taken so that those who choose to participate can talk meaningfully about the difficult situations that they have faced, and about their perceptions of how [the Company's] practices have influenced them.

If you find the project's objectives to be relevant and interesting, I hope that you will take the time to participate. I believe that the insights developed from the study will help [the Company] as we seek to continuously improve the management processes of the Company.

Sincerely yours,

*4*

# Using Electronic Media to Support
# Fieldwork in a Corporate Setting

## JOHN P. WORKMAN, JR.

Participant observation has typically called on the fieldworker to get close to those being studied and seek to come to an understanding of how they see the world. As Van Maanen (1988, p. 2) notes, "Fieldwork usually means living with and living like those who are studied." However, when those being studied are geographically dispersed and rely on electronic mail, telephones, faxes, and video conferences in order to communicate with one another, new approaches to fieldwork may be called for. This note, based on nine months of participant observation in a computer systems firm, considers some of the ways in which electronic communication forums may be utilized in a field study.

### Overview of Electronic Media

During the site access negotiations, insiders had informed me that a computer account would be essential for communicating with others

AUTHOR'S NOTE: Financial assistance to offset travel costs associated with the fieldwork was provided by Penn State's Institute for the Study of Business Markets.
NOTE: Originally appeared as a research note under the title "Use of Electronic Media in a Participant Observation Study" in *Qualitative Sociology*, Vol. 15, No. 4, 1992, pp. 419-425.

and thus I was assigned an account which allowed me to access "Zytek's" worldwide computer network from my PC at home. Although there was a broad range of on-line services available (e.g., daily corporate news, new product information, price lists, text of internal publications for the sales force), the services I spent the most time using were the electronic bulletin board system and the electronic mail system (E-mail system). The bulletin boards facilitated discussion among groups of people with common interests while the E-mail system facilitated sending information from one person to another.

The E-mail system, along with the ability to set up distribution lists, allowed for the rapid and widespread dissemination of information within Zytek. For example, one marketing manager had a list of over 1000 Zytek employees that she could forward messages to with less than ten keystrokes. However, this ease of communication also led to a considerable amount of unwanted information on the other end. For example, during the first week of my fieldwork, my sponsor's secretary mentioned that she'd gotten a little behind in handling the mail sent to him and there were over 1500 mail messages in his account. She said he typically received 150 to 200 messages a day, and I frequently ran into people who said they received more than one hundred E-mail messages a day.

In addition to the computer-based communication forums, Zytek also made extensive usage of audio and video conferences. The audio conferences linked individuals or groups by telephone, and the video conferences used satellite communications to either downlink a broadcast or to link two groups using both transmitting and receiving equipment. Audio conferences included phone calls using speaker phones on one or both ends, meetings using speaker phones to allow people at distant locations to take part, and conference calls where people at up to 30 or 40 different locations could take part. Because of the cost of satellite broadcasts, the video conferences were primarily used for large-scale training programs for the sales force or for large product introductions where customers were simultaneously present at dozens of locations. Additionally, many presentations were videotaped, and the corporate libraries had hundreds of videotapes. I viewed several tapes to learn the histories of specific projects and the evolution of some of the marketing strategies. With this overview of the various types of electronic media, I now discuss how this information was used on a daily basis.

## *How the Electronic Media Was Used in the Fieldwork*

Within the first few weeks of the fieldwork, I found people asking me for my electronic mail address and saying they would forward material to me that they thought might be of interest to me. I soon was checking my account several times a day and was finding it an essential part of my fieldwork. In this section, I discuss various ways in which I used the electronic communication system.

### Distribution Lists

My earliest exposure to the E-mail system came in the first week as I started attending the meetings for the projects I was assigned to. The product managers had set up distribution lists with the names and E-mail addresses of people interested in their products and used these distribution lists to announce the time and place for team meetings. These distribution lists were also used to send correspondence that might be of interest to team members, such as "product requirements" and "market requirements," proposed schedules, costs, planned intro-duction strategies, and text for brochures or advertisements. I asked to be placed on the distribution lists for these products and in this way automatically received notification of all team meetings as well as the same documents that team members received. As I started observing activities in other parts of the firm, I also asked to be placed on the distribution lists for these groups.

I was soon receiving an average of five to ten documents per day because of being on these various lists. Some messages were only one or two lines long, simply announcing the time and date of meetings; others were dozens of pages long, providing the full text of marketing or planning documents or asking for detailed information from others. I relied on the E-mail system to keep track of the meetings I was to attend, to learn of the agendas for these meetings, and to receive the written minutes for these meetings. Because I was soon following activities in a range of groups and was not able to attend all meetings, I found the minutes from meetings I did not attend a useful way to keep up with what was going on. I initially downloaded my mail and printed it out at home but soon found this too time consuming and instead routed it to a laser printer at corporate headquarters. In this way, I was able to save and file the thousands of pages of E-mail messages I received.

## Scheduling Interviews

In addition to automatically receiving mail by being on distribution lists, I also used the E-mail system to schedule interviews or to obtain permission to attend various activities. In the first week of the field-work, the vice president sponsoring me had one of his managers write a one-page memo describing my project and asking people to cooperate with me. I kept this memo in my computer account and over the course of the fieldwork sent it to over a hundred people when requesting an interview or asking for permission to attend a meeting.

Because of the geographic dispersion of the Zytek facilities (I visited over 20 facilities), in many cases I made my initial introduction via E-mail. I kept several introductory memos in my account and edited them as needed and forwarded them along with the VP's memo. All of the seven interviews I had with vice presidents at Zytek were arranged by E-mail and typically were set up two or three months in advance. For mid-level managers, it was typically necessary to schedule interviews two or three weeks ahead of time, and many interviews had to be rescheduled (some as many as 4 or 5 times) via E-mail. I typically sent reminders a few days in advance of an interview, and in some cases people asked for a short outline of topics I wanted to discuss with them.

## Monitoring Internal Debates

There were hundreds of electronic bulletin boards, facilitating dis-cussion of topics such as products (e.g., midsized systems, desktop systems, printers, networks), applications (e.g., desktop publishing, networking, graphics and imaging), organizational groups (e.g., mar-keting, field service, sales support), specific customer accounts, and competitors. There were additionally dozens of bulletin boards on non-work related topics such as current events, religion, parenting, relationships, skiing, entertainment, and hobbies. Anyone could post an initial question or topic for conversation. Initial postings were typically fairly short and either asked specific questions (e.g., "Are there any plans to introduce a color monitor in the next four months?") or asked general questions to provoke discussion (e.g., "What do you make out of the recent announcement by [Competitor R]?")

The more "interesting" bulletin boards might get five or six new topics a day, with dozens or even hundreds of responses to a given topic.

Most of these bulletin boards retained old correspondence (sometimes three and four years old), and in some cases, it was possible for me to go back and look at debates about strategic decisions made several years earlier. Although I never posted my own questions or comments on the bulletin boards, I did spend dozens of hours reviewing the content of many of these files and I found them useful for keeping abreast of developments in a wide range of groups that I would not have otherwise had easy access to. Although virtually everyone at Zytek claimed they monitored a handful of bulletin boards related to their interests, many people warned me to not take them too seriously. The limitation seemed to be that those in power tended not to participate while those who were the most active participants seemed to be the disenchanted. In this way, the bulletin boards tended to overstate marginal positions and understate mainstream positions.

**Communicating With Informants**

Finally, I used the E-mail system to directly correspond with key informants. My network of informants regularly forwarded me messages on topics they thought I might be interested in. It only took a few keystrokes to forward a message, and I received thousands of pages of messages, including several dozen messages that had worked their way down from the CEO. On many occasions, people sent me "historical memos," often several years old, on key strategic decisions. For one decision I was trying to unravel, a key informant sent several hundred page of original memos among the key decision makers that helped me chronicle the activities. Such background information was extremely valuable in preparing me for interviews, because I often knew a lot more about historical events than the people I interviewed realized.

In addition to receiving memos forwarded to me by informants, I also corresponded with them via E-mail. In some cases I would ask specific questions to clarify technical terms, to learn the history of certain projects, or to better understand some of the organizational politics. I was very concerned about not being seen as an information broker and passing things on, but I did forward what I considered to be nonsensitive mail to others on occasion (usually when discussion came up about a message I had received and another person did not have a copy). I continued to have access to the E-mail system for 15 months after the full-time fieldwork, and during this time I often sent messages to key informants to clarify certain issues. I also sent rough drafts of chapters via E-mail to 4 or 5 of my informants and received feedback from them on what I had written.

## Discussion

In this note I have outlined some of the ways electronic forums can be used when doing fieldwork. A few themes emerge as to how I utilized these media. First, I used the E-mail system just as insiders do to correspond with others and to learn of the time and place of meetings. Second, because of the ease of storing messages and forwarding them to others, there was a rich electronic paper trail that provided context to the activities I observed and that could be used to reconstruct the history of specific projects. Third, because most presentations to large groups were videotaped, I was able to watch presentations made years earlier or where I attended other activities because of scheduling conflicts. Finally, I took part in over a dozen meetings where the participants were geographically dispersed and were linked via audio and/or video conferencing. These activities included training sessions, product introduction events, and some product review meetings. Although the electronic media facilitated the fieldwork, it in no way replaced traditional participant observation activities. For example, most of my time in the field was still spent either attending meetings, conducting interviews, or chatting with people I ran into.

A few aspects of the Zytek setting seemed to make electronic media especially appropriate. First, the participants worked in a technical setting and were at ease in using E-mail and on-line systems for communicating with each other. Much of the communication between people was initially in an electronic (rather than paper) format. Second, because Zytek produces computers that can be easily interconnected, almost all employees could communicate with each other over a single worldwide network. Most organizations have computers from dozens of different vendors and their systems may not be networked in the way that the computers at Zytek were. Finally, the focus of my study was on the communication among groups in the firm as new products were developed, and the electronic media were the primary means by which these geographically dispersed groups were linked. If I had been focusing on activities of groups that were in the same physical place, the electronic media might have been a less central part of their lives.

Will future fieldworkers find electronic media appropriate for studying organizational groups? Computer vendors claim they are on the leading edge of a trend toward using computers and telecommunications to reorganize work processes among groups that no longer need to be physically close to one another. The activities of the 1992 presidential campaign whereby Bush, Clinton, and Perot used satellite conferences, "electronic town hall meetings," and electronic bulletin boards for position statements are similar to the activities I observed. I suspect that participant observers will find electronic media appropriate in their own fieldwork to the extent that those they are studying rely on it in their daily activities. In this note I have attempted to show a few of the ways in which electronic media can complement more traditional participation observation methods.

## Reference

Van Maanen, J. (1988). *Tales of the field: On writing ethnography*. Chicago: The University of Chicago Press.

# 5

# Tales From the Field

## Learning From Researchers' Accounts

### PAUL M. HIRSCH

I once enthusiastically told Erving Goffman I was studying business elites. "Have you slept with them?," he replied. "No, but I am getting in to talk with them," I proudly answered.

Some of the essays in this volume honestly address the issues of gaining access, struggling to decide if what you think you have learned is accurate, and reporting it as interestingly and creatively as possible, ideally extending or even creating a sociological theory. The Goffman challenge—Is our knowledge intimate enough to be genuinely reliable?—doubtless haunts every field researcher setting up to go into the field. Although ultimately we may never be positive that what we report is 100% correct, we will be satisfied to know that it is well-informed, carefully researched, close to accurate, and, if we are very fortunate, also as interesting in its descriptions and conceptualizations as exemplars by such mentors as Goffman, Becker, Gans, or Rieder.

In this essay, I highlight common technical strategies for achieving these goals noted by several other contributors to this volume, as well as by Hertz and Imber in their introduction. To the examples and experiences they report, I will add some from my own research and conclude with a few additional caveats and encouragements for those beginning their own research journeys.

## *Street Smarts and Critical Decision Points*

In reading Hertz and Imber's introduction, two key points to which I immediately resonate are (a) the importance of the field researcher's "street sense" and (b) noting the critical decision points at which it is time to shift focus.

### Street Smarts

I suspect a good correlation between the success of projects for those just starting out and their personal knowledge of or connections to the worlds about which they are writing. This is not only because critical access may become easier (through referrals, advise, personal contacts) but also because the investigator should have a stronger sense of what counts here. In my early work on the music industry (Hirsch, 1972), I benefited from being a New Yorker whose dad knew some record company staffers who became good initial informants. Although reluctant to "fess up" to such personal connections, field researchers whose "street smarts" lead them back to an area they already know something about often produce stronger studies than those who choose to avoid their own background to freshly learn about topics thoroughly new (and foreign) to them. Although what we can add our own street smarts to may seem like unchronicled "old news" to us, the study that results will be more authoritative and, quite likely, strike others in the discipline as more weighty and appropriately exotic.

Interestingly, the essays by Thomas, Useem, and Gamson all touch on the added credibility to which they also see such "street smarts" contributing in order to gain access and conduct interviews. Whether the product of personal contacts (early on) or experience (from having been around), each of these field researchers strongly emphasized the importance, of either (a) being referenced or recommended by persons trusted by the executives from whom we seek information and/or (b) sounding sufficiently knowledgeable and prepared once admitted, in increasing the likelihood of straight answers. Although the depth of background information requisite to pass these credibility tests may be lessened some if the access "fix" is in, the researcher's "street smarts" are always enhanced enormously by advance preparation (reading secondary reports, newspaper, trade press coverage, etc.). *It is virtually impossible to overprepare for an interview!*

## Critical Decision Points

Hertz and Imber also refer to the dilemma of collecting data whose
voices may make you change the project. I experienced exactly this
while at the University of Chicago Graduate School of Business. Professor Thomas Whisler and I had secured an NSF grant to personally
interview elite "walking interlocks"—directors on the boards of two or
more Fortune 1000 corporations—about their experiences as directors
and assessment of (what we translated from) sociological theories about
them. The responses we encountered could be a case study of Robert
Thomas's insightful formulation and reminder of the multiple roles and
persona of elite respondents. Once comfortable with the interviewers,
we found directors had no difficulty distinguishing their persona as
individuals with good careers, and as "company men and women" in
their roles as executives and CEO's, as well as "business statesmen" in
their external roles as representatives of the top managerial class.

As individuals with their own careers to attend to, these executives
honestly spoke of advancing on the prestige ordering of Fortune 1000
companies' boards ("trading up" onto companies with higher reputations). Where most sociological theories about interlocking directorates
(and as investigators we also expected) see these board members as
functionaries (doing the business of their companies or class), these
interviews added a very different perspective—a professional (careerist,
individual) persona that seemed more important to them, and a window
on a more collective culture that went beyond the individual companies
with which they were associated at that moment (Hirsch, 1982).[1]

A bigger surprise from these interviews was the early warning we
received about the wave of corporate takeovers about to convulse the
established corporate world during the 1980s. Our respondents were
very concerned about the takeovers that Wall Street was about to
unleash on large corporations. As more and more CEO's interviewed
steered our attention to the coming contests over corporate ownership,
I found our discussions turning to their *losing* much of the massive
power that our project (and discipline) assumed and expected to learn
more about. Their board memberships, for example, could soon depend
on which side would win a contest for ownership of "their" companies.
As these ownership dramas shaped up, I felt this might be a more
important field project to track than the interlocks we had come to study.

My fieldwork on "the language of takeovers" and "cockfights" (à la
Geertz) between corporations was born at this point, and it constituted

a clear decision point in which unexpected answers in field research deflected us from pursuing what we expected to find (more on interlocks) to where we wound up (the diffusion of takeovers as a deviant innovation, in Hirsch, 1986). The personal lesson for me bore out the inference that field researchers had better be prepared to follow their data into grounded theoretical avenues (à la Glaser and Strauss) other than the ones they began with. This was both very exciting and time consuming.[2] For the greater comfort of predictably analyzing a data set, secondary quantitative analysis is safer.

## Multiple Levels and Downward Executive Mobility

In this volume, chapters by both Yeager and Kram and by Useem provide dramatic reminders of disparities in information and perceptions between upper and lower levels of organizational hierarchies. If the researcher's purpose is to construct profiles of the business elite (only), this disparity may not pose any interpretive problems, but if the elite study is also designed to shed light on broader organizational phenomena, then the field research will run up against methodological problems. Reports from different levels of organization and society regularly find corresponding differences in the attitudes, understandings, and experiences of respondents occupying positions at each of these (respective) levels. In the changing automobile industry of the 1980s, top General Motors executives continued to take separate elevators from all the other employees, to their separate floors. Top Ford executives, on the other hand, "walked the talk" of their change efforts by visiting with plant workers on the production line and developing a reputation for taking seriously the company's rhetoric on improving both profitability and working conditions (Pascale, 1989).

As we move through the 1990s, one legacy of the recent wave of takeovers and corporate restructurings is a transformation of the world of work. Important field studies are beginning to appear,[3] and the changes rampant throughout this new environment are a sociological laboratory calling for many more. More significant, as the number of levels in organizational hierarchies declines, the boundaries between the ranks of upper, middle-upper, middle, and lower-middle managers, and the (higher and lower) rank and file become increasingly blurred, recalling Dahrendorf's (1959) important observation that all positions between the top and bottom of organizations are at risk and ambiguous. The confusion and rhetorical gyrations ("empowerment," "cross-functional teams") that result invite new field studies. Field sites, as Yeager and Kram note, should become more accessible as the pace of change accelerates—along with appropriate concerns over employees' levels of commitment, trust, and loyalty as job security and benefits decrease (Rousseau, 1995).

An important implication of these changes is that the composition of the business elite may change accordingly. While quantitative surveys will announce which skill sets become the new routes to the top, there will be a corresponding need for field studies to explore and compare the cultures, values, experience, and composition of this new business elite.

## *Fieldwork Operations, Tactics, and Judgment Calls*

An interesting consensus across contributors addressing interview formats here is a clear preference for using a *semi-structured* format or questionnaire. Aldridge observes high-level respondents are accustomed to expressing themselves on their own terms, if not controlling their interactions; hence, providing them the opportunity to add to and embellish on an answer is a necessary component for retaining rapport. Thomas agrees, though he also warns against giving total control (i.e., unstructured open-ended interviewing) to the elite respondent who, precisely because s/he is used to controlling an interview, can take it over completely unless the investigator retains some control. In conducting elite interviews, my best information has come from having a core set of key topics and issues to cover during the course of the interview. Although the order in which they arise is allowed to follow the course of a more general discussion, I make clear there is a core set of questions to be covered and retain license to ask them before the interview is formally ended if we have not already gotten to them more informally.

A related key point bearing on the ease of gathering good data is the mutual realization that the intellectual worlds of the interviewer and elite respondent barely intersect. I saw this demonstrated at a luncheon where a professor asked T. Boone Pickens if he had read some articles he'd sent about takeover strategies; Pickens politely allowed as how he was too busy doing them to have had time to examine the package.

Although usually very bright, the business elite are men and women of action ("doers"). They are neither theorists nor academics, and it is important to understand that the theoretical categories driving our research are largely irrelevant to their interests. It is for this reason, I think, that experienced field researchers so often speak of how their projects are "packaged" or "customized" for these respondents.

Most businesspeople—as Yeager and Kram observe—respond far more easily to concepts like "values," "culture," and "leadership" than to "sociology," "bureaucracy," or "ethical malfeasance." So long as our reports to colleagues can emphasize the latter topics, the "packaging" we are well advised to employ calls for utilizing the former terms to explain the project to potential respondents and pique their interest. A good model for this is Merton and Lazersfeld's utilization of a project for *Time* magazine to develop the concept of "cosmopolitans" and "locals" for the discipline, while providing a more applied study for the interested organization.

When elite respondents agree to invite the field researcher in for the interview, or to study their organizations, it is usually from a spirit of charitable "noblesse oblige" or good will toward universities, or because someone they know vouched for the project, or a reward for your patience and persistence. Once inside, if they like you and can see any benefits (e.g., as per Useem and Yeager & Kram's experience), they can be enormously helpful by publicly supporting the study if you are conducting further interviews inside their organization.

### Conclusion

This essay has reviewed "tales from the field" to highlight strategies and techniques for conceptualizing and operationalizing field research on business (and other) elites. In all field research, access and accuracy are problematic. I have emphasized the contributions of "street smarts" (prior experience in the area, contacts, preparation) and flexibility in allowing the data collected to recast the project (critical decision points). The insights from Hertz and Imber were illustrated with examples from my research on corporate boards and takeovers.

As large corporations restructure and downsize, there are enormous opportunities for field researchers to examine the transformation of work and employment, as well as the major associated social changes (unemployment, altered careers, increased alienation, utilization of new opportunities). The study of business elites will encounter new types of executives as well as downward executive mobility.

The execution of field research discussed throughout this book also emphasizes the value of semi-structured interviews and the explanation and "packaging" of research projects to respondents. These were discussed, as well as the question of why elites agree to be interviewed. Such technical considerations supplement the more strategic issues of generating and extending interesting theories about the elites that we study.

## Notes

1. For example, their status as CEO's would preclude them from the price-fixing that sociological theory about interlocks often infers could go on at board meetings. This was denied as *beneath their personal dignity,* now that they were directors. It was not denied as a potential practice at lower ranks in the company, but rather corrected as a misunderstanding of what the more exalted role of director should and should not be assumed to include.

2. It also led to the related further "detour" of interviews with middle managers adversely impacted by the takeover wave, in what became my more "practical" book, *Pack Your Own Parachute,* for which my original running title was "The Fire Sale of the Fortune 500."

3. Among such studies, on downsizings, Smith (1990) and Vonk (1994) provide first-rate contributions. In the literature of applied organization studies, job redefinitions are well analyzed in Galbraith, Lawler, and associates (1993), and large-scale organizational changes in Nadler, Gerstein, and Shaw (1993).

## References

Dahrendorf, R. (1959). *Class and class conflict in industrial society.* Stanford, CA: Stanford University Press.

Galbraith, J., Lawler, E., & associates. (1993). *Organizing for the future.* San Francisco: Jossey-Bass.

Hirsch, P. M. (1972). Processing fads and fashions: An organization set analysis of cultural industry systems. *American Journal of Sociology, 77*(4), 639-659.

Hirsch, P. M. (1982). *Network data versus personal accounts: The normative culture of interlocking directorates.* Paper presented to the annual meetings of the American Sociological Association, San Francisco.

Hirsch, P. M. (1986). *Pack your own parachute: How to survive mergers, takeovers, and other corporate disasters.* Reading, MA: Addison-Wesley.

Nadler, D., Gerstein, M., & Shaw, R. (1992). *Organizational architecture.* San Francisco: Jossey-Bass.

Pascale, R. (1989). *Managing on the edge.* New York: Simon and Schuster.

Rousseau, D. (1995). *Promises in action: Contracts in organizations.* Newbury Park, CA: Sage.

Smith, V. (1990). *Managing in the corporate interest: Control and resistance in an American bank.* Berkeley: University of California Press.

Vonk, T. (1994). *Exploring the results of restructuring: An ethnography of middle managers following force reductions.* Unpublished doctoral dissertation, Department of Organizational Behavior, Northwestern University, Evanston, IL.

# PART II

# Professional Elites

Access to professional elites is second in difficulty only to access to business elites. In the case of those types of occupations which straddle both professional and corporate statuses, the question of how the researcher establishes rapport remains critical. Joshua Gamson presents this case in his examination of the people who broker Hollywood celebrities. Theirs is a highly professionalized and competitive type of work. Conducting social research in such an environment illustrates, as Gamson remarks, the competition among elites: "Hollywood elites often see intellectual elites not only as competitive but also as threatening to their populist grounding." Gamson further recognizes the role dimensions of the researcher. He knew when and how to play the role of researcher: part of that is creating a "spontaneous" identity in response to the expected hostilities one may predictably encounter from those who believe their time is money. As he states about his own orientation: "Coping with research in the world of information commodities means, of course, continually positioning oneself in relationship to it. A self-presentation dilemma that holds true for any field research setting takes its own form here: the particular advantages of presenting as a knowledgeable insider trade off with those of presenting as a knowledge-pursuing outsider."

Jennifer Pierce, an outsider as both a sociologist and a woman in a male-dominated law firm, explores the significance of her status, arguing that it is insufficient to accept the standard belief about the superordination and subordination of researcher and subject. She describes what she terms her "outlaw" position in a setting where the demands upon her assume typically gender-defined forms: "The outlaw position is a multiple and discontinuous identity whose movement between positions proves to be a critical advantage in uncovering the regimes of power in the workplace." The formation of her identity as a researcher, she claims, enabled her to expose the intersection of gender and power.

Based on interviews with Anglican clergymen in England, Alan Aldridge's article addresses the status similarities between ministers and social scientists. Unlike the other articles that explore status inconsistencies, Aldridge's approach to gaining access, achieving rapport, and adopting an appropriate research methodology are all predicated upon the sociologist's understanding of the nature of the shared meanings between these two professions, particularly in terms of education and sex. By reconceptualizing prestige in a more fluid and open-ended way, Aldridge discovered that this elite was willing to confide in him precisely because he was taken to be their equal rather than a deferential outsider, which is a more common pose to gain confidence. His is the only article that remarks upon the significance of the sex of the researcher serving as the commonality that overshadows occupational differences.

Howard Becker's discovery of the "crock" illustrates the importance that elites attach to the creation of interesting cases. This parable, which Becker tells in his fieldwork classes, has become folklore among his students. We include it here as a reminder that the social researcher is constantly faced with reconciling status with interests. In his example of the fledgling physicians, Becker demonstrates how "professional" interest defines the status of patients. If one were to accept the formal expectations of this elite's professional interests, crocks would not exist. What Becker has uncovered through his field experience is the unexpected finding that professionals, like others, categorize among themselves informally what would otherwise be formally unacceptable to do. The study of elites is particularly well served by Becker's admonition that "Intuitions are great but they don't do much for us unless we follow them up with the detailed work that shows us what they really mean, what they can really account for."

# 6

# *Stopping the Spin and Becoming a Prop*

## *Fieldwork on Hollywood Elites*

### JOSHUA GAMSON

The slightly bizarre experience is often the most instructive. Midway through an interview with a Los Angeles entertainment publicist, in the midst of a project investigating the production of celebrity (Gamson, 1994), I inadvertently rolled my eyes.

I had suggested that his job seemed like a battle with editors and publishers for story control, and the publicist told me that his recent experience negotiating a magazine cover for a "controversial performer" was "very good training for negotiating a hostage release." "If we can do that," he continued, "we can get the hostages out of Lebanon." I pushed him. Doesn't public relations involve fabricating or manipulating an image? The publicist carefully suggested that his job is to "gift wrap the uniqueness" of a celebrity, emphasizing, for example, the "unique capacity" of one client, a popular and mannequin-like game show hostess, to "be very alluring to men, and not threatening to women." I rolled my eyes. He caught me, so I explained myself.

"These are such slippery answers," I said, smiling.

"But they're good ones," he returned with a we-both-know-this-is-a-game wink. I began to sense important data coming at me, as it so often does, through the cracks opened by rule-breaking behavior (a faux pas, an intrusion, a roll of the eyes). He asked me to turn off the tape recorder, and then, oddly, asked me to rank him in relation to other publicists I had interviewed.

"On a scale of zero to ten, ten being unctuous slipperiness and zero being absolute blunt candor," he asked, "where would I rank?" I ranked him somewhere in the middle, which seemed to satisfy him. I pressed the play button and continued, collecting answers both of us knew were "good" but not exactly believable. We continued as if it were a conversation, but knowing that it was a game (wink); he controlled the information by packaging it in what he must have thought was the form most useful and pleasing to me.

This extreme and self-conscious relation to information control on the part of entertainment industry elites—and the assumption that the scale is weighted toward the unctuous end—is a formidable obstacle for a researcher entering Hollywood,[1] but an unsurprising one. After all, the livelihood of many of these industry professionals rests largely on the shaping of public images and public stories, whether it's a journalist or program producer shaping images for sales or ratings, a celebrity team (celebrity, agent, manager) molding an image to increase a performer's value on the job market, or a publicist spinning a story to pitch to an editor.

Typically, information is traded by celebrity teams for access to media, or contained by media workers to secure exclusive access to a celebrity (Koch, 1991). But information in Hollywood is sometimes so fully commodified that it is more unseemly than unusual to literally sell it: to a tabloid, most commonly, or perhaps to a researcher. For example, after a written request (on University of California letterhead) for an interview with a local celebrity, whose claim to fame was the ongoing appearance of her name and image on Los Angeles billboards, I received the following message on my answering machine from her assistant:

> We got your letter, I'm looking it over, um, and she charges a hundred and fifty for interviews of this sort. Actually, she normally charges about five hundred, it's a flat fee, but she said for this project she could do it for like a hundred and fifty. You guys could meet and discuss, discuss the concepts and, you know, you can talk with her about it, 'cause frankly, you know, we get so many calls like this that, you know, she could spend the rest of her life just doing one interview right after another twenty-four hours a day.[2]

The extremely lucrative entertainment business hinges in large part on a management of words, images, and attention, and on the ongoing exchange of, sale of, and battle over partly true tidbits about celebrities that serve as the basis for attention-gathering.[3] Researchers, as information gatherers themselves, are easily sucked into this system.

Indeed, negotiating over information is a ritualized habit among the various elites vying to profit from celebrities and their attention-getting capacities. Producers and editors complain of it constantly: of demands to give up control of writer, content, and photo selection, in exchange for access to a celebrity. Perhaps more important, many of these participants see their effectiveness as dependent on the invisibility of negotiation and manipulation activities. From the point of view of many journalists, producers, and editors, getting caught compromising on information-gathering techniques (not to mention the compromise itself) is often seen as a damaging prospect, because sales rest on credibility.

Similarly, from the point of view of the winking publicist, "the best [publicity] campaigns are the ones that don't look like campaigns at all," because "the petri dish in which maybe romance grows is not always so clinically dissected, and maybe there's some moderate analogy to public relations." For some, the habit of control is so great it extends to any caller. After many attempts, for example, I got through to a husband-and-wife publicity team who handle several major movie stars. I explained the project (a Ph.D. dissertation about celebrity) and what I wanted to discuss (how they do what they do), and I offered them assurances of anonymity. Their defensiveness was stunning, as though I was asking them to endanger national security; their negotiating posture was immediate. He explained that they don't like talking about their work, because "they like to stay behind the scenes." She coldly agreed to meet with me but insisted that we would need to talk beforehand to "set some terms, of course." When I declined, suspecting that the phone call had already provided the most important data I would receive from them, they sounded surprised. What kind of creature was this that did not participate in the setting of terms for discussion?[4] Most members of the cultural elite[5] of Hollywood not only take information battles for granted but are used to sizing up how much power they have in any given negotiation—and, as elites in an information-based hierarchy, are used to having the upper hand with outsiders. I did not compute.

Buried in these strange experiences are important lessons about doing field research on Hollywood elites, or perhaps more accurately, on elites in industries of information and attention.[6] This environment, with its heavy emphasis on habitual packaging and control activities, puts its own particular cast on familiar fieldwork strategies: of gaining access, of managing insider-outsider roles. Moreover, the peculiar information-control habits in the celebrity industry are rooted in a heightened attention to audiences, to the spoken-to, and these roots point to another important implication for studying such commercial cultural elites: that they cannot be effectively studied apart from their relationship to their key audiences.

### Access and Candor in the Land of Information Commodities

The first key to coping with obstacles of access and candor in Hollywood, given the environment I've described, involves respecting a cliché: Hollywood, anyone will tell you, is all relationships. The entertainment business in notoriously risky, not the least because it deals in many intangible resources ("talent," for example, and "star quality") and with a hugely disproportionate ratio of financial misses to hits. Trust is scarce; put simply, everyone is pitching everyone else, and no one knows what succeeds (Prindle, 1993). Moreover, where a player fits on the Hollywood hierarchy is often measured by these relationships: the more restricted the access, the more important the stature. A true player calls from a car phone, on her way to somewhere else, and for most callers is "in a meeting," while those who will talk with any caller are marked as minor players. Relationships are indeed more central to the way things get done in Hollywood than in other more stable industries with more formalized roles. They are both the barrier and the facilitator to access.

Thus what is true of any research setting is even more true in Hollywood: an outside researcher who does not tap into a relationship network, and one with a powerful individual at its center, is going to have terribly restricted access to the higher-ups in the industry elite.[7] The flip side is that, once in, it is not difficult to ride a relationship circuit for quite some time. So, for example, I began with a *Los Angeles Times* reviewer, who met with me out of college loyalty, and whose name granted me access to numerous interviews. When the relationships became distant ("who did you say gave you my name?") or the contact less powerful (no favors owed), however, interviews and access became much more difficult for me to gain.[8]

One implication is that a researcher will do well to approach people without much power in the relationship circuit; they will take phone calls. In fact, those lower on the food chain, with less invested in protecting "trade secrets," do more freely offer candid insights into the way the system operates; it certainly pays to have friends in low places. For example, it was the underpaid assistant to a self-proclaimed "star maker" talent manager who told me of her boss's more explicit "product improvement" strategies (rubber bands around the nipples of one star at all photo sessions, the manager insisted, were the key to her success). Yet in general, a researcher who wants access at all levels of the hierarchy faces the problem not only of being a player without the status to break through the frenzy of phone calls and faxes, but also of being perceived as someone wanting a piece of the action for free, with nothing to trade.

The deeper difficulty, however, is not gaining access to an interview, but breaking through the habitual packaging of words and ideas. Anonymity does not necessarily do the trick, because it is not so much the attribution of words to the particular person but the interactional give-and-take of information commodities that is crucial. Coping with re-searching in the world of information commodities means, of course, continually positioning oneself in relationship to it. A self-presentation dilemma that holds true for any field research setting takes its own form here: the particular advantages of presenting as a knowledgeable insider trade off with those of presenting as a knowledge-pursuing outsider.[9]

On one hand, I can place myself as a newcomer to the game of information exchange, adopting an outside "learner" role (Lofland & Lofland, 1984, p. 26). This has the advantage, in general, of drawing out the subject's expertise while maintaining clear role boundaries between the researcher and the researched. Presenting as an outsider in Hollywood helps shift the lens, to keep the rules of the information-management game from kicking in: I am just a researcher, I just want to understand how things work.

Ironically, though, the "outsider" position that might promote candor is not easily maintained but is constantly pushed toward conversion into an "insider" one. Given access-driven pressures, the learner role is too comfortably subsumed into familiar industry roles. To begin with, industry connections are especially necessary, and in order to be effective, the subject must be convinced that one is known and trusted by the referring contact—an insider. Moreover, access often depends on the impression that one has something of value to offer (publicity, attention) in the economy of information: the book. The researcher then easily looks much like any journalist, eliciting customary responses ("she could spend the rest of her life just doing one interview right after another twenty-four hours a day"), triggering the information-control and negotiation routines built into the industry roles.

The "insider" role is easily adopted, too, given its own advantages: assuring the subject that she is talking to someone who understands her world, the knowing questioner can probe in areas the naive learner cannot. The risk in Hollywood, however, is that being able to "talk the talk" is again easily mistaken for genuine insiderness, covering over the researcher role. When the academic researcher disappears, another role takes its place in the interaction, usually the information-gathering and attention-bestowing journalist, and the customary wrapping of information is likely to begin again.

This is not always a bad thing, given that it reveals extremely important data: how publicists and journalists wrap their information, their negotiating customs, their conversational habits, and the pecking order of who will speak with whom about what. There are certainly times when triggering the package itself ("if we can do that, we can get the hostages out of Lebanon") or the typical postures ("we'll need to set some terms") can be significant and revealing. Yet once one has heard these, one wants to push past them, to get behind the standard lines and the measured words. In order to elicit candid and spontaneous responses, one must struggle to find a way to present as a learner while distinguishing oneself as not-a-journalist, as genuinely outside the conventions of the industry. The researcher must break out of the cycle.

The obvious strategy would seem to be a return to a self-conscious emphasis on the role of academic researcher, the true outsider who has no stake in "good" answers but only in honest ones. In many cases, in fact, this might offer an alternative access route: for many people of non-elite status, and for elites sharing the general perception of scholarship as a high status profession, the flattering attention of a member of a university elite can often open doors.

In Hollywood, however, it is no safe guarantee of access. This is a different kind of elite, one that derives its status from the provision of popular commodities. Members of the commercial-cultural elite are often unimpressed by a university credential and are sometimes openly hostile, given the (mostly accurate) perception that intellectuals are disrespectful of popular culture producers and out of touch with the population upon whose attention the status of pop-cultural elites relies.[10] As one interview subject put it,

If you want to know how America will react to something, ask someone in an elite university, and not in the natural sciences, and whatever they tell you take the opposite. If you want to know what the vast majority of women are feeling in America, ask any person in the women's studies department of an elite university and just do the opposite and that's it, end of issue.

Hollywood elites often see intellectual elites not only as competitive but also as threatening to their populist grounding. Advertising membership in an academic elite, then, while it highlights the researcher role in ways that can help one get behind the standard line, can also be risky in studying entertainment industry elites.

Interviewing commercial-cultural elites involves treading these various role-lines: between the disinterested outsider with nothing to give and the book-writing insider, between the novice who elicits information games and the expert who understands the games but will not play them, between the academic and the populist, between the well connected and the disconnected.

### Audiences and Studying Up Hollywood

The difficulties in interviewing celebrity industry elites clearly grow out of their everyday professional environments. In particular, they are rooted in a constant need on the part of those in the entertainment industry to keep audiences of various sorts in mind. More often than not, this is not the audience who will consume a program, film, or celebrity image, but rather another party in the Hollywood nexus itself. As one manager put it, "You can't worry about your [consuming] audience too much, because they don't do the hiring." Your audience is the entertainment industry itself: you worry about packaging an aspirant in a way that will allow them to fill a niche on the entertainment job market, give them a shot at a particular kind of role. Or you worry about the needs of a mass media gatekeeper, "what this person is going to look like on the cover," as one studio publicist said, and your direct audience is an *Entertainment Tonight* producer or a *People* editor. If you are the producer or the editor, of course, you worry more directly about viewers and readers—sales, ratings, demographics. But in any case, these professions breed an almost automatic tendency to adjust presentation with an eye to the audiences to whom one is beholden.

This behavior suggests, I think, that study of commercial cultural elites is dangerously incomplete if it does not directly investigate their various relationships to audiences. That can be done in part through interviews, simply by asking about perceptions of audiences, about formalized and informalized knowledge about audiences, about the most common sets of interactions for any given professional. But the interview data, exactly because they are so tightly adjusted to fit the perceived needs of the spoken-to (either the researcher or some imagined public for the researcher's writing), are constantly in need of checking.

Direct observation of the relationship to various audiences adds and checks the picture that comes across in discussion. In the celebrity industry, it was often possible for me to operate quite unobtrusively and anonymously, by closely watching the interactions at celebrity-based events such as film premieres and awards shows. Positioned by a helpful studio publicist along the receiving lines of a film premiere, I began to see in active form the choreography of information control and exchange, and battles over images: publicists dragging clients quickly up the carpet, or delivering them to particular journalists with whom they had made prior arrangements, or getting in the way of irritated photographers in order to prevent a particular shot; journalists air-kissing their sources. In fact, it was only by directly watching and hearing image-barter and word-management—the interactions between people who constituted one another's primary audiences in professional life—that I was able to make full sense of the language and habits of controlled information. Only through these interactions could I build the lens of audience considerations through which to analyze interviews.

Taking audiences carefully and actively into account, then, provides an opportunity to check words against actions, affords a more developed means of getting inside the mindset of those studied, and yields fodder for deeper interviewing; indeed, these are general capacities of ethnographic work. I want to suggest a more profound reason for paying close attention to audiences, in particular to popular consuming audiences (watchers, readers) in the study of Hollywood elites. Even when the consuming audiences are not the direct concern of industry professionals, they are always hovering in conversation, being held in the conversational wings to bring on as support for one action or another: they want this, they won't buy that. Although industry players have a range of contradictory theories about the mass consuming audience (Gamson, 1994, pp. 108-125), the (mythical) "American public" has a central place in the everyday work culture and conversation of the entertainment industry. The reasons are plain: buying publics are the source of the industry's survival, the key to the success of a particular product, and ultimately the source of the industry professionals' elite status.

In order to fully study members of such an elite, one must understand the place in their world not only of the directly targeted spoken-to audience (other Hollywood operators) but also of the publics to whom, and often for whom, the elite speaks. Doing so involves the recognition that those publics are accessible not only in the minds of elite interview subjects (most often as a broadly conceived audience-as-market) but also in their interactions with living, active audiences. Hanging out at film premieres, for example, I saw that audiences on the street are sometimes kept behind police barricades across the street from the glamour production line; "it's not just that we don't need the fans around," a publicist told me, "in fact, we don't *want* them around." Outside of an awards show, I found that the interactions between celebrities and celebrity-watchers are not simply those between adored and adoring, but are tempered by a good deal of irreverence toward celebrities and animosity toward the program managers dragging celebrities off to the next posing stop. At television program tapings, I was jolted by the discomfort of producers with audience silence during breaks, by the often incessant flattery and attention lavished on audiences, and by the enthusiastic willingness of audiences to be shaped into production props (playing themselves as happy, laughing, loving the show).[11]

One learns much not only about audiences from such experiences, but also about Hollywood elites. In particular, one learns about elites by taking the position of the audience in their daily lives. A gap between what commercial cultural elites claim is happening with audiences and the experience of being an audience member emerges full force to be analyzed. The activity of molding live publics into production props, for example—clap this way, laugh when you think it's supposed to be funny—calls attention to crucial factors of uncertainty, especially the "problem of knowing" (what do audiences want?) in the entertainment industry (Gitlin, 1983, p. 22); the happy studio audience serves to alert the at-home audience that this is where they should keep the dial. The instability and uncertainty of status in an industry of popularity reasserts itself, made visible by adopting the audience roles the industry requires. Alongside it, actions take the shape of coping mechanisms: attempts not only to gauge audience response but to control it, both in live settings and through the management of image and information.

Taking consuming audiences directly into account spotlights a final basic proposition: that researchers cannot study "up" only from their own position, or only from inside the elite world, but from the locale of those against whom "up" is defined. Studying Hollywood elites requires a willingness to take that position in as many situations as possible, to come face-to-face with Hollywood elites as a member of their intended market, public, or audience. There, inside the logic but outside the elite, acting as prop or getting in the way, Hollywood comes clear at its most strange, slippery, and candid.

## Notes

1. I adopt the conventional use of "Hollywood" as a synonym for the Los Angeles-area entertainment industry; it is not a geographical term but one describing, often in misleadingly mythical ways, a loose group of professional cultural workers. My discussion, it should be noted, is built on observations from work on the celebrity industry (Gamson, 1994), primarily with those working on getting and managing attention (performers, studio publicists, personal publicists, managers, and agents) and those keeping the gates of attention to celebrities (journalists, editors, producers, and talent bookers). Although it crosses segments of the entertainment industry (television, film, music), the dynamics are not precisely the same in those particular industry segments. Classic examples of studies of the entertainment industry range from Powdermaker (1950) to Gitlin (1983), but the most insightful recent study of Hollywood, I think, comes from outside of academia and outside of the documentary form: Robert Altman's 1992 film fiction, *The Player*.

2. I did eventually get an interview, simply by refusing to pay, and by making clear that this interview was desired but not essential. In terms of the discussion below, this positioning likely created a useful confusion of insider (I knew the game but had the upper hand in it because I did not need the interview for my celebrity-based product) and outsider (I did not know the game and was surprised and offended by the suggestion that I, an academic researcher, would pay for an interview).

3. For a full discussion of celebrity production, see Gamson (1994), Part 2.

4. Some programs and publications, such as the *Los Angeles Times*, have enough power and autonomy in the relationship to publicists that they can refuse to set terms. Nonetheless, many publicists are used to interactions with media professionals who are more dependent on celebrity access for their jobs, and thus to interactions in which publicists have a good deal of control. I was easily lumped into that category, because I was a non-player with nothing much to offer.

5. I use this term not in the ideological sense Dan Quayle made famous, nor in the society-page sense of those whose status is marked by consumption of high culture, but in the more literal sense, to mean those people in control of the production of American commercial culture.

6. Many of the dynamics discussed here are likely to be similar in other industries—electoral politics, for example (McGinnis, 1988)—in which success is heavily dependent on the management of images, information, and attention.

7. On the process of gaining access in fieldwork see, for example, Burgess (1984) and the firsthand accounts in Shaffir, Stebbins, and Turowetz (1980).

8. One effective alternative is to work with interpersonal connections in a single workplace. For example, one initial contact at Home Box Office was able to easily persuade her friends there to take time out to talk with me. This strategy removes the interactions from the more instrumental network of relationships.

It should also be noted that, quite logically, the further one gets away from image management professions, the fewer the obstacles to access and candor seem to be. Not everyone in Hollywood is equally protective of secrecy or equally tuned in to the market value of secrets. Gitlin (1983) found television producers willing and sometimes eager to speak to him openly and on the record.

9. On membership roles in fieldwork, see Adler and Adler (1987).

10. On this often hostile relationship, see Ross (1989), and on changes in the academic stature of popular culture, see Schudson (1991).

11. For analyses of these celebrity-watching events, see Gamson (1994), pp. 108-113, 129-141.

## References

Adler, P., & Adler, P. (1987). *Membership roles in field research*. Beverly Hills, CA: Sage.

Burgess, R. G. (1984). *In the field*. London: George Allen & Unwin.

Gamson, J. (1994). *Claims to fame: Celebrity in contemporary America*. Berkeley: University of California Press.

Gitlin, T. (1983). *Inside prime time*. New York: Pantheon.

Koch, N. (1991). The Hollywood treatment. *Columbia Journalism Review* (January/February), pp. 25-31.

Lofland, J., & Lofland, L. (1984). *Analyzing social settings*. Belmont, CA: Wadsworth.

McGinnis, J. (1988). *The selling of the president*. New York: Simon and Schuster.

Powdermaker, H. (1950). *Hollywood: The dream factory*. Boston: Little, Brown and Co.

Prindle, D. (1993). *Risky business: The political economy of Hollywood*. Boulder, CO: Westview.

Ross, A. (1989). *No respect: Intellectuals and popular culture*. New York: Routledge.

Schudson, M. (1991). The new validation of popular culture. In R. Avery & D. Eason (Eds.), *Critical perspectives on media and society* (pp. 49-68). New York: Guilford Press.

Shaffir, W. B., Stebbins, R. A., & Turowetz, A. (Eds.). (1980). *Fieldwork experience: Qualitative approaches to social research*. New York: St. Martin's Press.

7

# Reflections on Fieldwork in a Complex Organization

## Lawyers, Ethnographic Authority, and Lethal Weapons

JENNIFER L. PIERCE

Contemporary critical writing on ethnographic authority begins with the premise that ethnographers inescapably exercise textual and social authority over the people they study, particularly people who occupy subordinate social positions. Clifford (1988), for example, suggests that ethnographic texts produce subjectivities in an unequal exchange between anthropologists and "natives." Within this asymmetrical relationship, ethnographers typically provide the final, authoritative account.[1] Sociologists also acknowledge the inequality in the relationship between the researcher and her[2] subjects. As social scientists, we receive grants for our research and write publications that further legitimate our professional status, while the people we study often receive little in return for their participation (Blauner & Wellman, 1973, p. 316). Furthermore, as feminist scholar Wise has argued, "we are still operating in

AUTHOR'S NOTE: An earlier version of this paper was presented on the qualitative methods panel at the American Sociological Association Meeting in Miami, Florida (August, 1993). Special thanks to Lisa Bower, Lisa Disch, Martha Easton, Susanna Ferlito, and Barbara Laslett for their critical comments and suggestions on earlier drafts of this essay.

an environment where the ethic prevails that those who publish research are the experts and those who are written about are not" (1987, p. 76). In contrast to these formulations, I suggest that asymmetrical relations between researcher and her "objects" of study are not always so clear cut. In my own fieldwork, my positioning within this formulation at some times fit the researcher-dominant, subject-subordinate script, but at others, it did not. As a generic ethnographer, I exercised textual authority over those I studied. On the other hand, as a female ethnographer, conducting research on male litigators, I "studied up." Not only did I study an elite and powerful group of experts, but my research also focused on people who occupy the dominant gender position. As a woman studying men in a predominantly male profession,[3] sexist expectations and jokes, sexual innuendos and occasional outbursts of hostility served as constant reminders of my subordinate status. How does ethnographic authority play out in a field setting where the relations of power and authority between researcher and subjects are not so clear cut?

In this essay, I argue that the classic conception of ethnographic authority obscures the varied ways the researcher's power and authority can shift and change in differing relationships and situations in the field. As an ethnographer, I often had the power to define the reality of others, but as a woman, this authority was often challenged and (re)negotiated in interactions with the male elites I studied. This essay reflects upon this contested process by drawing from my fieldwork experiences in two San Francisco law firms where I spent over 15 months working as a paralegal in 1988 and 1989. Legal workers in both firms knew that I was a graduate student conducting interviews for a dissertation on occupational stress; however, they did not know that I was *also* doing fieldwork. My covert status as a fieldworker not only raises serious ethical questions,[4] but it also brought to light a tension between my feelings about exploiting the people—especially the very powerful people—I studied and my commitment to doing ethnographic research.

In the following, I explore these issues beginning with a discussion of my feelings about the unacknowledged exploitation of my research subjects. My early fieldwork experiences were marked by a pervasive feeling of guilt and anxiety about the potential betrayal of my subjects. However, as time went on, these feelings shifted from guilt to resentment and anger. Here, anger served as an "epiphanal moment"[5] in shifting my thinking about the nature of ethnographic authority. The tension between my subordinate gender positioning in the field and my authorial voice as a feminist sociologist strained and shifted and my authorial voice emerged as a "lethal weapon." The next section details a new move in my shifting positions in the field. Here, my ethnographic authority is acknowledged and I develop a new term for this position: the "outlaw." The outlaw position is a multiple and discontinuous identity whose movement between positions proves to be a critical advantage in uncovering the "regimes of power"[6] in the workplace. Further, I suggest that it is *through the responses I elicit in my movement between positions*—from female paralegal to outlaw—that I unveil the complex operations of gender and power in the field. Finally, I discuss how issues of inequality and exploitation become more complex when ethnographic authority does not follow the usual script. When women study men, what is a lethal weapon for some can be a potent methodological tool for researchers.

### Lawyers, Ethnographic Authority, and Lethal Weapons

My feelings about the potential exploitation of my subjects varied over the length of my duration in the field. Ironically, the longer I was in the field and the more I became involved in people's lives, the less I worried about this issue. By contrast, at the beginning I was acutely sensitive to the asymmetry in my relations with others. It was clear to me what I would get out of the research—a dissertation to fulfill my Ph.D. requirements and, eventually, a book—but what would they get out of it? Every early personal confidence drove me wild with anxiety. People readily confided their personal troubles to me. What was I to do with such personal information? Was I betraying them, even as I promised confidentiality?

The following excerpt from my field notes highlights the guilt and anxiety I experienced when one of my subjects revealed personal feelings about his work. Early in the field during a long car drive to an interview with a potential trial witness, Stan,[7] one of the lawyers I worked for, confided his fears about turning forty and his personal assessments about what he had accomplished in his career. In my notes, I recorded the following:

> After reviewing the background of the witness and discussing the possible testimony we might uncover to bolster our case, our conversation took a more

personal turn. Stan asked me what I would like to do if I wasn't in graduate school . . . I thought for a minute and said, "A rock-n-roll star." I explained it was a pretty far-fetched fantasy given that I am practically tone deaf, but I love to sing anyway. Then I returned the question. This opened a long discussion about his frustrations about being an attorney, how much work it was and how little the psychological pay-off is. "You do a great job, and no one cares. The client doesn't understand the intricacies of law well enough to know how well you've done. And, other lawyers bite the bullet in envy." At one point, he said his wife had told him that he shouldn't feel he has to prove himself so much to people, that he should learn to like himself as he is. He added that it was a "sweet thought," but that's not how law works. "In the real world, you have to keep on proving yourself if you want to stay on top." Thinking of the academic world, I felt inclined to agree, but I also sensed some truth in what his wife said. His constant need to prove himself didn't appear to result simply from some external pressure, but an inner insecurity which compelled him to prove himself again and again. I nodded assent, but said nothing. We drove the last ten minutes of the trip in silence.

Initially, I felt pleased that he had confided in me, but now, as I write this, I feel guilty. This was a highly personal revelation for someone who is typically emotionally closed and distant. He does not strike me as the type of person who makes such personal disclosures easily. On the other hand, why did he tell me? Am I just the sympathetic female ear? Or was he just in a funk, and I just happened to be the closest available body? (JLP field notes).

Although the conversation had given me insight into the pressures trial lawyers face, I continued to feel somewhat uncomfortable after such disclosures were made. People trusted me, yet I felt that my notetaking somehow betrayed that trust. This was further exacerbated by that fact that although most people knew I was doing a dissertation on occupational stress and the legal profession, they did not know that I was also doing participant observation. At least in interviews, the power relationship was somewhat apparent, but in fieldwork, it went unacknowledged.

Though early in my fieldwork I was acutely aware of my unacknowl-edged ethnographic authority, the longer I worked in the field, the less angst I experienced about this issue. Feelings of guilt and anxiety gradually shifted to feelings of frustration, resentment, and anger. This shift came about for several reasons. First, I entered the field as a novice. My expectations about fieldwork were idealistic and naive. The formulaic guides I had read on participant observation had not prepared me for the moment-to-moment ethical dilemmas that arose in the field.[8]

Second, as a novice, I also experienced confidences as personal. I assumed that people confided in me as another person—as an equal. Furthermore, in retrospect, I can also see that I responded to their problems and concerns as a traditional caretaking female. As a woman, I somehow felt responsible for taking care of their feelings.

What I began to realize over time is that male attorneys did not confide in me as a person, but rather as a position in an imagined relation—as a feminized Other (de Beauvoir, 1949). In de Beauvoir's formulation, women are expected to tend to the needs of men, becoming Other or "object" to his Self or "subject." Further, as de Beauvoir suggests, this positioning is not reciprocal but asymmetrical because women's subjectivity is denied. Here, my early suspicions about being "the female sympathetic ear" were on the mark. Male attorneys talked about their problems; I listened. As these realizations dawned on me, I began to feel less guilty and more resentful of their expectations. Anger often served as the epiphanal moment in this realization.

In *Reflections on Fieldwork in Morocco*, anthropologist Paul Rabinow (1977) also describes how anger became a crucial moment in his field research and in his thinking about the role of the ethnographer. After a long day with his key informant, a Moroccan male, Rabinow lost his temper and yelled at the man. Initially, he was concerned that it may have damaged the relationship. However, as it turned out, the opposite occurred. Rabinow's initial passive, "scientific" stance had been interpreted by his informant as a sign of weakness. Rabinow's subsequent angry outburst redefined his identity as a man of good character who would not submit to another man's efforts to dominate (1977, pp. 47-48). As a white female ethnographer in American society among largely white, male, middle-class lawyers, becoming angry did not have the same effect it did for the male anthropologist in Morocco. As the following examples illustrate, my slip into the "black hole" did not improve the quality of my relations with attorneys, though it did yield some insights about myself, the nature of ethnography, and the regimes of power governing work relations between female paralegals and male attorneys.

Todd, a young male associate, had the habit of hanging around in the office I shared with Pamela, another woman paralegal. He appeared to want and need attention. Whereas Pamela lavished him with attention, I found his personality and behavior childish and irritating and typically ignored him. One day when Pamela was at the courthouse, Todd sauntered into the office. We exchanged greetings and then I asked him what he needed. "Oh nothing, I just came in to hang out," he responded with a broad smile. I said pointedly that I was working and returned to the stack of depositions sitting on my desk. He remained seated on Pamela's desk. I continued to do my work. After a moment or two of silence, he said, "You don't like me, do you Jennifer?"

> I looked up briefly and said, "That's right Todd, I don't like you." I heard him kind of laugh/gasp. Then he said, "Well, I'm completely crushed. That wasn't the response I was expecting at all." I looked up and smiled and laughed. Then I saw his face. He had this look of genuine surprise and he was blushing. He quickly exited (JLP field notes).

As I described the incident later in my field notes, I began to feel guilty. I knew Todd was not a particularly malicious person, he was just insecure and wanted my attention. On the other hand, I had grown tired of his pointless interruptions. Personally, I did not like him and I wanted to be left alone. Further, I resented the assumption that I, as a woman paralegal, should be interested in devoting personal attention to him. Although this conversation did not improve my relations with Todd, at least from his perspective, it did from mine. Thenceforth, he left me alone and I was able to complete my work without interruption. Additionally, the incident helped me to understand the importance emotional norms play for the work lives of women paralegals. Todd clearly expected me, as a female paralegal, to pay attention to him. When I did not, he asked a question to remind me of my appropriate role—"You don't like me, do you, Jennifer?"—a question that suggested I had behaved inappropriately and at the same time invited reassurance. In other words, he not only expected me to apologize for not being friendlier to his overtures, but also to tell him that I liked him. In this light, my response can be read as a disruption of social norms. By refusing to play the role of the feminized Other, I subverted the informal norm for female paralegal behavior.

The reaction my anger elicited also underscores the differences between Rabinow's fieldwork experience and my own. For Rabinow, an angry outburst served to consolidate his masculinity, marking him as a man of strong character who refuses to let another take advantage of him. It also helped to build, rather than damage, rapport with his informant. By contrast, my anger challenged Todd's traditional conceptions of femininity. My refusal to accept his understanding of appropriate feminine behavior not only served to unsettle, rather than consolidate, my "femininity," but it also created distance in our relationship. My confrontation with such sexist expectations marks the distinctiveness between my fieldwork experience and that of the male anthropologist. By virtue of being female, I was compelled to contend with attitudes and behavior that Rabinow was not. Our divergent gender positionings not only gave rise to differential experiences but also explain why our common reaction—anger—was perceived in different ways. Anger is acceptable behavior for men but not for women.

A similar epiphany of anger occurred on a long work day with another male lawyer. On a particularly grueling day, the attorney I worked for had to file ten motions *in limine* by 5 p.m. Our "team"—three paralegals, two associates, and two secretaries—began the day at 6 a.m. Some of the motions had been written the previous day, but six remained to be completed. I had serious doubts that our team would be able to finish them, but, by 4:30 in the afternoon, all but one of the motions were printed out and ready to go. The remaining motion was still being revised by Daniel, the partner working on the case. Another paralegal and I sat waiting nervously for the pleading. At about ten minutes to five, Daniel came running into the room, threw the motion at us and screamed as we ran out the door to catch a cab to the courthouse: "And, don't fuck up!"

The cabbie drove us through rush hour traffic from the financial district to the courthouse. As we ran down the long hallway to the county clerk's office, the clock chimed five o'clock and the office doors closed. I banged on the door and we pleaded—more "emotional labor"[9] —with the clerk to let us file the motions even though we were technically five minutes late. The clerk finally relented, but only after chastising us severely. The other paralegal was so angry he decided not to return to the office. I rode the cab back alone.

When I got back to the office, I went into Mark's office (one of the associates on our team) and lay on the floor—my back was killing me—and relayed the story. I was very tired and still very angry. He went off to get me something to drink. He returned with Daniel who asked pleasantly how things had gone. I said icily: "We didn't fuck up." He looked surprised, but said nothing and left. Mark laughed and told me that I'd probably get into trouble for a comment like that.

Mark was right. The next day at our "team meeting," Daniel brought in gag gifts for all of us because we had done such a "great job." The associate

[Mark] who smoked [but was trying to quit] received a torch shaped cigarette lighter, the other paralegal got a miniature basketball hoop with a foam rubber basketball and I received a plastic gun which shot bright orange ping pong balls called "The Big Ball Blaster." Everyone, including Daniel, thought this was very funny. Although it was done as a joke, the joke was at my expense and the message was clear—women paralegals who aren't nice are "ball blasters" (JLP field notes).

Again, my icy retort did not improve my relationship with the attorney. However, my behavior did reveal informal norms about gender appropriate emotional labor for paralegals. By telling the attorney that "we didn't fuck up," I once again resisted the appropriate feminized position. I did not play the role of the supportive and good female paralegal, but rather that of a "ball blaster." Daniel, consciously or not, appeared to recognize my attempt to disrupt power relations. The gag gifts he presented to us, an unusual display of "gratitude" on his part, reveal in a somewhat disguised form his actual intentions. First, because the gifts are gags, they are not genuine demonstrations of gratitude or appreciation, but jokes. The joke serves to reframe the moment as "humor," setting it apart from our ongoing, more serious work lives. And, as Freud (1905/1963) suggested, jokes often contain an element of aggression. Presenting me with a toy gun and Mark who is trying to quit smoking with a large cigarette lighter are hardly gracious gestures, but aggressive moves. Daniel's anger with me for talking back to him and with Mark for witnessing his loss of face is returned to us symbolically in the form of gag gifts. Second, as anthropologist Mauss (1954) suggests, by giving us gifts Daniel attempted to reinstall his authority.

The meaning of my gift adds another twist to Mauss's analysis. "Ball blaster" is a pejorative term for a woman who acts like a man, or more accurately, a woman who castrates men and hence disempowers them. By giving me the gift, Daniel at once reclaims his authority and confers abject status upon me signaling the inappropriateness of my behavior. Further, as Mauss suggests, gift giving is a means of cementing social relationships. To refuse the gift demonstrates not only ingratitude but also withdrawal from social intercourse. In that moment as a member of the "team," I could not refuse. The possibility of my withdrawal is also foreclosed by the frame of the joke—if I did not accept the gift and laugh at the joke, I become the ball blasting bitch. And yet, to laugh along and "to accept without returning or repaying more is to face subordination" (Mauss, 1954, p. 63).

Though I accepted the gift, I did not accept subordination. Here, power relations shifted again and my authorial voice returned from the void of the repressed. I marched straight back to my office and attached the cardboard "ball blaster" box top to my office door beneath my name plate—an attempt in Butler's (1993) terms to reappropriate my abject status and claim a new and affirmative meaning.[10] After all, ball blasters are powerful women. One of the paralegals who admired my new name plate added her own graffiti to the cardboard box top. Beneath the giant letters "BIG BALL BLASTER," it read in tiny print "shoots safe ping pong balls." She crossed this out with a big black "X" and wrote above it in ominous black letters: "LETHAL WEAPON."

### The Outlaw Position

The power I had in defining the reality of others did not always go unacknowledged. Toward the end of my stint at the first field site, I ran into a situation where one of the attorneys clearly recognized that my critical and sociological understanding of working relations in the law firm was inconsistent with his own. At some point this particular attorney, Michael, expressed interest in my dissertation prospectus. I naively assumed that he might find it interesting and provided a copy for him. As I discovered, he was highly offended by my "literature review." Here is a synopsis of events from my field notes:

He was really hurt because my prospectus, in his words, "portrays all these wonderful secretaries and paralegals who support these asshole attorneys." And how did I think he would respond, but to take it personally because (he raises his voice) "wasn't this really about me and Jane [his secretary] and Debbie [a paralegal]?" He added sneeringly "And, it's so well-written and polished. All these footnotes and references. You must have spent a lot of time working on this." I said that I was sorry that I had hurt his feelings, but that had not been my intention at all. I tried to explain that I was interested in how the structure of the legal profession necessitated certain kinds of behavior and I was interested in what the consequences were for people who were involved in such occupations. . . . I further explained that all interviews would be confidential as were the names of the law firms where they worked.
  He continued to say how much I had hurt his feelings. . . . Then he started talking about what a good interviewer I was. It's a "special skill." "Stan [attorney] calls six people and no one tells him anything. You call one person and we get everything we need to know." He went on to say that it was a

valuable, but *dangerous* skill because people feel so comfortable talking to me that they might reveal a confidence they would later regret. (I think he was talking about himself here.) I told him that yes I am a good interviewer and people do enjoy talking to me, but my dissertation interviews are confidential.

And, to top it off, as I am leaving he tells me to never discuss our conversation with my thesis adviser. (Is this a sign of his guilt or embarrassment?) (JLP field notes; emphasis in original throughout).

Over the weekend I brooded about Michael's behavior. Although I had an inkling of why he was upset—he didn't like being an object of study—I couldn't figure out how a fairly straightforward literature review had produced this reaction. Moreover, I felt he had been down-right mean—the sneer about "it's so well-written" suggested that he had not perceived me as a skilled and competent researcher before he read the prospectus. Furthermore, his "orders" about what I could or could not say to my thesis adviser struck as extremely controlling. His response strongly resembled adversarial tactics—the intimidation, the attempt to control and direct the witness (me). The more I thought about it the more angry I became. After talking to my thesis adviser and a number of other people, I decided that it was time to leave the field site and find a new one. I had already accumulated voluminous field notes, and I was concerned that I might contaminate the field if I stayed any longer. At the end of the weekend, I talked to the paralegal coordinator and told her I would finish the projects I had begun, but I was planning to quit.

[On Monday] when I came into the office, Michael did his best "charm" routine, lots of big smiles, "how are you's" and so on. When everyone else left the meeting, he said he had heard that I was angry with him. I said, "That's right." He said he'd like to talk to me about it later in the day . . .

When I met with Michael, he said he wanted to "clear the air." He was sorry if he had offended me and hoped we could be friendly. He repeated several times that he really liked me—*as if that were the issue.* "You are such a good paralegal." How could my feelings be hurt, he had said such glowing things about my research skills. I explained why [his insinuation that I wasn't smart was insulting and ordering me around . . . ]. Rather than apologize again, he said, "Well, attorneys have feelings too." He tried to conclude on an upbeat note saying he was willing to put this behind us, they really need me for the upcoming trial and everyone knows how much work I did interviewing all those witnesses. [I interviewed almost 40 witnesses in a 3-month period.]

I said that if I stayed, I would be very friendly and professional. I had no problems with that. However, I thought he should know that he was currently on my shit list. And [I added] people who are on my shit list have to do *lots* of penance to get off. He laughed in an overly hearty voice . . . (JLP field notes; emphasis in original throughout).

This encounter highlights at once the lawyer's recognition of my authority and my disruption of norms. By problematizing what he took for granted as natural, the work relationships and the nature of work in the law firm, I had hurt his feelings, made him feel angry, and betrayed his trust. My critical view also violated my subordinate status as a woman paralegal. Women legal assistants are supposed to be nice and supportive of attorneys. My prospectus and my role as researcher demonstrated that I was critical, detached, and even instrumental. Not surprisingly, the attorney perceived this point of view as threatening. Michael's anger at me, however, gives way to a new step in this dance of shifting power and authority. After berating me on Friday, on Monday his strategy is to call me in to talk to me and to smooth things over. He apologizes for offending me and hopes we "could be friendly." He compliments my work and appeals to me personally—"he really liked me." Beneath the carefully scripted lines—his "charm routine"—is not only an effort to win me back—after all, "they need me for the trial"— but an attempt to reinstate the status quo. By courting me back into the fold, he attempts to put me back in my proper place, the position of female paralegal.

I did not return to my proper place, however. Here, as in the ball blaster story, I resisted his attempts to make me do so. Though I tell Michael that I will continue to be friendly and professional, I also put him on notice by telling him that he's currently on my "shit list." In this way, I disrupt the status quo he is attempting to reinstate and reassert my authorial voice—this time verbally. After all, what could be a more graphic representation of my ethnographic authority than telling him that I will pen him in on my "shit list" with a "pocket signifier?" In reclaiming the pen, I reclaim, as French feminist Cixous (1981) suggests, the phallus. My bid for the phallus is further cemented by putting his behavior on notice—he has to do "*lots* of penance to get off"—such a move not only displaces his authority, but serves to position me as the final arbiter of appropriate behavior.

Although some lawyers viewed my research as threatening, secretaries and paralegals had an entirely different reaction. When I casually mentioned my dissertation topic, many eagerly volunteered to be interviewed. One woman accosted me in the bathroom providing a list of reasons for why I should interview her. Others completely rejected the notion of confidentiality. As one secretary said repeatedly, "Use my real name. I want you to use my real name in your book." (Their bid for visibility in my text posed a stark contrast to the lawyers, many of whom refused to be tape recorded in their interviews and worried excessively about confidentiality.) These women legal workers also expressed curiosity about my written work. Much later, after an interview with one paralegal, she asked to see my prospectus/literature review. I was reluctant and explained why. However, because I had already done the interview and no longer worked in the firm where she did, I decided that it couldn't blow up in my face. She called me a week later and said, "No offense Jennifer, but this thing is boring. How did Michael ever get riled up over this damn thing?"

The difference between the paralegal's response and Michael's is suggestive of their own positioning within regimes of power as well as my own. Paralegals and lawyers occupy differential locations in the law firm hierarchy. Paralegals, unlike lawyers, saw my critical view as compatible with their own view from below. Many of the women I interviewed attempted to disrupt the status quo through their own strategies of resistance. It was another paralegal who penned "lethal weapon" on my nameplate.[11] Further, these differing perceptions are also related to my positioning in the script on ethnographic authority. In relation to male attorneys, I am "studying up" from the subordinate gender position. At the same time, as the author, I pen the story. My efforts to write a story against theirs is, not surprisingly, read as threatening and/or offensive.

The transgressive moves I make in my fieldwork and have described thus far arc not intended simply as provocative stories, but rather, as Easton suggests, as "a way to explore and explode the discursive structuring of expected gender behavior" (1994, p. 20). In other words, by disrupting norms—unwittingly or not—I uncovered regimes of power governing gendered working relations in these law firms. Further, as Easton suggests, "special knowledges" are to be gained when it is women, and not men, who do research on men. "When men hold the researcher position . . . the constructions of power behind masculinity are conflated with and obscured by the positional power of the researcher. However, when women hold the researcher position, there is a strange inversion of and disruption of power by the researcher. . . ."

(Easton, 1994, p. 22). In my own work, the "strange inversion" and "disruption of power" plays out in the dissonance between my subordinate gender position and my authoritative researcher position. Given this positioning, my identities are at once multiple—female/paralegal/researcher/ball blaster/feminist—and, at times, discontinuous—female paralegal doing research who is not seen as a researcher. For instance, even though Michael knew that I was doing research for my dissertation, it was not until he actually read my prospectus that he saw me as anything other than a female paralegal. The critical advantage of this multiple subject or "outlaw"[12] position lies in its creative and strategic movement in and around the roles of researcher, paralegal, feminist, and ball blaster. Furthermore, *it is through the reactions I elicit* in my movement between positions—from female paralegal to outlaw—*that I unsettle the boundaries between gender and power.* Michael's reaction to my prospectus not only reveals for him a new way of seeing me—my ethnographic authority is unveiled—but it also lays bare his expectations about appropriate behavior for female paralegals. His surprise at my expertise and skill as a sociologist suggests that these skills are incommensurate with his expectations of the typical female paralegal role.

Some sociologists may object to my "outlaw position" in doing ethnography. Indeed, the outlaw breaks not only the rules in the field but also the rules of a positivistic social science—detachment, neutrality, and objectivity. Ethnographers who become overly involved with the people they study are considered not only disruptive, but biased, partisan, and potentially contaminative influences in the field. However, to paraphrase Kleinman and Copp (1994), the crucial question in qualitative research is not did the researcher influence the study, but *how did the researcher influence the study?* My tales of the field not only articulate many of the ways my presence influenced the people I studied, but they also yield important insights about gender, power, and knowledge. Through male lawyers' reactions to my outlaw position, I uncover the operations of power and privilege that are never formally stated.[13] Todd's response to my unfriendliness, for example, is to ask me a question reminding me of my appropriate role—"You don't like me, do you, Jennifer?"—a question at once suggesting that I behaved inappropriately and inviting reassurance. My reaction—"No, I don't like you"—in turn produces yet another step in this dance—"that wasn't the response I was expecting at all"—thus bringing the norm I have broken into bold relief. Similarly, Daniel's gag gift, his response to my "talking back," reveals at once his attempt to name my behavior as inappropriate and to reinstall the status quo.

Still others may object that the outlaw position is somehow sneaky, immoral, or unethical. Certainly, I do not always treat attorneys with great reverence or respect, and my behavior as well as what I had written did embarrass and offend some lawyers. But here again, we have to think critically about my gender position in relation to those I study. European American social scientists, for instance, have been criticized for their exploitative research on communities of color. But what if the tables are turned—what if African Americans studied white communities? And, what if women studied men? In a society strongly stratified by race and gender, the tables cannot be turned with an equivalent force. White women as well as women and men of color—even as researchers— are embedded within raced and gendered matrices of domination and privilege that have consequences for the responses their multiple subject positions—researcher, female, and/or person of color—provoke. In contrast to the experiences of white male researchers, these researchers are likely to encounter racism and sexism. Such incidences are far from respectful. And yet, at the same time, these incidences also serve to reveal the complex and shifting operations of power in the field, thereby providing important clues in cracking the code of power and domination.

Finally, the outlaw position challenges both new ethnographers and feminist scholars who despair the achievement of egalitarian research fieldwork methods. They are correct in arguing that the dilemma of ethnographic authority is unavoidable. However, this dilemma and its particular regime of power—researcher-dominant, subject-subordinate— must be considered in relation to other matrices of domination that may intersect with them, matrices shaped by race and gender relations. When the dilemma of ethnographic authority is an inversion, as Easton suggests, concerns about inequality and exploitation become more complicated. Lawyers may feel threatened, even exploited, by what I have written. At the same time, however, as a female researcher and a paralegal—a subordinate—I have felt exploited by their attempts to put me in my "proper place." Being screamed at—"don't fuck up," being treated as less intelligent—"the sneer about it being so well written" and being bullied—"never discuss our conversation with your thesis adviser!"—are not empowering experiences. When we privilege the usual script on ethnographic authority—(white) male as author—these shifting and changing regimes of power in the field are obscured. By contrast, the outlaw position brings these shifts and changes into bold relief. Indeed, it is precisely the multiple and shifting nature of the outlaw position in the field that renders my work empowering to some ("I want my real name in your book"), boring to others ("No offense Jennifer, but this thing is boring!"), and a "lethal weapon" to still others.

## Notes

1. Recent feminist discussions of ethnographic practice have explored fieldwork and rhetorical strategies that attempt to disrupt these asymmetrical power relations (Abu-Lughod, 1993; Kondo, 1990; Minh-ha, 1989; Stacey, 1988, 1990). For example, in her book *Brave New Families*, Stacey describes her attempts to involve the white working-class women she studied in reading and commenting upon her book-length manuscript about their lives. Though these women have criticisms of the text, they cede that the book is hers—not theirs—thus relinquishing authority to Stacey's voice.

2. I have used the female pronoun throughout the text when referring to "the researcher" to challenge the assumption that ethnographers are men.

3. My research was on litigators. Compared to other specialties within law, litigation has the highest percentage of men, 88% (Menkel-Meadow, 1989).

4. There are two sets of ethical questions related to my fieldwork. The first concerns the issue of covert versus overt fieldwork which I discuss in the introductory chapter of my book, *Gender Trials: Emotional Lives in Contemporary Law Firms* (Pierce, in press). The second set of concerns revolve around the more personal ethical dilemmas of the moment. For instance, though I promised confidentiality to my subjects, writing about their personal confidences—even in a disguised form—sometimes felt like betrayal. This essay focuses on this second set of concerns.

5. See Kondo (1990) for an interesting discussion of how an epiphanal moment in her fieldwork in Japan led her to shift the focus of her study.

6. I am using "regimes of power" in Butler's (1990) sense of the term. Butler rejects the notion that power is simply an exchange between individuals—a constant inversion between oppressor and oppressed. By contrast she conceptualized power in a Foucaultian sense wherein power is dispersed through all social relationships. In this sense, power can neither be withdrawn nor refused, but only redeployed. Such an understanding highlights the ways that power is diffuse, shifting and changing.

7. I have used pseudonyms throughout this essay to protect the confidentiality of subjects in this study.

8. Some of the works I had read as a graduate student included Whyte's (1943/1993) methodological appendix to his classic book *Streetcorner Society*, McCall and Simmons's (1969) anthology on participant observation, Hughes (1960), and Burgess (1982). Many of the more reflexive works written by feminist scholars that address these issues had not yet been published (e.g., Stacey, 1990; Krieger, 1991).

9. In Hochschild's conception of the term, emotional labor requires workers "to induce or suppress feeling in order to sustain the outward countenance that produces the

proper state of mind in others" (1983, p. 7). Just as the flight attendants in Hochschild's study are expected to hide feelings of irritation with difficult passengers and display feelings of concern for their welfare, paralegals are expected to be deferential to trial lawyers and to provide emotional support for them. On the other hand, the work of trial lawyers requires not only skills in legal research and writing but also an emotional presentation of self as intimidating or strategically friendly.

10. In her recent book *Bodies That Matter*, Judith Butler (1993) makes this argument with respect to gay and lesbian activists who have reappropriated the stigmatized term "queer" as a positive and affirmative political identity. Butler suggests, however, that such reappropriations do not always work for progressive political ends. See, for example, her discussion of the pejorative and racist epithet, "nigger."

11. Many paralegals and secretaries I interviewed expressed a critical perspective on the gendered division of labor within law firms. In chapter 6, "Gendering Consent and Resistance in Paralegal Work," of my book *Gender Trials*, I discuss a number of strategies female paralegals employ to resist degradation on the job (Pierce, in press).

12. Here I am drawing from critical race theorist Austin's (1989) concept of the "black outlaw." The black outlaw also has multiple and discontinuous identities that serve to destabilize the way legal doctrines attempt to "fix" racial classifications.

13. In my research, typical paralegal job descriptions do not list the feminized emotional dimensions of the job. See my discussion of job descriptions in chapter 4, "Mothering Paralegals: Emotional Labor in a Feminized Occupation" in *Gender Trials: Emotional Lives in Contemporary Law Firms* (Pierce, in press).

## References

Abu-Lughod, L. (1993). *Writing women's worlds: Bedouin stories.* Berkeley: University of California Press.

Austin, R. (1989). Sapphire bound. *Wisconsin Law Review, 3,* 539-578.

Blauner, R., & Wellman, D. (1973). Toward the decolonization of social research. In J. Ladner (Ed.), *The death of white sociology* (pp. 310-330). New York: Vintage Books.

Burgess, R. (1982). *Field research: A sourcebook and field manual.* London: Unwin.

Butler, J. (1990). *Gender trouble: Feminism and the subversion of identity.* New York: Routledge.

Butler, J. (1993). *Bodies that matter: On the discursive limits of sex.* New York: Routledge.

Cixous, H. (1981). The laugh of Medusa. In E. Marks & I. de Courtivron (Eds.), *New French feminisms* (pp. 90-98). New York: Schocken Books.

Clifford, J. (1988). *The predicament of culture.* Cambridge, MA: Harvard University Press.

de Beauvoir, S. (1949). *The second sex.* New York: Knopf.

Easton, M. (1994). *Knowing gender in an unknowable world: The possibilities of post-structuralism for research on gender.* Unpublished paper, Department of Sociology, University of Minnesota.

Freud, S. (1963). *Jokes and their relation to the unconscious.* New York: Norton. (Original work published 1905)

Hochschild, A. (1983). *The managed heart: Commercialization and human feeling.* Berkeley: University of California Press.

Hughes, E. (1960). Introduction: The place of field work in the social sciences. In B. H. Junker (Ed.), *Fieldwork: An introduction to the social sciences* (pp. v-xv). Chicago: University of Chicago Press.

Kleinman, S., & Copp, M. (1994). *Emotions and fieldwork* (Qualitative Research Series 28). Thousand Oaks, CA: Sage.

Kondo, D. (1990). *Crafting selves: Power, gender and discourse of identity in a Japanese workplace.* Chicago: University of Chicago Press.

Krieger, S. (1991). *Social science and the self.* New Brunswick, NJ: Rutgers University Press.

Mauss, M. (1954). *The gift.* Glencoe, IL: The Free Press.

McCall, G., & Simmons, J. (1969). *Issues in participant observation.* New York: Addison-Wesley.

Menkel-Meadow, C. (1989). Feminization of the legal profession: The comparative sociology of women lawyers. In R. Abel & P. Lewis (Eds.), *Lawyers in society. Volume III: Comparative theories* (pp. 196-255). Berkeley: University of California Press.

Minh-ha, T. (1989). *Woman, native, other: Writing, postcoloniality, and feminism.* Bloomington: Indiana University Press.

Pierce, J. (in press). *Gender trials: Emotional lives in contemporary law firms.* Berkeley: University of California Press.

Rabinow, P. (1977). *Reflections on fieldwork in Morocco.* Berkeley: University of California Press.

Stacey, J. (1988). Can there be a feminist ethnography? *Women's Studies International Forum, 11*, 21-27.

Stacey, J. (1990). *Brave new families.* New York: Basic Books.

Whyte, W. (1993). *Streetcorner society* (4th ed.). Chicago: University of Chicago Press. (Original work published 1943)

Wise, S. (1987). A framework of discussing ethical issues in feminist research: A review of the literature. In *Writing feminist biographies. 2: Using life histories* (Studies in Sexual Politics, No. 19, pp. 47-88). Department of Sociology, University of Manchester.

*8*

# Negotiating Status

## Social Scientists and Anglican Clergy

### ALAN ALDRIDGE

The elite status of the clergy of the Church of England, like that of any
social group, is the product of complex social interactions. This article
argues that it is necessary to move beyond the sociologically dominant
but intellectually dubious model of a consensually agreed unidimensional prestige hierarchy. Occupational cognition is, it is contended
here, multivalent, fluid, and context dependent. In researching Anglican
clergy, rapport is achieved not through orienting to the relative standing
of clergy and academics on a one-dimensional scale of occupational
prestige but by affirming both commonalities and divergencies of values, objectives, occupational culture, and professional competence.

### The Elite Status of the Anglican Clergy

That the clergy of the Church of England are members of a social elite
is, on the face of it, self-evident. Theirs is an ancient profession steeped
in history. The Church of England is the church "by law established"

NOTE: Reprinted from a special issue, "Fieldwork in Elite Settings," edited by Rosanna Hertz
and Jonathan B. Imber for the *Journal of Contemporary Ethnography*, Vol. 22, No. 1, 1993,
pp. 97-112. Copyright 1993 by Sage Publications, Inc.

and enjoys legal privileges reserved to it alone. Church leaders move in the same rarefied social milieu as members of the Royal Family and senior politicians. At supreme moments of national crisis, the Church of England bears the prime responsibility for expressing "civil religion." The Church is the custodian not only of the Faith but of a wider cultural heritage including priceless documents (e.g., the Magna Carta and the Mappa Mundi), Thomas Cranmer's unsurpassed liturgy, a rich and flourishing musical tradition, and an abundance of architecturally significant churches and cathedrals.

The "establishment" of the Church of England had two dimensions: the legal and the cultural (Archbishop's Commission, 1970). On the other hand, the Church enjoys an official, legally defined relationship to the state. Arguably, the specifically legal dimension of establishment has become less significant in the 20th century. Even so, at least two aspects of it are of continuing importance. First, the representation of Anglican bishops in the House of Lords, the (unelected) upper chamber of the British Parliament, retains of actual and symbolic significance. After the Reformation, bishops continued to enjoy the privilege of representation in the Lords. In 1847, the maximum number was fixed at 26, made up of the archbishops of Canterbury and York, the three senior bishops—of London, Durham, and Winchester— and 21 others according to their seniority of appointment. This arrangement provides the Church of England with a political platform at times of national crisis. Second, the link with the monarchy is very close. The Sovereign is required to be in communion with the Church of England, of which she or he is the "Supreme Governor." During the coronation ceremony the monarch takes an oath to uphold "the Protestant reformed religion established by law" and to "maintain and preserve inviolably the settlement of the Church of England, and the doctrine, worship, discipline and government thereof, as by law established in England."

In addition to its legal implications, establishment has a wider cultural significance. In this sense of establishment, the clergy are members of an elite stratum of top people: socially well connected, highly educated, enjoying links to the aristocracy and the monarchy, and engaged in professional practice rather than socially inferior occupations in commerce, trade, and industry. The clerical profession in England has retained the elements of "status professionalism": It is characterized by status-cultural knowledge based on lifestyle, exclusive cultural stylistics, and social networking rather than on the monopolization of abstract utilitarian knowledge that defines and is the principal power resource of the fully modernized profession (Murphy, 1988). The legal and cultural dimensions of establishment are interrelated. So, for example, as the present Archbishop of York has argued, "the mystique of the Crown has irreducibly religious roots" (Habgood, 1983, p. 109). Both the Church and the monarchy are at the heart of "civil religion" in Britain. Following Bellah (1975), it is important to note that this enables the Church to call the nation to judgment. Establishment does not necessarily entail sacralization of the status quo. In the aftermath of the Falklands war, the Church of England—to the dismay of the government—refused to orchestrate a triumphant victory celebration for the nation.

The fact that the Church of England is established is important to many clergymen and informs their orientation to their work. Central to this is the conception of the Anglican clergy having responsibility for the whole population in their parish regardless of people's religious or other affiliations (Ranson, Bryman, & Hinings, 1977, pp. 46-51). There is some evidence to suggest that establishment plays a key role not only in preserving the quintessentially English quality of the Church of England but also in preventing its evolution into a sectarian type of organization (Aldridge, 1986, pp. 372-376).

At the individual level, the personal integrity of clergymen and clergywomen is taken for granted. They enjoy a style of life that grants them a high degree of control over their own time. Despite the growing pressure of bureaucratization in the Church, clergy are professionals with considerable autonomy, without either the alienated labor of the factory or the bureaucratic routines of the modern office. English society, which is notoriously status-ridden, accords to Anglican clergy an unassailably high standing. There is, in particular, a powerful diffusion effect from church leaders to the clerical rank and file. As Towler and Coxon (1979) said in their major study of the Anglican clergy,

If the clergy are part of the cream, the bishops are most certainly part of the *crème de la crème*. They come from the most privileged of homes and, if no longer princes except in the Church, they rank beside government ministers and High Court Judges, and have immediate access, granted as of right, to every privilege our culture has to offer. The top rank of every occupational group, save perhaps the armed forces and the Law, are left standing by the presence of the Rt Revd the Lord Bishop of anywhere. And of course it is the standing of their own highest rank which does so much for the clergy as a whole, so long as a credible proportion of them continue to come from the public schools and from Oxford and Cambridge. (p. 183)

The historical development of English universities is intimately connected to the Anglican Church. At the beginning of the 19th century, virtually all the dons in Oxford and Cambridge were in the holy orders of the Church of England. As Engel (1983) said, "The Oxford don was by profession a clergyman, not a university teacher" (p. 4). Many of the undergraduates came from clerical families and were themselves destined for a career in the Church's ministry. Until 1854, the University of Oxford was governed by statutes laid down by Archbishop Laud in the early 17th century. From 1850 to 1881, a series of government commissions produced radical revisions of college and university statutes. University teaching became a permanent career in its own right, rather than simply a step toward a Church incumbency. So it was for men; for women, the struggle for recognition was delayed. The first women's colleges at Oxford were founded in the 1870s and were admitted into full membership of the university only in 1920. The parallel with women's struggle for equality in the Church of England is significant.

In their wide-ranging survey of the academic profession in Britain, Halsey and Trow (1971) identified the English ideal of the university, an ideal deeply influenced by the model of Oxford and Cambridge. The English vision of the university embraces the following elements: It is an ancient foundation; its students are not locally based but are drawn from a national and international pool; recruitment is highly selective; it offers education for life, not training for a job; it is a small-scale residential community; the ratio of staff to students is high; it is politically autonomous; and its organization is collegiate.

This ideal is antithetical to rationalization and bureaucratization. The history of the English university system in the 20th century is characterized by rearguard actions against growing pressures from successive governments for rationalization. Similarly, the Church of England has proved extremely resistant to the rationalization of its structure and operations (Aldridge, forthcoming; Russell, 1980; Thompson, 1970).

## The Relative Standing of Clergy and Academics

The main contentions of this article are two: that there is a high degree of congruence between the status of Anglican clergy and that of academic sociologists and that, in researching the clerical profession, this congruence has to be socially negotiated and confirmed in the research process itself.

However, as soon as we inquire about the relative standing in English society of academic social researchers, on one hand, and ministers of religion, on the other, it might appear that the first contention is false. From the findings of the major investigation of social mobility conducted by sociologists at Oxford in the 1970s, academics possess a markedly higher social standing than clergy (Goldthorpe & Hope, 1974). On the Goldthorpe-Hope scale, university faculty are rated in the 4th category out of 124, but parochial clergy are far lower, in the 34th group. In the collapsed version of the scale, which comprises 36 categories, university academics are placed in Category 2 (salaried professionals), whereas parochial clergy are found in Category 9 (salaried professionals: lower grade). Finally, in the sevenfold schema of class positions adopted by the Oxford research, university faculty are assigned to Class 1: the higher and intermediate levels of the "service class." This is defined as "the class of those exercising authority and expertise on behalf of corporate bodies—plus such elements of the classic bourgeoisie (independent businessmen and 'free' professionals) as are not yet assimilated into this new formation" (Goldthorpe, Llewellyn, & Payne, 1987, p. 41). Parochial clergy are assigned to Class 2: the subaltern or cadet levels of the service class. Although they are categorized as members of the same broad "service" stratum as academics, clergy are clearly identified as relatively lowly members of it.

In ranking parochial clergy lower than university academics in all their scales and classificatory schemata, the Oxford researchers were echoing the findings of an earlier British study conducted by Glass (1954), titled *Social Mobility in Britain*. This study, carried out in the era of postwar socialist reconstruction and conducted by a team of researchers based at the London School of Economics and Political Science, placed university faculty in Category 1 of the Hall-Jones sevenfold scale of occupational prestige. This category, labeled "professional and high administrative," included "all occupations calling for highly specialized experience, and frequently the possession of a degree or comparable professional qualification necessitating a long period of education and training" (p. 31). Ministers of religion were located in Category 2, bearing the label "managerial and executive" and described as including "those responsible for initiating and/or implementing policy" (p. 34). Even if the location of ministers of religion in a lower category than academics is accepted, the category description itself is surely very odd. It bears a curious relation to the work of Anglican clergy, who are most commonly and plausibly viewed not as managers or executives but as professionals. By itself, this labeling of clergy as managerial and executive is enough to cast doubt on the validity of the scale.

### Prestige, Deference, and Symbolic Power

At the outset of their work, the Oxford researchers went to great lengths to produce a scale based on a strict interpretation of occupational prestige. Following a seminal paper by Shils (1968), they conceptualized prestige as symbolic social power and advantage giving rise to structured relationships of deference, acceptance, and derogation. Prestige as a form of power manifests itself in several modes: It creates favorable presumptions, it is a basis for exerting influence, and it confers an ability to determine standards, tastes, and styles of life.

In this strict sense, prestige depends on a shared universe of meaning: a set of traditional beliefs and values grounded in social interaction in a *gemeinschaftlich* social order. The "parson" takes his place with other social actors—the squire, the village blacksmith, the farm laborer—in a stable social order with a consensually agreed prestige hierarchy of symbolic power governing all aspects of social life.

In spite of their efforts, the Oxford team reported failure. They were unable to elicit from their respondents a scale of occupational prestige in this strict sense. What they produced instead was a ranking of occupations in terms of their "general desirability," derived from respondents' aggregate judgments of the relative costs and benefits typically experienced by members of an occupation.

Reflecting on their failure to construct a scale of occupational prestige, Goldthorpe and Hope (1974) argued that "it may well be that in modern societies no sufficiently integrated and stable ordering of prestige relationships exists to make the prestige rating of occupations (or other roles or positions) at all a feasible proposition" (p. 60n).

### Prestige in Social Context

From this it does not follow, however, that prestige qua symbolic power is a concept of no utility in analyzing contemporary social processes. Jettisoning societal scales of occupational prestige does not entail abandoning the concept of prestige itself. If prestige is conceptualized as multivalent, fluid, and context dependent, it has, I shall argue, considerable explanatory power in the analysis of relations between academic social researchers and members of elite occupations.

In their seminal work on occupational cognition, Coxon, Davies, and Jones (1986) mounted a sustained critique of attempts by British and American social scientists to construct a consensual prestige ranking of the occupational structure. Such attempts fail, the authors argued, through a combination of theoretical incoherence and methodological confusion. They identified and sought to refute the four fundamental claims that constitute the structural-functional fallacy. These claims are as follows:

1. *Methodological invariance*: that a similar hierarchy of occupational prestige is disclosed in social scientific studies, despite the wide variety of research methods employed and populations sampled.
2. *Linearity*: that occupational prestige rankings form a unidimensional continuum.
3. *Evaluative consensus*: that occupational prestige rankings represent a single, stable viewpoint from which there are no systematic social deviations.
4. *Cross-national uniformity*: that there is a high degree of conformity in occupational prestige rankings despite apparent cultural diversity between industrial societies.

Their own research, which is eclectic and more fine-grained, pointed to different conclusions: that prestige is multidimensional, fluid, and context dependent. In contrast to the prevailing static and context-free model of prestige, they argued for an approach to occupational cognition that is dynamic and grounded in a social context: "Occupational discourse is inherently contextual." Rather than possessing one dominant "image" of occupational standing, people employ a repertoire of such images in different contexts for different purposes.

There follows a conclusion of crucial importance for research into elite occupations: Occupational prestige is not given but negotiated. To gain access and secure cooperation, to achieve rapport, to gather sensitive information—all rely on the successful negotiation of the prestige relationship between researcher and informant. In Shils's (1968) terms, what is sought is the appropriate blend of deference and acceptance in relations between the participants in the research process.

### Negotiating Status With Anglican Clergy

In contrast to conventional sociological wisdom, Coxon, Davies, and Jones (1986) found strong evidence of occupational egoism. There was a marked tendency for respondents to enhance their evaluations of their own occupations and ones deemed similar to it. This is, as they say, "clearly a phenomenon of major importance." Its implications for the research process are profound.

What, then, is likely to determine perceived similarity? Coxon, Davies, and Jones identified two salient criteria: the degree of formal education demanded by the occupation and the degree to which it requires its members to work with people rather than with things. Dichotomizing and combining the two criteria generates a fourfold typology. From their own data, as well as from a priori judgment, ministers of religion are located in the quadrant that contains occupations requiring a high degree of formal education and involving work directly with other people. This is also, of course, the quadrant in which professional sociologists are located.

I would argue that it is this congruence that explains the high rates of response that social researchers typically achieve in studies of the Church of England and other mainline Christian denominations in the United Kingdom. For example, a mail questionnaire I distributed to parish clergymen in 1983 had an 82% response (Aldridge, 1986), and a later mail questionnaire to women deacons (Aldridge, 1991) achieved 86%. Ranson, Bryman, and Hinings (1977) had a 79% response to a mail questionnaire, and a follow-up by Bryman (1989) achieved 73%. It is not that clergy have plenty of spare time on their hands and nothing better to do. Contrary to popular mythology, they are massively burdened with professional commitments. Rather, they respond to social research because they see in it and its practitioners a set of aims and objectives similar to their own. Questionnaires still have to be properly designed, of course!

I contend that, in the research act, what the social scientist has to accomplish is a successful negotiation of relations of prestige—of deference, acceptance, and derogation. In the case of my own work with Anglican clergymen and women, I consciously sought to emphasize the elements of congruence, in particular similarities of occupational culture and habitus (Bourdieu, 1984).

The success of my research depended on establishing my own independence from internal Church affairs. I tried to do everything possible to confirm my identity as a sociologist at the University of Nottingham conducting independent academic research. For example, in a cover letter accompanying a mail questionnaire, I stated, "This is a piece of individual academic research and is not being carried out on behalf of any organization or interest group inside or outside the Church." Despite this, one respondent—a prominent (Anglo-Catholic) figure in the national affairs of the Church—wrote to me asking whether I was an associate of the (Evangelical) principal of a nearby theological college. He also wanted an assurance that I had no connection with MOW, the Movement for the Ordination of Women. My personal assurance on both of these matters secured me a successful, frank, and highly revealing interview. Another respondent inquired, ostensibly as a joke, whether I was a spy from the archdeacon. Given that this respondent reported acute personal problems affecting his ministry, his question was pointed and poignant.

The Church of England has many of the qualities of a club for gentlemen. It is exempt from the provisions of the Sex Discrimination Act of 1975 and thus is legally entitled to continue to exclude women from the priesthood. Women have found great difficulty in securing acceptance into the structures of decision making at the parish level; conventional gender roles predominate (Aldridge, 1987, 1989). Female researchers might well have found it harder to achieve rapport with some of the clergymen I interviewed.

In conversation with me, and even during the tape-recording of interviews, many respondents were apparently unabashed at passing manifestly sexist remarks. I was initially very surprised because I had imagined that, given my efforts to remain neutral, they would project onto me the characteristics stereotypically ascribed to sociologists in English culture, including progressive leftist opinions. I had forgotten the congruence of clerical and academic occupational cultures. The English university has been and remains a predominantly patriarchal institution, where senior management positions are a virtual male monopoly, whereas women, as in the Church, predominate in lower-status roles—cleaning university offices and Church brass, for example. It is only in the past 20 years that British sociology has seriously addressed the problem of sexism within the profession, entirely as a result of pressure from feminist colleagues. In the university community more generally, equal opportunities policies are typically of even more recent origin. So when one respondent, opposed to women's entry into the priesthood, said that he relished the Church's "atmosphere of a man's club, perhaps. It's actually quite a safe place not to be nagged at," he was expressing views not uncharacteristic of the faculty club at the university.

I had expected difficulty in achieving rapport with female respondents, but this proved not to be a problem. At no point did any interviewee make an adverse comment about the fact that I was asking questions about women's issues, including their own experiences of discrimination and their own aspirations to the priesthood. After one interview was concluded, one woman addressed the issue explicitly—but this was to compliment me on empathizing with women's issues.

Again, I attribute this to occupational culture. Women in the ministry of the Church are working in a man's world: They are used to dealing with men and answering questions from them. Few female ministers adopt an overtly challenging stance, and few identify themselves as feminist; rather, they seek to persuade by example. The Christian virtues of humility and forbearance are operative factors, as is women's lack of authority over men within Church structures. My female informants appeared more than content to use my research as a vehicle to tell their story, a story that has been largely hidden from history.

All professions have a corpus of sacred discourse. Access to this discourse is closely guarded by licensed practitioners and their professional associations. One or two key words typically signal the boundary between the sacred discourse of the profession and profane discourse accessible to laypeople. In the case of my work on those in the clergy, the key word was "theology." It frequently happened during interviews that a respondent would spontaneously label an argument "theological." For example, when discussing the hotly contested issue of women's exclusion from the priesthood, it was common for respondents to specify that their arguments were theological and not simply "practical." Not only was this a means of signaling the importance of the argument, it was also a way of claiming expertise and authority in propounding it. Very often, the respondent would draw a contrast not just between theology and practicality but between theology and sociology. The implication was clear: Theology was their main expert domain, sociology mine. When they offered "sociological" arguments, they invariably indicated that they were mere amateurs, whereas I, as a professional, would probably find their reasoning faulty or ill-founded. Conversely, it was clear that I was not to profess expertise in theology, although I was expected to acknowledge the primacy of theological arguments. When I interviewed women—who at the time were deaconesses and therefore technically lay women rather than professional clergy—they typically disclaimed theological expertise. Theology—the theoretical heart of professional knowledge in the Church—has been a male preserve. When I approached deaconesses to request an interview, I often had to reassure them that their own experience and opinions would be valuable to me; this was never the case with the men, who simply took it for granted that their professional opinions would be of value. In the interviews themselves, whereas clergymen offered opinions, women tended to report experience, reflecting the differential location of women and men in the authority structure of the Church.

In regard to theology, then, my role was to be deferential. I gave no indication of familiarity with technical theological writing. On the other hand, I felt it necessary to ensure, in advance of my interviews, that I understood the formal organization of the Church of England, had learned its technical vocabulary, and was au courant with contemporary issues in the Church. This partly accounts for the fact that all my respondents appeared to assume (incorrectly) that I am a communicant member of the Church of England.

In one sense, they were simply surprised that anyone could be so conversant with Church affairs without being a participant in them. Even so, it is surely revealing that they expected a sociologist interested in the Church to be a Christian. This contradicts the (distinctively British) stereotype of the sociologist as an immoralist, a view most sharply portrayed in Malcolm Bradbury's novel *The History Man*. Perhaps the parallel between clergy and sociologists is again relevant: Sociologists as a secular priesthood may have replaced the clergy as an object of satire in the English novel.

In terms of their mutual relations, sociology and theology in Britain have indeed been allies, not opponents. Among the social sciences, it is not sociology but psychology and economics that are the principal heirs of freethinking Enlightenment rationalism. Far from being aggressively reductionist, British sociology of religion has been dominated by the Weberian paradigm of humanistic *verstehende Soziologie*.

In my research, I was careful to avoid any impression that my practice of sociology was scientistic. Hence my interviews were semistructured, allowing respondents to develop their own reflections with only gentle guidance from me. If I had presented myself with a highly structured interview schedule, I am sure it would have endangered rapport. Clergymen are used to being in a position of authority, leading discussion rather than following it. They are also used to conducting interviews with their own clientele, and these will not be highly structured. A structured interview would have created a symbolic opposition between sociology as science and theology as nonscience. I was seeking to signal the congruence between sociology and theology, sociologist and theologian, researcher and researched.

Owing to its length, my mail questionnaire to parish clergy consisted mainly of closed, forced-choice questions. I was careful, therefore, to allow ample space for respondents to write additional comments, and my cover letter emphasized that I planned to conduct follow-up interviews "to explore the issues in more depth." Preliminary piloting of the questionnaire had indicated that respondents were likely to react unfavorably to any research instrument that appeared to be designed to pigeonhole them and their opinions into predefined categories. Even (especially?) in a mail questionnaire, it was necessary to emphasize the underlying humanistic approach. Without this, respondents would have been less likely to see the sociological researcher as sharing with them a location in Coxon and colleagues' "people oriented" quadrant.

### Concluding Remarks

The history and contemporary condition of university academics and professional clergy in Great Britain, and more specifically in England, have many points of similarity. The academic profession evolved out of the clerical, and the ideal of the English university is infused with religious connotations. Both professions have retained significant elements of 19th-century "status professionalism," resisting the full impact of processes of rationalization that have transformed other professions.

Similarly, both professions are under threat. On one hand, the "statistics of decline" endanger the economic viability of the Church of England as presently organized and are corrosive of morale in the clerical profession. On the other hand, universities are confronting a major but underfunded expansion of student numbers. In this period of rapid change, the ancient professions, including universities and the Church of England, have come under attack from the radical right for alleged failures to recognize and adapt to contemporary realities.

Viewed in this sociocultural context, to conceptualize the research relationship between social scientist and cleric merely in terms of a one-dimensional hierarchy of occupational prestige is superficial and of little practical use to either party. Rather the contextualization and

negotiation of status in its full Weberian sense is an integral part of the
research relationship in the study of the clerical, as of any other,
profession.

## References

Aldridge, A. E. (1986). Slaves to no sect: The Anglican clergy and liturgical change. *Sociological Review, 34*(2), 357-380.
Aldridge, A. E. (1987). In the absence of the minister: Structures of subordination in the role of deaconess in the Church of England. *Sociology, 21*(3), 377-392.
Aldridge, A. E. (1989). Men, women and clergymen: Opinion and authority in a sacred organization. *Sociological Review, 37*(1), 43-64.
Aldridge, A. E. (1991). Women's experience of diaconate. In *Deacons now.* London: Advisory Council for the Church's Ministry.
Aldridge, A. E. (Forthcoming). Discourse on women in the clerical profession: The diaconate and language-games in the Church of England. *Sociology, 21*(1).
Archbishop's Commission. (1970). *Church and state: The Chadwick report.* London: Church Information Office.
Bellah, R. N. (1975). *The broken covenant: American civil religion in time of trial.* New York: Seabury.
Bourdieu, P. (1984). *Distinction: A social critique of the judgement of taste.* London: Routledge & Kegan Paul.
Bryman, A. (1989). The value of re-studies in sociology: The case of clergy and ministers, 1971 to 1985. *Sociology, 23*(1), 31-53.
Coxon, A. P. M., Davies, P. M., & Jones, C. L. (1986). *Images of social stratification.* London: Sage.
Engel, A. J. (1983). *From clergyman to don.* Oxford: Clarendon.
Glass, D. V. (1954). *Social mobility in Britain.* London: Routledge & Kegan Paul.
Goldthorpe, J. H., & Hope, K. (1974). *The social grading of occupations.* Oxford: Clarendon.
Goldthorpe, J. H., Llewellyn, C., & Payne, C. (1987). *Social mobility and class structure in modern Britain* (2nd ed.). Oxford: Clarendon.
Habgood, J. (1983). *Church and nation in a secular age.* London: Darton, Longman & Todd.
Halsey, A. H., & Trow, M. A. (1971). *The British academics.* London: Faber & Faber.
Murphy, R. (1988). *Social closure.* Oxford: Oxford University Press.
Ranson, S., Bryman, A., & Hinings, B. (1977). *Clergy, ministers and priests.* London: Routledge & Kegan Paul.
Russell, A. (1980). *The clerical profession.* London: SPCK.
Shils, E. (1968). Deference. In J. A. Jackson (Ed.), *Social stratification.* Cambridge: Cambridge University Press.
Thompson, K. A. (1970). *Bureaucracy and church reform.* Oxford: Oxford University Press.
Towler, R., & Coxon, A. P. M. (1979). *The fate of the Anglican clergy.* London: Macmillan.

*9*

# *How I Learned What a Crock Was*

## HOWARD S. BECKER

In Fall 1955, I moved to Kansas City to begin fieldwork at the University of Kansas Medical School as the first field-worker in a project led by Everett Hughes, part of a team that eventually also included Blanche Geer and Anselm Strauss.[1] We were going to study medical students and medical education, but, to be truthful, I had very little idea of what I was going to do beyond "hanging around with the students," going to classes, and whatever else presented itself.

I had even less idea what the problem was that we were going to investigate. There was a field of sociology called "socialization," and Robert Merton and his students had been studying the socialization of medical students to the role of doctor. My dissertation, a study of schoolteachers' careers, could have been said to be in the "sociology of education," but that didn't prepare me to study medical students. As far as I had gone in conceptualizing my problem was to say to myself that these kids came in at one end and 4 years later came out at the other end and that something certainly must have happened to them in between.

In any event, I was more concerned with our family's move from Urbana (what a relief to get out of there!) to Kansas City (which I hoped, and it turned out to be true, would provide a better place to practice my

NOTE: Reprinted from a special issue, "Fieldwork in Elite Settings," edited by Rosanna Hertz and Jonathan B. Imber for the *Journal of Contemporary Ethnography*, Vol. 22, No. 1, 1993, pp. 28-35. Copyright 1993 by Sage Publications, Inc.

other trade of piano playing) and with getting to know my way around what appeared to me enormous buildings that were the University of Kansas Medical Center.

I knew next to nothing about the organization of medical education and consoled myself about my ignorance with "wisdom" that told me that therefore I would have no prejudices either. How scientific! I didn't even know, and had to be told, that the first 2 years of the 4-year medical course were mostly academic; only during the last 2 "clinical" years did students actually work on hospital wards, attending to patients.

Fortunately, the dean of the school took me in hand and decided that I should begin my investigations with a group of third-year students in the Internal Medicine Department. There were two third-year student groups, superintended by different faculty members, and he took care that I ended up with the one run by the "benign" doctor. I learned soon enough that the other was one of those legendary terrors who cowed students, house staff, and most of his patients with his temper.

I didn't know what internal medicine was but learned quickly enough that it had to do with everything that wasn't surgery or pediatrics or obstetrics or any of a lot of other named specialties. I soon learned too that the people who practiced internal medicine considered themselves, and were considered by others, to be the intellectuals of the medical business, as opposed to the surgeons, who were thought to be money-grubbing brutes, or the psychiatrists, who were thought to be crazy themselves.

With no problem to orient myself to, no theoretically defined puzzle I was trying to solve, I concentrated on finding out what the hell was going on, who all these people were, what they were doing, what they were talking about, finding my way around and, most of all, getting to know the six students with whom I was going to spend the next 6 weeks. I was a Jewish smart aleck from the University of Chicago and they were several varieties of small-town and larger-city Kansans and Missourians, but we got on well from the start. They were interested in what I was doing and curious about my work and job ("How much do they pay you to do this?" they wanted to know). They thought it was nice that I got paid to study them and did not doubt that they were worth the trouble.

None of us was sure what I was "allowed" to do or which things they did that were "private" while others were OK for me to follow along on. Clearly, I could go to class with them or make rounds of the patients with them and the attending physician. But the first time one of the students got up and said, "Well, I have to go examine a patient now," I could see that I had to take matters into my own hands and set the right precedent.

Neither the dean nor anyone else had said I could watch while students examined patients. On the other hand, no one had said I couldn't do that. My presence during a physical examination might have been construed as a violation of patient privacy except that it would be a joke to raise that matter in a medical school, where such intimate procedures as rectal and vaginal exams were often carried out before a sizable audience. The student, being new at examining patients, wasn't too eager to have me watch him fumble. But if I let the situation get defined as "the sociologist can't watch us examine patients" I'd be cut off from one of the major things students did. So I said, with a confidence I didn't feel, "OK. I'll come with you." He must have thought I knew something he didn't and so did not argue the point.

Making rounds worked like this. The physician whose group I was working with had a "service," a number of beds occupied by his patients. A resident or two and an intern worked on the service, and six students were assigned to it. Every patient was assigned to a student, who was responsible for doing a physical exam, taking a history, ordering diagnostic tests, making a diagnosis, and planning a course of treatment. Mind you, all that work was done again by an intern, a resident, and the physician.

Every morning the whole group assembled and walked around to see all the patients on the service; that was making rounds. At each bed, the physician talked to the patient, asked the house staff about any developments since yesterday, and then made that patient the occasion for an informal quiz of the student to whom he or she had been assigned. The quiz could be about anything, and students were nervous about what might come up.

During my first week in the school, while I followed the students and others through the ritual of making rounds, I made my discovery. It wasn't the "ah-ha" that researchers often report. Rather, it was a piece of detective work that took me and several of the students most of the next week. Its ramifications occupied me and my colleagues for the duration of the project.

One morning as we made rounds, we saw a very talkative patient, who had multiple complaints to tell the doctor about—all sorts of aches, pains, and unusual events. I could see that no one was taking her very seriously, and on the way out, one of the students said, "Boy, she's really a crock!" I understood this, in part, as shorthand for "crock of shit." It was obviously invidious. But what was he talking about? What was wrong with her having all those complaints? Wasn't that interesting? (By the way, this first patient was a woman and the "non-crock" that followed was a man, which exactly suited the medical stereotypes that said crocks were overwhelmingly women.)

As I've already said, my discovery of what the word "crock" meant was not a lightning bolt of intuition. On the contrary, it was guided by sociological theorizing every step of the way. Like this. When I heard Chet call the patient a crock, I engaged in a quick but deep theoretical analysis. I had a piece of theory ready to put to work here. To put it most pretentiously, when members of one status category make invidious distinctions among the members of another status category with whom they regularly deal, the distinction will reflect the interests of the members of the first category in the relationship. More specifically, perhaps less forbiddingly, the invidious distinctions that students made between classes of patients would show what interests they were trying to maximize in that relationship, what they hoped to get out of it.

So, when Chet called the patient a crock, I made this theoretical analysis in a flash and then came up with a profoundly theoretical question: "What's a crock?" He looked at me as if to say that any damn fool would know that. So I said, "Seriously, when you called her a crock, what did you mean?" He looked a little confused. He had known what he meant when he said it but wasn't sure he could explain it. After fumbling for a while, he said it referred to someone with psychosomatic illness. That let him off the hook for the moment by partially satisfying my curiosity, though I still wanted to know what interest of his as a student was violated by a patient with psychosomatic illness.

But, as a good scientist, I wanted to check my finding out further, so I held my tongue. The next patient we saw, as it turned out, had a gastric ulcer, and the attending physician made him the occasion for a short lecture on psychosomatic illness, with ulcer the example at hand. It was quite interesting, and, when we left the room, I tried out my new knowledge and said to Chet, "Crock, huh?" He looked at me as though I were a fool and said, "No, he's not a crock." I said, "Why not? He has psychosomatic disease, doesn't he? Didn't you just tell me that's what a crock is? Didn't we just spend 10 minutes discussing it?" He looked more confused than before, and another student, eavesdropping on our discussion, undertook to clear it up: "No, he's not a crock. He really has an ulcer."

I don't remember all the details of what followed. What I do remember is that I got all the students interested in the question, and, between us, with me asking a lot of questions and applying the results to succeeding cases, we ended up defining a crock as a patient who had multiple complaints but no discernible physical pathology. That definition was robust and held up under many further tests.

But my problem was only half solved. I still had to find out why students thought crocks were bad. What interest of theirs was compromised by a patient with many complaints and no pathology? When I asked them, students said that you couldn't learn anything from crocks that would be useful in your future medical practice. That told me that what students wanted to maximize in school, not surprisingly, was the chance to learn things that would be useful when they entered practice. But if that was true, then it seemed contradictory to devalue crocks because there were many such patients. In fact, the attending physicians liked to point out that most of the patients a physician saw in an ordinary practice would be like that. So a crock ought to provide excellent training for practice.

When I pursued that paradox, students told me that you might have a lot of patients like that later on, but you couldn't learn anything from seeing them here in school. Not what they wanted to learn, anyway. Which was what? They explained that all their teachers ever said about what to do with crocks was that you should talk to them, that talking made crocks feel better. The students felt they had learned that with the first one. Succeeding crocks did not add to their knowledge of crockdom, its differential diagnosis, or its treatment. A crock presented no medical puzzles to be solved.

What they wanted to learn, students said, was a certain kind of knowledge that could not be learned from books. They studied their books dutifully, preparing for the quizzes that punctuated rounds and other such events, but believed that the most important knowledge they would acquire in school was not in those books. What was most worth learning was what my colleagues and I eventually summarized as "clinical experience"—the sights, sounds, and smells of disease in a living person: what a heart murmur really sounded like when you had your stethoscope against a patient's chest as opposed to its sound on a recording, how patients whose hearts sounded that way looked and talked about how they felt, what a diabetic or a person who had just suffered a heart attack looked like.

You could only learn those things from people who had real physical pathologies. You learn nothing about cardiac disease from a patient who is sure he's having heart attacks every day but has no murmurs to listen to, no unusual EKG findings, no heart disease. So crocks disappointed students by having no pathology you could observe firsthand. That showed me an important and characteristic feature of contemporary medical practice: the preference for personal experience over scientific publications as a source of the wisdom you used to guide your practice. We eventually called this the "clinical experience" perspective and found its traces everywhere. Perhaps most important, even faculty who themselves published scientific papers would say, in response to a student question about something reported in a medical journal, "I know that's what people have found but I've tried that procedure and it didn't work for me, so I don't care what the journals say."

Crocks had other irritating characteristics, which students eventually explained under my barrage of questions. Students, perpetually over-worked, always had new patients to work up, classes to go to, books and articles to read, and notes to record in patients' charts. Examining patients always took time, but examining crocks took forever. Crocks had dozens of symptoms to describe and were sure that every detail was important. They wanted to describe their many previous illnesses in similar detail. Many of them had been able to persuade physicians (who, the students thought, should have been less pliable) to perform multiple surgeries—which they also wanted to describe fully. (I remember a patient who had had so many abdominal surgeries that her navel had been completely obliterated. She made a deep impression on all of us.)

So crocks took much more of your time than other patients and gave you much less of anything you wanted for your trouble. That showed me another important feature of medical school life: Everything was a trade-off of time, the scarcest commodity for a student or house officer, for other valuable things. We found the traces of that proposition everywhere too. For instance, students often traded patients with each other. Why? Well, if I've had three patients with myocardial infarcts (as I learned, with the students, to call a heart attack) and you've had three patients with diabetes, it's obviously mutually advantageous for us to trade, so that neither of us wastes our time learning the same facts three times while missing another equally useful set of facts altogether.

Students disliked crocks, I eventually learned, for still a third reason. Like their teachers, students hoped to perform medical miracles and heal the sick, if not actually raise the dead. They knew that wasn't easy to do and that they wouldn't always be successful, but one of the real payoffs of medical practice for them was to "do something" and watch a sick person get well. But you can't perform a medical miracle on someone who was never sick in the first place. Because crocks, in the student view, weren't "really sick," they were useless as the raw material of medical miracles.

We eventually called this attitude the "medical responsibility" perspective and saw its traces everywhere too. Perhaps its most bizarre outcropping was the idea that you weren't fully operating as a doctor unless what you did could, if done wrong, kill people. This was enshrined in a putdown of the specialty of dermatology we heard several times: "You can't kill anybody and you can't cure anybody." A more accurate rendition of the general principle involved would have been "You can't cure anyone *unless* you can kill them."

Learning what a crock was was thus a matter of carefully unraveling the multiple meanings built into that simple word, rather than the Big Ah-Ha social scientists sometimes describe. This little ah-ha may have a lesson for us when we experience the Big Ah-Ha. Intuitions are great but they don't do much for us unless we follow them up with the detailed work that shows us what they really mean, what they can really account for.

### Note

1. The study was reported in full in Howard S. Becker, Blanche Geer, Everett Hughes, and Anselm Strauss, *Boys in White* (Chicago: University of Chicago Press, 1961). A one-paragraph description of the discovery of the meaning of "crock" appears in Howard S. Becker, "Problems of inference and proof in participant observation," *American Sociological Review, 23*(December, 1958), 658.

# PART III

# Community and Political Elites

Despite the public visibility of community and political elites, the authors in this section present the hurdles they had to overcome in defining themselves as researchers in relation to those who have power in communities and politics. Each of them tells a different story about how they came to understand the unique contexts in which their identities as researchers became as important to define as the subjects of the studies themselves. What worked in one context may not necessarily work in another.

Susan Ostrander discusses her past work on upper-class women and several non-profit agencies including her present research on a radical philanthropic organization. From her point of view, the problem of conducting such research does not center so much on gaining access but rather on penetrating the class culture sufficiently to expose the "real" concerns and viewpoints of her subjects. Researchers need to recognize their inclination to defer in such settings which may result in simultaneously overestimating what their subjects know about their organizations and underestimating the researcher's ability to achieve a more candid and informative interview.

By paying attention to how nonverbal cues may subtly define the interview situation, she explains why directing the interview can counter the elite's inclination to "just talk," which is part of their class culture repertoire. By recognizing these repertoires, she effectively neutralizes her subjects' social class position, thus placing herself on equal footing with them, if only momentarily.

Albert Hunter envisions the social researcher as a mediator between the haves and the have nots. His approach focuses as much on the ironic, debunking mission of conducting research as on the methodological problems inherent in getting "backstage." In studying local politics in a variety of communities, he emphasizes the difficulties of establishing the appropriate identity of researcher. He capitalizes not only on his shared status as a local himself but also on his professional status as a professor. One dilemma he points out is that elites expect researchers to know something and to have done their homework. The extent to which this preparation is displayed may have consequences for being dismissed or taken seriously by community elites.

Hanna Herzog offers a cross-cultural examination of women in local politics. Because so few women enter politics, Herzog was given access to their networks as someone who was an expert and "who possesses relevant knowledge about the subjects." Unlike her counterparts who study American political elites, Herzog describes an inverse status relation in which her presence validated their attempts to imagine themselves as real political players. One of the implications of a feminist methodology is that a researcher may contribute to the coherence that takes shape within groups that have felt historically disenfranchised. As she concludes, "the research situation [should] be considered not as a one-dimensional power situation, but as a multi-level interaction."

Hugh Gusterson's major concern is with the ethics of writing critically about those who have consented to be studied and whose viewpoints are not shared by the researcher. This political tension, he argues, is part of the liberal legacy; researchers invoke "cultural relativism to bracket any moral disagreements we may have with informants." But, he continues, this is much easier to accomplish with cultures especially different from our own: the headhunter poses fewer personal difficulties for the researcher than does the nuclear weapons designer who lives next door. The study of nuclear issues has consistently represented the voice of protest rather than the official voices against which protest is directed. The unwillingness to scrutinize the activities of nuclear elites, Gusterson believes, inadvertently reinforces their professional and political power. Further, he offers suggestions to social scientists for a kind of ethnographic writing that is at once more critical and more balanced.

# 10

# "Surely You're Not in This Just to Be Helpful"

## Access, Rapport, and Interviews in Three Studies of Elites

### SUSAN A. OSTRANDER

Social scientists too rarely "study up." The list of names of sociologists who have written about upper-class elites is too short and too easily recalled. A documentation of research methods used in studying elites, like the present special issue, should facilitate more of this kind of work. Because it is my own view that a lack of knowledge about elites contributes to obscuring and therefore maintaining their position in society, a better understanding of methodologies for elite study may also play a part in challenging that position.

From the mid-1970s to the present, I have conducted three distinct projects that include or focus entirely on elites. The first was based on in-depth qualitative interviews with traditional married women of the old upper class. I was most interested in how the family and community activities of these women and the meaning they gave to them contrib-

NOTE: Reprinted from a special issue, "Fieldwork in Elite Settings," edited by Rosanna Hertz and Jonathan B. Imber for the *Journal of Contemporary Ethnography*, Vol. 22, No. 1, 1993, pp. 7-27. Copyright 1993 by Sage Publications, Inc.

uted to maintaining the position of their class, this in spite of clear and important contradictions between their class and gender positions (Ostrander, 1980a, 1980b, 1984).

In 1983 and 1984, I conducted a field study of three old, established nongovernmental, nonprofit family and child welfare agencies using the multiple methods of observation, documentary analysis, and focused qualitative interviews (Ostrander, 1985, 1987, 1989). These agencies were themselves elites in their field and were so described by members of the human service community. I was interested generally in how they were coping with the governmental cutbacks in social welfare spending. A focus of that work was to see how board members who were social and business elites exercised their influence at this critical time in these agencies' history. I was also interested in how that influence was challenged by nonelites and some elites, and in how beliefs and practices of elites became established as uncontested taken-for-granted realities and institutionalized formal policies.

My present project is a study of Haymarket Peoples' Fund, a small charitable foundation in Boston that supports only grassroots organizing efforts for social change (Ostrander, 1993, 1995). Haymarket was founded in 1974 by a group of young people of inherited wealth who wanted to use some of their money for radical causes. It is a founding member of a national network of similar foundations called the Funding Exchange. One of my primary interests in this project is to see what possibilities there are in the way that Haymarket practices fund-raising and grant making for building alliances across class, race, and gender to work together for social change. In this project, I am again using the multiple methods of observation, documentary analysis, and focused qualitative interviews.

My research on elites has, therefore, covered a rather wide range of ways of understanding their place and their relationships with others in the class structure and in the structure of organizations. Across this range, I have found a number of methodological issues in common. This article focuses especially on two issues: gaining access and techniques of interviewing. I also consider some ways to gain and establish the rapport necessary for studying elites, a rapport that consists of both trust and respect. A few points are also made about dealing with the status difference between elite subjects and the researcher and about protecting the interests and integrity of the research and the researcher, given the power of elite subjects.

### Gaining Access, Establishing Rapport, and Protecting the Research

My experience suggests that the difficulties of gaining access and establishing the rapport necessary to study elites have been exaggerated, whereas the difficulties of protecting the research and the researcher have been rarely discussed. Well-thought-out strategies for access and rapport are often useful or necessary. However, luck and a willingness to take advantage of opportunities as they arise have proven just as valuable. Because I believe that one reason why social scientists are hesitant to study elites is because they expect difficulty at this stage of the project, I present my experience in some detail. The strategies I discuss include using your own circles and activities to put you in touch with subjects; doing preparatory background work with people "in the know" before attempting to enter the field; making the right contacts, often in the right order; being appreciative of subjects' willingness to participate but not deferential and never obsequious; taking extra time to meet directly with people who have concerns and respond actively to those concerns while at the same time maintaining clear control of the research; being aware that gaining access is not the same as establishing the trust required for getting useful data and that there will likely be an ongoing process of being "checked out"; putting agreements in writing; and providing feedback and, when appropriate, opportunities for subjects to respond to and engage in dialogue about written proposals and interim and final reports or working papers as part of the research.

For a period of months before beginning my project on upper-class women, a project that began as my Ph.D. dissertation, I talked with my fellow graduate students and professors about my plans. One day, a fellow graduate student told me she had worked on an electoral campaign with a woman she thought met the criteria for upper-class membership that I was intending to use (Baltzell, 1958, 1964; Domhoff, 1970). I contacted this woman and told her of my interest in "learning about the role of women in some of the old and influential families in town." As is often true of first contacts, this woman was somewhat marginal to her class, being of more liberal political views (Vidich, 1955, p. 357). She nonetheless met the criteria of upper-class membership, and, even more important, was known and respected by others so that she could serve as an informant about entrée as well as a subject. She told me that it was important to "go in the right order. You have to start at the top." By this she meant starting with the oldest grandes dames who would then—if they liked me—provide me with access to others. She offered to call three of these women for me and arrange their consent. She was successful, and I interviewed them, explaining my project by telling them that people knew a great deal about what men in families like theirs did with their lives but that very little was known about what women did. At the end of the interviews, I asked if they could refer me to other women like themselves, with similar backgrounds, and if I could use their names. They agreed and offered to call the women they mentioned to say they had spoken with me. I was in. Issues of rapport are considered in more depth in the section on interviewing.

Gaining access and establishing rapport in the three family and child welfare agencies I selected for my next major project was more challenging. These agencies were described by others as "elite," by which people meant having been around for over a century, having relatively large operating budgets, and being supported by local social and business elites. I spent a number of months locating and doing background preparatory interviews with people "in the know" about the human service community in the city, asking them what they saw as the important issues and questions and seeking their advice on what agencies would provide the best settings for the kinds of issues I was interested in. I also learned who to approach and how and in what order and who to avoid or expect might present difficulty. The process that each agency put me through before agreeing to participate told me something about how the agency worked and who made decisions and how. Gaining entrée is the first source of valuable data in any field research project.

As I began to contact agencies for this project, I followed the earlier advice to "start at the top." The first agency I selected was the oldest and the biggest, the one that others referred to as the Cadillac of child and family agencies. In my letter to the executive director, I said, "Everyone I have thus far talked with speaks of [your agency] as a prime example of a successful voluntary agency." I enclosed a copy of a three-page, single-spaced research proposal spelling out as clearly as I could the rationale for the project, goals and objectives, methodology, and my credentials for doing the work. The next week I made the follow-up telephone call as promised in the letter. A meeting was set up by the executive director, including himself, two directors of programs, and the chair of the board of directors. This was a much more formal process than later occurred in the other two agencies.

In preparation for the meeting, I made notes to myself on two topics I expected to be of concern. One was how I thought my project might be useful to them. This included helping them to assess priorities for future decision making and planning. I had done my homework—essential for establishing the respect necessary for doing research with elites—and I knew some of the issues currently facing them, and I mentioned those. I also talked about how I could find out more about their organization in ways their own staff might not have the luxury to do by conducting interviews, attending meetings where I could reflect on the larger picture, and analyzing the data they collected on clients for trends and potential problems. I spoke of the value of my being able to gather frank opinions from people at all levels in the organization because I would assure each respondent confidentiality. I quoted from an unnamed person from another agency who saw my project as a help to "make up our minds about some hard issues." I also spoke about the kind of time commitment I would need to do the work from various people in the agency, that I would need access to records and reports, and that I would want to attend meetings at every level and take notes. I said I would provide them with a final report, comparing them in a number of measures to the other two agencies, obscuring each one with a fictitious name that I would reveal only to each agency about itself. I was not assessing quality of performance and would not be able to provide definitive answers to problems. This kind of setting of the boundaries of the research—what it can do and what it cannot—is in my experience important to establishing trust because it avoids creating expectations that the research cannot meet. Finally, I said I would expect to publish several articles in professional journals from the data I collected. This was important to protecting my own interests in regard to the research.

They queried me about my overall goals for the work. The chair of the board added in what I have come to appreciate as the common forthrightness of many elites, "Surely you're not in this just to be helpful." She accepted my repeating my goals essentially as I had stated them in the written proposal. The executive director asked me if I knew of others doing similar studies, and I did and he knew them too. This is a form of "checking out" that has occurred in all my research with elites. You get in and get useful data from them if you know others that they know and respect. The program directors were concerned that it was a bad time for the agency to be involved in a research project because "we're just now ourselves beginning to talk about how we want to use research." I said I felt no time pressure regarding their decision, that I could easily cycle through the other two agencies first and come to them several months later. I have more than once found that elites will respond to a request that suggests, politely of course, that I have other important work to do while they decide when or whether to talk with me. This makes a point about my own status, and it establishes the attitude of mutual respect that I have found essential in dealing with elites.

Toward the end of the meeting, the executive director raised a question about the phrase "self-perpetuating elite" that I had used in my written proposal in regard to board membership and questions I had about it. He asked if I would want to look at their board nominating process and I said yes, knowing it was important to be honest with them about all of the aims of my research even if it meant I didn't get in. If they let me in but didn't go along with what I was after, I knew the data I got would not be of much value. He continued to frown, and I kept quiet. The chair of the board broke in. She said supportively, "It's very much an issue," implying that I would, of course, want to look at it. Two weeks later, one of the program directors called me to say they had agreed to participate and that she would be my liaison to the agency.

I approached the next agency with another letter to the executive director and the same three-page, single-spaced research proposal, calling again the next week for an appointment. The director was intrigued by my project. During the meeting, he asked that "no students" be involved in gathering data. He said he would "clear" the project with the board at the next meeting and that he expected "no problems." A short while later, his secretary called to say they were interested in the project and I could "go ahead." Because I planned to go into this agency first, I drafted a memorandum that I requested appear in the agency newsletter introducing me and saying that in the next 2 months or so, I would be attending and taking notes at many of the board and staff meetings and that individuals in the agency might be contacted by me to request interviews. The memo explained what I was doing was in no way an evaluation or assessment. It said that I had been provided with lists of names of staff, that I would contact some of them for interviews on my own, that they would not be identified in any way, that their participation in the project was purely voluntary, and that staff had management's permission to meet with me during working hours.

About 8 months later, after spending time in both of the first two agencies, I contacted the third, saying in my letter to its executive director that the agencies I had been working in "tell me they have found my work useful to them." A meeting was set up with the executive director, the assistant director, and the head of the major program. They were agreeable to participating after "approval" by the board and other staff, which was accomplished in a couple of weeks. I began my work in the agency shortly thereafter. In a meeting with the assistant director several weeks into the project, she dropped what felt to me initially like a small bomb. She asked that the agency be provided the opportunity to "sign off" on any written reports that would be circulated or papers I might prepare for publication. Because this agency was smaller and in more financial difficulty than the other two, I could understand why its staff might be more concerned about what I would have to say about them, so I was willing to extend some protection to them. Still, I clearly could not allow the integrity of my research to be threatened by agency staff exercising control over what I could and could not write. After several conversations to try to understand the concerns more clearly, I drafted a memo "to confirm the verbal agreement made between us." I loosely interpreted her request to "sign off" as "the opportunity to review and comment on any final written reports or papers deriving from observations." I set a time limit of 10 working days for receiving such comment, and I said that I understood "that a primary reason for this agreement is to allow you to correct any errors that I may inadvertently make. In that spirit, I welcome your comment and agree to make the necessary corrections." After several conversations back and forth, a written agreement was finalized and signed by the assistant director and myself.

During this period of negotiation, I was carrying out my research in the agency on a day-to-day basis, trying not to hold my breath. When I submitted a draft of the final report 4 months later for "review and comment," there were indeed a number of changes this agency wanted made, and I had to reiterate more than once that it was only factual errors I had agreed to correct, not interpretations or conclusions. The written agreement we had signed was essential in the process. In the long run, I think the process enhanced trust between myself and people at the agency, perhaps enabling me to obtain better and fuller access to data. The few changes I did agree to clarified and thus improved my writing.

The request by this agency to have some control over what I wrote and to whom I circulated it raises the concern of protecting the integrity of the research and the researcher when studying elites. This includes the importance of assuring access to the research—making the work public. It comes up especially in elite research because of the power of elite subjects to shield themselves from exposure or criticism. In my initial negotiations with all three agencies in this study, I had made it clear, for example, that I intended to provide copies of the final report simultaneously to on-line staff as well as to administrators and board members. This became especially important in two of the agencies where there was a fair amount of conflict between management and employees. I had to gain the trust of staff members before they would talk frankly with me about these conflicts. One staff member said as I interviewed her, "I hope this study does not end up just giving more information to administrators. Staff need to know what's going on." She appeared pleased when I told her of my arrangement and asked her advice as to who would be appropriate staff members to receive the report.

Another occasion when protecting the integrity of the research became an issue had to do with the timing of publications from my early work on upper-class women. On finishing that project, I took a position in an organization in the same city where I had conducted my interviews. My boss knew of my research and, while generally supportive of it, asked me if I would be willing to not publish it for the time being as several of the women I had interviewed were on the board of this organization and he thought they might not be pleased with what I had to say. Because I needed the job, I agreed and kept my bargain. This explains in part why the book from that project was not published until a number of years had passed and I had left the city. Researchers interested in studying elites need to be aware of this kind of risk that would not occur in studies of the less powerful. Even at Haymarket Peoples' Fund, where elites are engaged in efforts to challenge the power of their own class, I have been aware of the risk that is always there of offending powerful people. To my mind, this risk is just part of studying elites.

Gaining access and developing the rapport needed to do the research at Haymarket Peoples' Fund, a project in which I am still involved, has been both similar to and different from my two previous studies of elites. The initial "getting in" at Haymarket was, on the surface, so easy that I had been "in the field" for a couple of months before I realized, first, that I had unintentionally been engaged for a number of years in carrying out the same kind of entrée work I had done in the previous study and, second, that getting in was not the same as gaining real access and establishing the kinds of relationships essential to getting useful information. Some parts of Haymarket were harder to get into than others. I discovered that my work in the progressive and feminist community in Boston and the people I met there and talked with over the years about my research interests had unintentionally fulfilled the same requirements of doing preparatory background work and making the right contacts that I had done in other research. When I approached the only staff member I knew at Haymarket with my idea for a research project, she was immediately enthusiastic. She was not a woman I knew well, but I had met her in my work in the feminist community and we knew a number of the same people. After she "checked" with other staff at a meeting where I was not present, I was in faster than I could say "But isn't there something you want from me?" I quickly prepared a letter outlining what I planned to do and what I understood they had agreed to. The letter was sent to board members and the Donor Committee, and I was introduced at the next meetings of these groups. I said very little and few questions were asked, and frankly I was puzzled about how it all happened.

Several situations that occurred over the next few weeks and months appeared to me to reveal that gaining access to Haymarket was actually an ongoing process. One day, a staff member introduced me to someone who came into the office to meet with him. It was a woman I knew from my own activist work. He shrugged and laughed and said—about me—"She knows everybody!" The next situation occurred at the Haymarket annual meeting a few weeks later. It called into question any assumptions I might have had about Haymarket being open to just anyone. A person hired by the staff but unknown to the group of about 40 people in the meeting room began to take pictures. Someone from the group immediately stood up to ask who he was and what he was going to do with the pictures. Why, I wondered to myself, had no one questioned me after I had introduced myself simply as "doing research about Haymarket" and as I sat for nearly 2 days taking notes that were almost a running transcript of the proceedings? That evening I paid special attention to what happened when I had a conversation with someone I had not met previously. What happened was they "checked me out." Who did I know? They found out I knew people they knew "in the movement." On various occasions over the next weeks and months, I have also been aware of people telling me things in confidence and then paying attention to see if I could be trusted to keep their confidence or whether I would reveal, even by my nonverbal behavior, that I had a certain piece of information they had shared with me.

So, in my present research especially, gaining access and establishing rapport has been an ongoing process over time, checking me out, testing me and finding I could be trusted, gradually letting me in to different parts of the organization. It was not until I had been at Haymarket for over a year that I began—through the staff—to have access to meetings of the planning committees for conferences that Haymarket holds for people of inherited wealth and extra earned income, and it was only as a workshop leader that I could attend one of those conferences. "Anonymity" of wealthy donors is an important operating principle at Haymarket. Although I have attended meetings of the Donor Committee since the beginning of my project, access to and relationships with donors who are not as active at Haymarket took much longer to obtain. It occurred through my establishing connections with a few donors initially at meetings and, especially I believe, in early interviews, which donors perceived as being personally valuable in sorting out a number of issues. These donors told this to others who then wanted to be interviewed. I consider this further in the next part of this article.

### Interviewing Elites, Continuing Rapport

Interviewing elites, in my experience, is indeed different from interviewing nonelites. Both my project in the three family and child welfare agencies and my present project at Haymarket provide opportunities to conduct interviews with people from a range of class backgrounds using the same interview guide. I am, then, able to make some comparisons of how class elites respond differently to the same interview situations.

In my research on upper-class women, I identified a number of issues: how the lower-status interviewer can establish the kind of relationship and control of the interview situation most effective for getting good data; how to deal with upper-class persons' tendencies to converse easily, freely, and at great length but not necessarily with the kind of substantive content the researcher requires; and how to ask threatening questions of powerful people and not only get away with it but get solid and clear answers. The other two studies I have done that include elites have allowed me to spell out further what is involved in these issues and how to deal with them.

I would suggest that all three of these issues arise out of a particular social context within which research on elites takes place and a particular kind of presentation of self to which upper-class people are typically raised. They are taught from a very early age social graces that set them apart from others but do so in a way that, on the surface, conveys an impression that they are like others. This can be both intimidating and confusing to the uninitiated researcher. In his book *Old Money*, Aldrich (1988) characterized the ability of his own class to put others at ease and make them feel good about themselves as a "gift: that the upper classes could close, even as they marked, the social distance between themselves and others" (p. 86). He described how upper-class social graces convey, on one hand, the message "Why, you're as good as I am!" (p. 85). On the other hand, this acquired demeanor, this "sense of composure, as though they were perfectly integrated" also brings out in others a sense of not being able to achieve this kind of natural, effortless, easy, confident sense of oneself (p. 83). Aldrich laid this out in stunning detail, showing how "by their easy, natural, and democratic manners [upper-class persons] should remind everyone else of what they are missing" (p. 86).

It appears relatively clear how this demeanor that Aldrich described so well can have the effect of intimidating others, including researchers who study elites. In addition to feeling intimidated, a sense of real confusion can arise from a simultaneous sense of being put in one's place by elites at the same time that they are being warm, friendly, open, and communicative. Both the intimidation and the confusion can, in my experience, be mitigated by understanding what is going on and where it is coming from, and seeing one's own responses as part of the data to be made visible and brought into the work rather than something that has to be erased entirely. The successful researcher has to meet these issues head on and develop clear and explicit strategies for dealing with them. Let me consider each of these issues in turn.

Elites are used to being in charge, and they are used to having others defer to them. They are also used to being asked what they think and having what they think matter in other people's lives. These social facts can result in the researcher being too deferential and overly concerned about establishing positive rapport. They can also result in the researcher overestimating the importance of what elites have to say, assuming, for example, that they necessarily know more and better what is going on in an organization. I have found that these common assumptions on the part of both the elite subject and the nonelite interviewer need to be actively challenged from the outset of the interview so that both can work together to construct a useful interview. In my experience, nonverbal strategies work best. I have found it important for the interviewer to establish some visible control of the situation at the very beginning, even if the elite subject is momentarily set off balance. This came to my attention especially on one occasion when an elite board member of one of the family and child welfare agencies I was studying suggested that I meet him for our interview at 7:30 in the morning at an elegant downtown restaurant where he had a table in his name and breakfasted daily. I agreed and wondered aloud to a friend how I would convey the message from the outset—to myself as well as to him—that I was going to structure the social situation in which we found ourselves, even though we were clearly in his social space and not mine. My friend suggested that I begin by arriving early and be sitting at his table when he came in. That would give me some time to get accustomed to the space and claim some of it as my own before he arrived. It worked like a charm. He appeared briefly taken aback and began by deferring to me and my research interests. It was a very successful interview, frank and substantive.

In my earlier work interviewing upper-class women, I stumbled onto the technique of using the placement of my tape recorder as an excuse to make the decision about where in the room we would sit. Arriving at the women's homes with clipboard and tape recorder in hand conveyed the message that I was there to work and expected the same of my subjects. I also learned after a few mistakes not to behave like a guest because being a guest set the wrong tone and led us into "socializing." Not behaving like a guest meant that I stopped accepting offers of tea and cookies in the afternoon, although I would accept offers of morning coffee. It meant that I did not comment on the elegant surroundings, and, although I certainly thanked my subjects for their time, I did not engage in the kind of gratitude that one extends to a hostess who has invited you to her home for a social occasion. I consciously assumed an expectation that the women would answer my questions as fully and directly as they could, following a journalist's "right to know." Others have emphasized the importance of these expectations on the part of the researcher, especially if one's subjects are superordinates (Gorden, 1969).

Establishing control over the interview situation from the outset in these ways can temporarily disrupt elites' taken-for-granted realities in the manner of ethnomethodological interpretations (Garfinkel, 1964).

Indeed, it was based on what appeared to me nonverbal expressions of some surprise—a momentary raised eyebrow or a quick wide-eyed glance—that led me to discover and make intentional these strategies. Being used to being in charge and having that challenged meant that the terms of the interview interaction had to be negotiated and the expectations restructured differently from a more typical social contact between persons of higher and lower status.

Maintaining an appropriate level of control over the interview requires contesting elite inclinations to "just talk"—easily, freely, and at length, but not necessarily to the issues in which the researcher is most interested. I have been especially struck in my recent work at Haymarket by how differently elites approach an interview situation from nonelites, even though I present the situation the same. In this project (unlike my upper-class women project), interviews are not the only source of data. As was also true in my study of family and child welfare agencies, interviews are intended to supplement extensive on-site observations. Whether I am interviewing a (nonelite) community activist board member, a staff member, or a wealthy (elite) donor at Haymarket, I ask for about an hour and a half in terms of time. I bring the same set of questions, typed out on a page in front of me, and I introduce the interview in much the same way, saying I like to have everyone address the same issues so I can compare but that we need not do that in any particular order. I explain that I take notes rather than taping because of the exorbitant amount of time that transcribing taped interviews takes, because I am focusing in on particular issues and don't need a full transcript, and because I've learned to take notes well enough. The implication here is that subjects should speak rather slowly and succinctly and address particular questions.

Interviews with Haymarket nonelites are usually closely timed, answers are brief, and follow-up questions on my part are often required. A particular order in the questions is followed, and subjects sometimes ask where we are in the schedule. In contrast, wealthy donors I have interviewed often begin talking immediately after my introduction before I have asked a particular question, and they often talk at some length. Sometimes, what they have to say is of interest to the particular project in which I am engaged; sometimes, it's not. When it's not, one of the things I do is stop writing. Usually, they notice after a while and stop talking and wait for me to ask a question. I don't shift topics abruptly but rather use something they have already said to get into the issues with which I am most concerned. Sometimes, I just let it go, depending on what they're saying and how important it appears to them and to me, and ask questions directed at having them elaborate their concerns. I think that this has made a difference in my gaining access to talk with other Haymarket donors because the first donors I talked with found they could speak with me in confidence about issues of concern to them and that I would listen and ask the kinds of questions that helped them clarify their own thoughts and feelings.

In general, I think that the tendency of elites to "just talk" has everything to do with their being used to having others interested in what they have to say and in having what they say make a difference in the lives of others. This is an accurate reading on their part of their social status and power, not simply a personal sense of self-centeredness or a distorted self-importance. I think it's useful for researchers to understand that. It is also important for the researcher to structure the talking in a way that enables her to get the kind of data that will be most useful, especially if the project is not a general ethnography or life-history account but, as is true in my own work, has more focused aims. I would advise not approaching interviews with elites with an expectation of following what is to the researcher a logical progression of fixed questions. A checklist of issues to be covered is more appropriate, which is the approach I followed more with my upper-class women. At Haymarket and in the agency study, I quickly began to use my questions in this way when I interviewed elite subjects (Zuckerman, 1972). It has worked well for me to stop at various points in the interview and say that I need a moment to see where we are and what issues we have covered and that I'd like to cover in the time we have left. Periodic time checks are also useful when the interview is going on longer than expected to see if the subject wants to spend a longer time and to ensure that all issues are covered. I have found I need to be sure myself to not schedule anything after an interview of this kind. The use of pointed questions, asking for specific examples, occasionally interrupting while explaining why one is doing so, and other approaches I discuss below are also useful.

The final issue to be considered here is asking threatening questions of elites and getting clear and solid answers. All that I have said above about establishing some control over the interview from the outset and about structuring respondents' answers so they don't "just talk" lays a groundwork for dealing with this challenge. I have developed three strategies for asking hard questions that elites might perceive as threatening. The first is learning their language so I can ask in terms they find more acceptable and will understand. The second is explicitly stretching the bounds of etiquette and defining the interview situation as different from daily social intercourse. The third is basing difficult questions on particular situations and events known to me from independent sources that I could use to query or challenge elites' knowledge or point of view.

One instance where learning the language proved useful was in my study of upper-class women in being able to ask about issues of class. Although I have argued that these women are highly "class conscious," that does not mean that they used the same words sociologists use to talk about class (Ostrander, 1980a). I had to learn the terms they used that actually referred to their own class. When I asked them, for example, who they felt they represented on the boards of local institutions on which they served, their most common answer was "the community." Initially, I thought they meant they represented the community at large, the general public who was served by the hospitals, universities, social service agencies, and cultural institutions we were talking about. Fairly soon I found that they made a distinction between what they called "client" or "consumer" representation on boards—and which they for the most part opposed—and other kinds of representation. So I began to ask them what they meant when they said they represented "the community." It became evident that they meant persons like themselves, people from, as one woman said, "a certain part of the community." Another said, "I represent an old-line family." The word "community" in this context apparently referred, then, to their own class. This was acknowledged by the woman who said, "I'd like to represent the community at large, but of course I can't know the thinking of people I'm not in contact with" (Ostrander, 1984, pp. 133-134).

Stretching the bounds of etiquette in various ways is useful, especially at those points in an interview where an elite person begins to appear obviously uncomfortable. It is helpful to acknowledge that their discomfort is not inappropriate, that I am in fact asking questions that might not be considered "polite." I might say, for example, "That's not a question I would ask you if we met socially, but my purposes here are quite different." I have also found that it is possible to get valuable information from elites by giving them the opportunity to respond directly to criticisms that others may have made about their actions. The "others" need not be very clearly defined. For example, I have sometimes said something like "Well, you know some people would say that having clubs where membership is purely invitational is elitist. What would you say to that?" I have used a similar question in regard to board membership. Both of these approaches have allowed me to press quite hard in interviews, asking elites to spell out their thinking and acting in rather precise ways.

Finally, having an independent source of information that I can use in developing later queries for elites has been valuable. Being present at a meeting where elites take a stance on a particular issue or when there is a challenge to elite influence provides me with concrete situations that I can later ask subjects about in interviews. Information from organizational documents or, especially if the study is based only on interviews, public sources such as the local newspaper can also be used in this way. On one occasion, for example, I was interviewing a board member from one of the agencies I was studying and I knew from reading board minutes that this person had opposed the agency's becoming a member of a local human service coalition. I asked why and gained some very valuable information on this person's views about why social service agencies ought not be involved in advocacy. On another occasion, I knew that a board member abstained from voting on cutting the budget of a particular program in the agency. Giving this person an opportunity to elaborate on that gave me some vital data on not only this person's reasoning but also that of people favoring the cuts. At Haymarket, I have been present as one wealthy donor and a particularly outspoken activist board member worked out their differences and came together on issues about expanding the funding base to include more middle- and working-class people and about blurring the distinctions between donors and activists. It has been valuable to speak to both of these people in interviews about how they felt about what was going on between them, and I have begun in my writing to see their interaction as an example of how relationships across class and race and gender can be established.

### Conclusion

The three research projects I have conducted that include or focus entirely on elite subjects suggest that there are special strategies and techniques that work well when studying elites and several points of caution to watch out for. The strategies and techniques discussed here address especially gaining access, establishing rapport, and conducting successful interviewing, as well as some concerns having to do with protecting the integrity of the research and the researcher.

My experiences imply that, in regard to getting in and developing ongoing trust and respect, taking advantage of chance meetings or of one's own social contacts may be as important as careful planning. Going in the right order when contacting elites may be important, often starting at the top. Doing background work and knowing at least some of the pressing issues before going into the field is important because elites may check you out by asking hard questions. They will also check you out by seeing if you know people they think you should know and by asking what you expect to gain from the research as well as what you intend to give back to them. It is best to be straightforward, and you can expect elites to do the same. You should not assume that just because they have agreed to the research that the checking out stops. It continues and is necessary to ongoing trust and rapport essential to getting valid data.

I have suggested that it is a mistake to be too deferential to elites, that gaining respect and confronting the status difference between researcher and elite subject require that the researcher make clear his or her own goals and conditions for doing the research and establish some control over the research situation from the outset. It may be important to give elites time to decide if they are willing to work with you and to let them know that you have other things to do in the meantime. Whereas compromise in terms of timing of the release of publications may sometimes be necessary, the researcher should not compromise the integrity of the work by allowing elites to have a voice in deciding what is published or where. My experiences indicate that researchers need not be so overly concerned about rapport that challenging questions are avoided. Being able to ask pointed questions is an issue especially when studying elites because they may wish to protect their position and have the power to do so. This kind of questioning is also a concern because elites converse so easily and at such length that the researcher may not be initially aware that what they are saying as they just "talk" is not specifically relevant to the goals of the research. The naive researcher may be dazzled by their ease and confidence and may then be hesitant to break in or to structure the interview in the way that is needed to get the most useful data. I have suggested some ways to deal with this, including not behaving like a guest, claiming your own space in the interview setting, and having a typed set of questions in front of you but being flexible about the order and time of the questions. Explicitly acknowledging stretching the bounds of etiquette enables the researcher to ask more threatening questions than might otherwise be possible. I have noted the value of having one's own independent source for events and situations that can be used to formulate specific questions for elites. A researcher who has these kinds of strategies under command can, I believe, conduct successful research projects with elite subjects. Research that spells out what elites do, how they think about it, and what meaning it has for the larger society is essential to complete our understanding. Much more of it needs to be done.

## References

Aldrich, N. W., Jr. (1988). *Old money: The mythology of America's upper class*. New York: Vintage.

Baltzell, D. (1958). *Philadelphia gentlemen*. Glencoe, IL: Free Press.

Baltzell, D. (1964). *The Protestant establishment*. New York: Random House.

Domhoff, G. W. (1970). *Who rules America?* Englewood Cliffs, NJ: Prentice-Hall.

Garfinkel, H. (1964). Studies of the routine grounds of everyday activities. *Social Problems, 11*, 225-250.

Gorden, R. (1969). *Interviewing: Strategy, techniques, and tactics*. Homewood, IL: Dorsey.

Ostrander, S. A. (1980a). Upper class women: Class consciousness as conduct and meaning. In G. W. Domhoff (Ed.), *Power structure research* (pp. 73-96). Beverly Hills, CA: Sage.

Ostrander, S. A. (1980b). Upper class women: The feminine side of privilege. *Qualitative Sociology, 1*(2), 23-44.

Ostrander, S. A. (1984). *Women of the upper class*. Philadelphia, PA: Temple University Press.

Ostrander, S. A. (1985). Voluntary social service agencies in the United States. *Social Service Review, 59*(3), 435-454.

Ostrander, S. A. (1987). Elite dominance in private social service agencies: How it happens and how it is challenged. In G. W. Domhoff & Thomas R. Dye (Eds.), *Power elites and organizations* (pp. 85-102). Newbury Park, CA: Sage.

Ostrander, S. A. (1989). Private social services: Obstacles to the welfare state? *Nonprofit and Voluntary Sector Quarterly, 18*(2), 25-45.

Ostrander, S. A. (1993). Diversity and democratization at Haymarket Peoples' Fund: Doing philanthropy as social change. In R. Hollister, D. Young, & V. Hodgkinson (Eds.), *Governing, leading, and managing nonprofit organizations: New insights from research and practice* (pp. 193-213). San Francisco: Jossey-Bass.

Ostrander, S. A. (1995). *Money for change: Social movement philanthropy at Haymarket Peoples' Fund*. Philadelphia, PA: Temple University Press.

Vidich, A. J. (1955). Participant observation and the collection and interpretation of data. *American Journal of Sociology, 60*, 354-360.

Zuckerman, H. (1972). Interviewing an ultra-elite. *Public Opinion Quarterly, 36*(2), 159-175.

lected in the steel and glass buildings and impressed in the concrete
he physical development of the local community. Logan and Molotch's
987) award-winning *Urban Fortunes* speaks to the significant role
yed by local developers, corporate headquarters, and public agencies
assembling parcels of land, private capital, and personal power.
milarly, Suttles (1990), in *The Man-Made City*, focused on the physi-
development of Chicago as the primary indicator of the interweaving
private power and public planning in that city. Perhaps the most
quent expression of the significance of the physical structure of a
mmunity as an indicator of its power structure is F. Hunter's (1980)
mment in his restudy of Atlanta:

My task in restudying the power structure actually lay in finding out whether
or not the new building surge was reflected in the composition of the power
structure. . . . A first step in such study would be . . . to begin, not altogether
with the words of men, but with a closer examination of what they have built
around themselves physically and to what purposes. (p. 7)

Although the public frontstage may reflect the power of local elites,
is in the backstages where the power itself is most often wielded. The
ckstages of elites are carefully guarded from public view, and they
ve the power to protect them. For community elites, perhaps the most
gnificant backstages are their exclusive clubs. In Pittsburgh, while
ing field research I happened to be wandering without purpose one
rly evening in the downtown area near the "Golden Triangle." I
ticed a large gray stone building into which people were entering, and
hought it might be an upscale nightclub of sorts. I saw no identifying
gn on the building, so I walked up the steps and entered into the lobby
d stood looking around. A doorman immediately appeared and asked
he could assist me, and I asked, "What is this place?" He replied,
This is the Duquesne club, and I'm sorry, sir, but it's *for members
ly.*" And with that, he took me guidingly by the arm and turned me
ack out the door. I later realized that this was one of the elite private
ty clubs about which Baltzell (1958) had written in *Philadelphia
entleman*. A similar elite city club, called The University Club, was
ported by one informant in a different community I was studying as
important venue for lunchtime meetings among local economic,
overnmental, and university elites. I was never able to penetrate this
nner sanctum. Years later, I was taken there by the provost of the
niversity for an administrative luncheon meeting and realized, too late,

## 11

# Local Knowledge and Local Power

## Notes on the Ethnography
## of Local Community Elites

### ALBERT HUNTER

### The Relationship Between Knowledge and Power

Knowledge and power are intimately related. Differences in the
distribution of knowledge are a source of power, and power may be used
to generate and maintain differences in the distribution of knowledge.
Knowledge, then, is a scarce resource. To invoke Harold Lasswell
(1958) in his little primer, *Politics: Who Gets What, When, How*, elites
are those who have more of whatever scarce values there are in a society,
while the rest, who get less, are the masses. To be ignorant is to be
powerless. The study of elites therefore is ipso facto a political act
insofar as researchers attempt to acquire knowledge from and about
elites and to distribute it more broadly in a public domain to the masses.

Now the research relationship, especially the ethnographic research
relationship, is also a power relationship between researcher and subject. In the actual act of studying elites the ethnographer cannot ignore
the elite's power and must not ignore his or her own power in the

NOTE: Reprinted from a special issue, "Fieldwork in Elite Settings," edited by Rosanna Hertz
and Jonathan B. Imber for the *Journal of Contemporary Ethnography*, Vol. 22, No. 1, 1993,
pp. 36-58. Copyright 1993 by Sage Publications, Inc.

151

relationship. Academically based researchers, especially, are wittingly or unwittingly likely to be drawing on their own human capital (advanced degrees, for example) and their institution's power and prestige in these relationships. Ethnographers must be self-reflexively sensitive to the fact that power relationships enter into the very process of studying power itself.

## Local Elites and Local Knowledge

The study of local community elites, and especially the concern with the structure or network of relationships among them and the local issues with which they are concerned, requires an intimate knowledge of the community context itself. The actions and reputations of local elites reflect not only their formal positional statuses or their organizational roles, as is more likely to be the case with many other elites. The study of local elites requires in addition a knowledge of their embeddedness within a broader or more wide-ranging set of community dimensions that include the physical ecology of the community, both its internal variation and its position within metropolitan and regional structures; a continuum of social structures that range from formal to informal, from local government and corporate and economic organizations to the neighboring, family, and friendship structures that make up the routines of everyday life; and a knowledge of the local culture consisting of different values, norms, symbols, and collective rituals that give meaning to everyday life. Local elites, their "power structures" and the "issues" with which they deal, do not stand apart from their communal context but are woven into the very fabric of the everyday life of the community. Reputations are made and broken, heroes made and villains vilified through the gossip in local coffee shops and the social notes in the local press. To study local elites requires, in Geertz's (1973, 1983) words, a "thick description" of "local knowledge."

In this article, I attempt to show how field research into the study of local community elites can benefit from the ethnographer's heightened sensitivity to and dense exploration of the communal context of elites— their ecological, structural, and cultural milieus. Specifically, I suggest how sensitivity to the local physical settings, social relationships, and symbolic systems of local elites are not only the subject of investigation but also, and more important for the purposes of this article, how these three dimensions of the elites' communal context enter into and reflexively structure the process of field research itself.

The examples in this article are drawn from a num local community elites both by others and by myse review is neither systematic nor exhaustive, but it is, to highlight what appear to be recurrent and import issues in the study of local community elites. Firsth my own research conducted over the past two decades atic comparative study of the power structure among l suburbs of Chicago, a study of local community leader neighborhood in Chicago, an early piece of field rese Italian elites who dominated the political life of a sm town, and a comparative study of local leaders in thre (White, integrated, and Black) in a Chicago suburb. Th graphic techniques were multimethod (Brewer & H approach, consisting variously of participant observatio more formal in-depth interviews with elite informants, of elites, and analysis of archives.

## The Physical Ecology of Elite Ethnography

### Even Backstages Have Backstages

Erving Goffman (1959) made a powerful distinctio frontstage and backstage settings for social behavior. penetrate to the more exclusive backstage, where inti behavior, sometimes "deviant" to public demeanor, take taken by ethnographers as a sign that they are now abl ironic, debunking mission of research. For example, as H and colleagues (see Becker, Geer, Hughes, & Strauss among the medical students they were studying, "The bes our presence did not noticeably alter their behavior lies they were willing to engage in behavior the faculty disapp in our presence" (p. 26). Among elites, however, adm backstage must be evaluated skeptically as even backsta other backstages. This is not to suggest the "infinite regre acy theories" of elites, but one must maintain a cynical even the most "private revelations" and never underestim capacity for secrecy.

The front stages of local community elites are often t and substance of their power, for the power structure is

I had now entered the backstage which had previously been closed to me. Again, like the Duquesne Club, there are no publicly identifying signs on the entrance. To know where it is is to belong; not to know is to be an outsider, one of the mass of pedestrians ignorantly passing on the sidewalk. Again, F. Hunter (1980) noted how the older, exclusive Capital City Club, the power center of an older generation of Atlantans, had been supplanted by the newer Commerce Club made up of "the majority of comers, climbers, and strivers of the power structure. . . . Changing power structures may periodically, in keeping with the times, change their architectural skins" (pp. 20-21).

Perhaps the most ubiquitous of private clubs are the country clubs that dot metropolitan areas, and the golf course is a perfect setting for off-the-record informal conversation where small cliques of elites may propose and discuss different courses of action. In a number of different communities several informants mentioned to me that this was the ideal setting where issues were "ironed out" before being presented as a smooth consensus in more public settings, such as city council meetings where many of the "influentials" would not even be present. Galaskiewicz (1987) similarly noted the importance of such exclusive clubs in defining the elite of Minneapolis: "To get a second measure of elite-corporate linkages we scanned the roster of the area's three major metropolitan clubs (the Minnesota Club, the Minneapolis Club, and the Women's Club) and the two most prestigious country clubs (Woodhill Country Club and Somerset Country Club) for the names of our elite" (p. 158; for a detailed account of his research, see Galaskiewicz, 1985).

On several occasions I was exposed to the fact that my presence among the elite drew a veil about conversations that would be dealt with backstage. This most clearly happened at one suburb's council meeting, when it was obvious I was an outsider, being the only White person in the room. The board members took their seats at the front table and looked around, and after some murmuring the mayor announced that they were adjourning into "executive session" and they proceeded to file out into the next room. A half-hour later they returned and announced that because of unforeseen circumstances all business was being postponed for 1 week and the meeting was summarily adjourned.

On another occasion in a different community, in a more informal, exclusive gathering of elites I learned that even this seeming backstage had yet other backstages. While listening to three men in conversation discussing an issue, one of the three suddenly turned to another and said, "I think we'd better talk about this later." The two others immediately turned, looked at me, and haltingly and jocularly proceeded to change the subject.

Perhaps the clearest example of backstages having backstages occurred while interviewing a man about his World War II heroics in the Office of Strategic Services (OSS) that had made him a living legend in the local Italian community. Among his exploits had been a parachute drop into Sicily behind enemy lines to coordinate the Resistance prior to the Allied invasion. When I asked why he was picked for this mission, he replied calmly, "You don't want to know." Mistakenly thinking he was merely being modest, I repeated "No, I really would like to know." It was then that he leaned forward across the desk, stared me straight in the eyes, and said in a slow steely voice, "You don't understand. You . . . don't . . . want . . . to . . . know." My immediate suspicion was confirmed a few years later when I learned from reading a history of the OSS that the invasion of Sicily was coordinated in part by cooperation between the American and Sicilian Mafia.

### The Community Ecological Context

Most elites have some major institutional affiliation; that is, in Weber's terminology, they occupy an "office." The office is ambiguously both a bureaucratic position and a physical setting. Where one conducts an interview will have consequence for its degree of formality or informality, and this form will, in part, also shape the content of the interview. If elite interviews are conducted in "the office," the informant is more likely to be operating with this formal position as a master operating status. Furthermore, the accoutrements of power manifest in the office may directly impinge on the research. In his study of corporate philanthropy in Minneapolis, for example, Galaskiewicz (1987) recounted the laborious process of being screened through secretaries jealously guarding their boss's time and how "in one company, at least, I had to go through a preliminary interview with a vice-president" (p. 157). Most often when setting up interviews with elites, I offer the option of meeting them at their office or at home, usually in the evening. I recall interviewing one part-time suburban councilman in his central-city "Loop" law office. Both he and I were out of our "community context" and the interview contained a surprising element of mutual camaraderie when discussing "our hometown."

The separation of home and work, often into different communities, which the above example illustrates, speaks to the many microlevel impacts of the larger metropolitan environment within which local communities and their local elites are embedded. Merton (1957) was one of the earliest to note the still relevant distinction between local and cosmopolitan bases of elite status within a community. In my previous work (A. Hunter, 1974, 1987), I noted the degree to which there exists a "hierarchy of symbolic communities" running from the local social block on up through the local community to larger metropolitan regions. The increasing "regionalism" of local community elites has been noted by a number of researchers; for example, Troustine and Christensen (1982) in *Movers and Shakers*, their comparative study of San Jose, California, and Indianapolis, Indiana, highlighted that the "new guard" of local elites tends to be a regional and even national corporate elite in contrast to the old guard made up of local industrial and financial elites.

I have found in the study of elites that it is important to understand their conceptions of and their linkages to this larger environment and the importance of how one positions oneself as a researcher within these different levels as either an insider or an outsider. In doing this, I am likely to ask elites about surrounding communities and how they would place their community in comparison with it (A. Hunter, 1984). I have also made a point of explicitly looking at larger, more formal structures that may encompass and yet extend beyond the local community. For example, in a study of selected suburban elites in Chicago, I have drawn on an annual seminar that I conduct at the Northwest Municipal Conference, a federation of suburbs that, among other things, offers a training program for newly elected officials. By defining myself as a "resident" of, and researcher interested in, the region, not simply any single local community, I am able to explore how these elites view themselves comparatively and how they use their social, economic, and political links with surrounding communities. Again, being defined as an "expert" in this setting, and by shifting my own "community of reference" to a scale that encompasses both myself and them as mutual members of "the same community," has given me access to many of the elites that I have been able to call upon.

In a similar vein, but at a smaller scale, I have also at times specifically asked elites to describe the different subsections or neighborhoods of their local communities and to compare their own area to others. I have generally plotted the residence of elites and, if interviewing them at home, have noted characteristics of the neighborhoods in which they live. Such observations are qualitatively different from—yet complementary to—whatever census data I can routinely collect on the community. Such data provide a contexted set of interests of elites that may in fact bear upon larger issues. For example, one councilman in a suburb sadly related how a local issue of a special tax assessment to be levied on one neighborhood for the instillation of new streets and sidewalks led to interpersonal "rancorous conflict" (Gamson, 1966) between leaders from that area and the rest of the community. He shook his head as he said, "Friendships were broken, and neighbors ended up not speaking to one another." F. Hunter (1980) described how the "revitalization" of downtown Atlanta was purchased at the price of a continued segregation between Blacks and Whites in both power structures and neighborhoods.

In sum, the micro- and macroecology, the physical and spatial setting of local elites within their community context, both reflect the content of their power and affect the conduct of field research itself. Sensitivity to this ecology of elites, and the various scales of their physical settings, ranging from boardrooms and private clubs to downtowns, neighborhoods, and whole communities and regions, is essential to providing a thick description and deeper understanding of the stages on which the elite enact their power plays.

### *Mingling in the Social Milieu:*
### *Social and Research Relationships*

Ethnographic fieldwork often consists of entering into the ongoing social relationships of participants. In the ethnography of elites in which I have engaged, I have generally gone into settings with the full knowledge among participants that I am a professor studying the group or the community. As I observe and participate, my status and role cannot but help enter into the field relationships. Rather than seeing this simply as "intrusive measurement error," however, one may reconceptualize it as a catalytic, quasi-experimental effect that can elucidate subtle aspects of power relationships among participants in a setting. The dominance of the interview and reputational method in the study of local community elites requires candid disclosures from researchers in order to elicit candid disclosures from informants. Troustine and Christensen (1982) noted the fine line the researcher must walk to dig behind elites' guarded public pronouncements:

Respondents may be reluctant at first to offer candid views of their peers. . . . Sometimes a respondent will balk at virtually every question, finding it increasingly uncomfortable to share the inside views we are asking him or her to reveal. This won't happen often, but when it does we should be persistent but not belligerent. After all, . . . the respondent could, if he or she is well-connected, make things difficult for us with just a phone call or two. (p. 70)

Participant observer studies of local community elites are more rare and disclose more tension in negotiating the research relationship. In his study of Chicago's land-use elite, Suttles (1990) told how he attended meetings and gradually became absorbed as a participant: "Not until I was well into the first year of these observations, however, did I begin to keep systematic field notes. I did so without telling anyone" (p. 281). He later described elites' reactions when he did disclose his observer role: "After I told two members that I was writing a book on Chicago planning, I was not reappointed to the Local Planning Committee. I understand their apprehensions" (p. 284).

Ongoing relationships existing among the elite are often the very data one is attempting to gather to discern something about the local "power structure." A sensitivity to these power relationships can also be used to aid the conduct of the research itself, especially for gaining entry. The very title of Rakove's (1979) study of local political leaders in Chicago, *We Don't Want Nobody Nobody Sent*, attests to the power of the personal voucher as a means of entry into elite power circles. Similarly, Galaskiewicz (1987), in his study of corporate philanthropy in Minneapolis, told how he dealt with elite "recalcitrants" who did not want to be interviewed: "We sent a list of those people whom we did interview in order to indicate to the recalcitrants that others were willing to take the time for the interview and that we were 'OK to talk to.' Also this would give the reluctant respondent a list of people to call if she or he doubted our credibility" (p. 162). Suttles (1990), in his study of Chicago's land-use elite, similarly described how he was introduced into his participant observer role by a fellow academic already operating in these circles:

Morris Janowitz stuck his head in my office . . . and said, "Let's go. I want to show you something." . . . Before I really knew what was happening, Morris and I were sitting around the conference table at the Chicago Metropolitan Housing and Planning Council. . . . It then dawned on me what Morris was up to. He was bringing me into contact with some of the most knowledgeable people in the city, people who collectively seemed to know what was happening to every plot of land in Chicago. Morris was also farming me out to one of his many roles, but I was to learn that later as I replaced him on the local planning committee. (p. 279)

On two different occasions, it happened in field settings that a key informant, acting as shepherd and host, proudly introduced me to fellow elites as "the professor" from the nearby university who was interested in studying their community. On one of these occasions, my host, a highly respected éminence grise in the community, on seeing me enter the room rushed over to me, grabbed me by the arm, and led me to the front of the receiving line where he proudly introduced me in a formal voice sufficiently loud for all around to hear as "Professor Albert Hunter of Northwestern University," to which the Mexican Consul in Chicago responded with a reserved graciousness, "Ah, sociology, one of my favorite subjects"—and, turning to my host, added approvingly, "Very good, José." Later that same evening, my host also gave me a more public "introduction" from the dais in Spanish, and his grown son sitting at the family banquet table leaned over to me and whispered, "He said you're writing a book about us. Watch out. Now everyone will want to talk to you." By observing how I was defined and used as an "object" within these interactions, subtleties of power and deference were revealed that would have been masked had I self-consciously ignored "the self" as but an intrusive methodological error.

I have found that public gatherings of elites, especially festive occasions like banquets, can be extremely valuable for a number of reasons, and I routinely try to get myself invited to them (aside from the intrinsic fun and food they may provide). On these occasions, one may simultaneously be exposed to both the formal and informal social relationships among elites. For example, more formally, one can note who is present/ who is absent and who is sitting at the head table/who is not, and one can analyze the content of a printed program if available; more informally, one can observe the networks of interactions and the deference and demeanor displayed in introductions. One can also make a point to collect names and foreshadow later potential interviews. Such gatherings can be used also as a "topic" for establishing rapport and for elucidating more detailed information in later interviews. Again, I have usually found it invaluable to have my host act as a "key informant," giving me running commentary and answering questions when possible about the unfolding drama. Finally, I suspect that vague recollections of my presence at such gatherings may serve to familiarize the elite with me, if not legitimate me. Suttles (1990) also noted his attendance at such

public gatherings: "I went to public hearings, press conferences, unveil-
ings, ribbon cuttings, and topping-off ceremonies" (p. 281).

It is often assumed that by getting individuals alone, away from the
presence of others, that one is more likely to get the inside dope, the
"truth" unsanctioned by significant others. This is often an underlying
assumption of the "private" elite interview, and it is for that reason
invaluable. I would suggest, however, that joint or group interviews can
also be equally revealing and have their own "truths" to offer. For
example, while interviewing a councilman at his home in a wealthy
suburb of Chicago, his wife came in, was introduced, and proceeded to
sit down and join us. After listening briefly as an observer, she began
to add asides and commentary on her husband's responses. Slowly, what
had been heretofore a very focused and somewhat formal interview
about issues and politics soon became transformed into a three-way
conversation about particular persons among the elite. The wife was
adding more "social commentary" about people, who got along with
whom, who was respected or not, and the interview was transformed
into a very informative and revealing "gossip session."

I have often found that elites are particularly interested in knowing
"who else have you talked to?" and are not likely to be put off easily by
some general noncommittal response. Again, one can use this to advantage, first by offering specific names and then noting their reactions and
responses and how they position themselves with respect to others.
Also, one can return the question in the best interviewing tradition by
asking who they think you should talk to; it is equally important to note
who is omitted. I have even had elites go so far as to say helpfully,
"Don't waste your time talking to _____. They don't know anything!"

### Learning the Local Patois:
### Studying the Culture of Your "Own" Community

I have been a firm believer throughout my career that the community
in which one resides, wherever that is, offers unique opportunities for
study. By being a natural participant one is clearly fulfilling the partici-
pant/observer role and thus brings to the study all of the subtle fore-
knowledge that living in the milieu provides. It is as if one had followed
the advice of Voltaire: "We must cultivate our garden." Some might
object to this "bias" on a number of grounds: that it raises innumerable
ethical and political issues or that it is unduly restricting and parochial.

Like W. H. Auden (1958), they would rather praise the cosmopolitan
individual who first challenged "the local ford demon":

> how squalid existence would be,
> tethered for life to some hut village,

> afraid of the local snake
> or the local ford demon,

> speaking the local patois
> of some three hundred words

> (from "HORAE CANONICAE:
> Immolatus Vicerit-Sext")

Though undoubtedly limited as are all case studies, there need be no
limit to the theoretical significance of a good piece of field research.
Learning the local culture and its symbol system (even if the local patois
is only 300 words) is the meat of the ethnographer's sandwich; the bread
and garnishings of theory make it handy to ingest and professionally
palatable. Learning the local culture requires attention to vocabulary
and absorption in the milieu. Suttles (1990), for example, noted this
osmosis: "It was only later . . . as I began to absorb the lore of those
attending these meetings . . ."; but F. Hunter (1980) once again cau-
tioned us to see beyond or dig behind the local patois:

One comes to understand in community life that hearing what men say is often
less important than observing what they do. Clichés tend, in many instances,
to be stated as great unshakable truths. . . . American businessmen, especially,
operate in syndromes of action in which great injustices are perpetrated in the
name of astute decision-making and many disastrous results of such activities
are covered by pious pronouncements rather than deeds of restitution. . . . A
whole language-set accompanies all this: "You win a few and lose a few."
"It's a whole new ball game." "It's how the ball bounces!" (Possible remarks
after "driving another to the wall"—bankruptcy.) (pp. 6-7)

In the limited space available, I cannot possibly address the full range
of significance that the local culture has for the elites and for the
ethnographer studying them. Here, I will more narrowly address an
often overlooked reflexive aspect of the ethnography of elites: the
nature and degree of preexisting knowledge existing in the culture of

the local community and its elites that relates to the ethnographer's field research itself.

## Preexisting Knowledge *of* the Elite

I have found that one of the best sources of routine everyday knowledge about the community and about its elite is the local community press (Janowitz, 1967). In contrast to metropolitan dailies, the local press is much more likely to focus on local events and especially local personalities rather than on larger, more abstract "issues." I have yet to find a study of local community power that does not make reference to using the local newspaper as a data source. Some may exist, but their rarity underscores the point.

Not only is "information" from the local press useful as "data" in and of itself, it is also useful in interviewing and in informal conversations with elites. Such information, by definition, is public, and so, routinely, my interviews with elites will include some reference to "I read where. . . ." I will then ask them to comment, and their corroboration (rare) or expansion and edification (much more likely) are often very revealing, much like a Rorschach test. I also make a point to interview local journalists and editors (the latter themselves often classified as "members of the elite"). They are "knowledgeable informants" and enjoy demonstrating their professional knowledgeability by relating facts and conjectures that lie behind the stories and that would never make it into print.

The blurred boundary between journalism and ethnography has plagued field researchers for years, yet such a blurring may in fact be useful within the field setting as a more readily understood "investigative role." Troustine and Christensen's (1982) comparative study of San Jose and Indianapolis was actually done in part as a merger between a local newspaper's journalists and a local university's social scientists as an example of the new "precision journalism," and Suttles (1990), perhaps harking back to Robert Park's earlier career as a journalist, said of his own research:

> In this case, research—my kind of research—is never just a test of theory. It is a kind of journalism which recovers what we already know, remaking it into contemporary language, redrawing the connection between past experience and present examples. In this kind of journalism, the search for some match between instrumental and moral rhetorics continues although one hopes that it does so within narrowed factual limits. (p. 294)

In addition to the local press, I also usually make a point of ransacking the archives of local libraries and local historical societies. These archives are very informative about the history of the community, and they are especially likely to contain detailed histories and biographies of leading individuals and families that compose the elite. Such data can be used as background to prepare oneself for more informed in-depth interviews with the elite and, as well, to "triangulate" (Brewer & Hunter, 1989, pp. 17-18) with data from other sources, such as interviews and observations. It is important to realize, as well, that these local institutions of local knowledge usually have boards and a voluntary staff that are themselves among the local "social elite." Getting to know these guardians of the local lore is itself, of course, part of doing fieldwork among the elite. But, given their interests and roles, these individuals may also be recruited as key informants, and they are often proudly willing to participate more actively in the research process by searching out records and even writing up reports.

### Preexisting Knowledge *by* the Elite

Ethnographers have a fine line to walk, especially when interviewing elites, as to how much preexisting mutual knowledge about one another exists and will be acknowledged. To show that one lacks knowledge is, of course, the raison d'être for doing the research in the first place and is often the basis for convincing informants that they should take the time to inform you of what they know. However, to be too ignorant of the setting and current affairs, to be a total ingenue, may convince elites that you are too unconcerned or uninterested to have done your homework for them to waste their time with you. Galaskiewicz (1987), in reflecting about what he would have done differently, noted, "We believe our introduction to the elite was much too haphazard. First, prior to the funding stage we should have compiled all the newspaper and magazine articles written on the Twin Cities business community from 1970 to 1980" (p. 160).

I have suggested repeatedly that knowledge is, in part, a basis of elites' power. One of the things I have discovered over the years is that the elite are usually well educated and well read, and such knowledge extends into the realm of some expertise about social science research itself. Therefore, the ethnographer studying elites must be aware of at least a superficial understanding by elites of what you are all about. The clearest example of elites having preexisting social science knowledge was brought home by the city manager of one suburb, who at the beginning of the interview asked, "Are you using Hunter's reputational technique?" He then proceeded to pull out a study done some 5 years before by a graduate student from a different department at my same university. With a satisfied smile, he pointed out that he ranked about 12th on the list, just about where a city manager should be—but still high enough to count. F. Hunter himself noted in his follow-up study (*Community Power Succession*, 1980) to his classic *Community Power Structure* (1953) how various members of the Atlanta elite welcomed him back with comparative commentary based on their reading and understanding of his earlier study.

In one very wealthy suburb, I went to observe a city council meeting precisely because one of the hot issues about which I had been interviewing dealt with citizens' reactions to a proposal to locate metropolitan-wide dispersed-site public housing in their community. The voluntary chair of research for the local League of Women Voters presented to the council a detailed statistical analysis that she had performed on a highly sophisticated sample survey of residents. It turned out she had a Ph.D. in marketing research, and the knowledgeable questions and comments from the council members turned the meeting into what appeared more like a dissertation defense than a political debate. At a later interview with one of the councilmen, when I asked for a copy of the report, he gave it to me with the proviso that I send him my brief evaluation of the research and its conclusions.

### Discussion and Conclusion

Ethnographic study in general, the ethnographic study of elites in particular, and the ethnographic study of local community elites more specifically have all reached a self-reflective phase in their development. This self-consciousness means that researchers have moved beyond mere questions of technique to seeing their research in larger epistemological contexts. Let us briefly address these unfolding contextual questions, beginning with the particular and moving to the general.

I have shown above that the ethnography of local community elites must take into consideration the communal context within which elites exist. The communal context of elites will shape the conduct of field research, and, in turn, both will shape the content of the analysis that follows. Rather than viewing the ecological, social, and cultural contexts solely as constraints, the good ethnographer is sensitive and resourceful in learning how to use fieldwork itself as a catalytic tool that may be used to elucidate the structuration (Giddens, 1987) of elite power that these community contexts create.

There is a "positivistic" analytic tendency within the study of local elites and community power to wrench both the structures and the issues out of their communal context. This is most clearly seen in quantitative comparative studies of large numbers or samples of communities where selected variables of the elites (e.g., network relationships) and the communities (e.g., demographic characteristics, such as size and diversity) are isolated and subjected to a variety of multivariate analyses from multiple regression to "logit" analysis. These are fine as far as they go, and they have resulted in a cumulative and valid set of nomothetic generalizations (see Bonjean, Clark, and Lineberry, 1971, for an exemplary collection of such studies). However, the variance "unexplained" in such models and the numerous caveats of ceteris paribus both speak to the limitations of this approach.

The contexted study of local community elites is most clearly seen in the classical community case studies—Warner (1963) in Yankee City and the Lynds (1929) in Middletown—and in other "wholistic" community studies, such as Gans (1967) in Levittown and Vidich and Bensman (1958) in Springdale. Elites were not the sole nor even the primary focus in these studies, and yet the rich ethnographic accounts of these communities contain the most subtle and manifold understanding of elites in vitro. The good community field researcher collects data whenever and however possible within ethical limits and cost constraints, and this was the source of the analytical power of these earlier community studies that earned them their enduring status as classics. They were for this reason rhetorically convincing (A. Hunter, 1990), not merely in their well-crafted prose but in the use of different methods, diverse data, and alternative analyses that converged to heighten the credibility of their conclusions.

These "wholistic" naturalistic accounts highlight a central characteristic of community elites, and that is that the status of being an elite is a system property, not a personal proclivity. Local elites arise from within a local system, operate through a local system, and wield their power on the local system. To more completely understand elites, it is therefore necessary to understand the systemic properties of their communal context.

As "community power" itself became a subfield within the social sciences, the community case study was adapted and altered to focus more narrowly and explicitly on the questions of power: Who has it? How is it structured? On which issues is it expended? F. Hunter's (1953) study of the power structure of Regional City (Atlanta), Dahl's (1961) response in his study of New Haven, and Banfield's (1960) account of the machinations of power in Chicago represent the classic exemplars of this case study approach to community power. It is interesting to note that Hunter, a sociologist, gave a more comprehensive account of the elite's community context than did either of the political scientists, Dahl and Banfield. This "bias" was noted by Walton (1966) in his reanalysis of the extensive literature in community power studies. He discovered that sociologists tend to use a reputational approach, to study smaller communities, and to find pyramidal power elites, whereas political scientists are more likely to use an issue approach, study larger cities, and find pluralistic power elites. Reflecting their ancestry, the methods that sociologists use to study local elites appear to be biased toward taking into account the more complex and embedded social arrangements of elites that are more readily researched in a smaller community context. It is at the level of community that the myriad institutions of social life may be seen in their interdependent and contingent complexity. Ethnographic accounts of local community elites are especially adept at capturing this institutional complexity and the embedded community context of elite power.

The ethnographic study of elites, more generally, highlights the importance of power itself as a context within which such research occurs. Many have noted that academics more readily study minorities—for example, the poor and the powerless—than they do the rich and the powerful—the elite. This imbalance in research focus is often benignly motivated and legitimated in terms of the need for knowledge to develop ameliorative and reformist programs to solve whatever are at the moment defined as the prevailing social problems of the masses. Rarely is it acknowledged that the masses are more likely to be studied simply because they are powerless, and many of their problems may, in fact, stem from this relational position with respect to the elite. Elites are, by contrast, relatively unstudied, not because they do not have or are not part of existing social problems but precisely because they are powerful and can more readily resist the intrusive inquisition of social research. This concern with the asymmetry of who is studied by whom was eloquently raised by Becker (1967) in his article "Whose Side Are We On?" and by Lynd (1939) in his little book, *Knowledge for What?* (one of the subquestions of which might be "Knowledge for Whom?").

If, as Gans (1962) suggested, social science serves as a vehicle for the continuing dialogue between elites and masses, then it may further contribute to the asymmetry of this dialogue by providing elites with knowledge about the masses. Rarely, however, does social science knowledge flow the other way. In large part, this asymmetry is reflected in and reproduced by large-scale research programs that are most often funded by elite institutions. The ethnographer has the potential to play an important political role in the distribution of knowledge. Even if the ethnographer is a solitary practitioner engaged in small-scale, under-funded research, armed with little more than an ingratiating smile and an inquisitive sensibility, elites remain vulnerable to disclosure; this is especially the case if the ethnographer, like Baltzell (1958), is among their numbers. But all ethnographic researchers should be aware that they can draw on the prestige of their academic status, their cultural capital, to create a greater symmetry in the power relationship between elites and themselves.

This brings us to the broadest epistemological context of ethno-graphic research, the recognition that social research is part of a larger social and scientific dialogue that must address the question of who is the audience for ethnographic accounts. One must be as conscious of the audience of one's research as one is of the subjects selected for study. Consciousness of the rhetorical context of ethnographic research reframes questions of scientific validity into questions of rhetorical credibility (Brown, 1987; A. Hunter, 1990). One great strength of ethnographic research lies in its ability to provide detailed accounts that make social life not only understandable but also accessible and believ-able to a wider audience. I have shown that power relations of the researcher must be understood and consciously used in the nitty-gritty conduct of research on the power of elites. Similarly, the rhetorical power of ethnographic accounts must be understood and used to distrib-ute knowledge of elites and masses alike to all sectors of the society. In this way, ethnography can contribute to making knowledge, and its correlated power, a democratic part of the broader community.

## References

Auden, W. H. (1958). *Selected poetry of W. H. Auden.* New York: Random House.

Baltzell, E. D. (1958). *Philadelphia gentleman.* Glencoe, IL: Free Press.

Banfield, E. C. (1960). *Political influence.* Glencoe, IL: Free Press.

Becker, H. S. (1967). Whose side are we on? *Social Problems, 14,* 239-247.

Becker, H. S., Geer, B., Hughes, E., & Strauss, A. (1961). *Boys in white.* Chicago: University of Chicago Press.

Bonjean, C. M., Clark, T. N., & Lineberry, R. L. (1971). *Community politics.* New York: Free Press.

Brewer, J., & Hunter, A. (1989). *Multimethod research: A synthesis of styles.* Newbury Park, CA: Sage.

Brown, R. H. (1987). *Society as text.* Chicago: University of Chicago Press.

Dahl, R. H. (1961). *Who governs?* New Haven, CT: Yale University Press.

Galaskiewicz, J. (1985). *Social organization of an urban grants economy: A study of business philanthropy and nonprofit organizations.* Orlando, FL: Academic Press.

Galaskiewicz, J. (1987). The study of a business elite and corporate philanthropy in a United States metropolitan area. In G. Moyser & M. Wagstaffe (Eds.), *Research methods for elite studies.* London: Allen & Unwin.

Gamson, W. (1966). Rancorous conflict in community politics. *American Sociological Review, 31,* 71-81.

Gans, H. J. (1962). *The urban villagers.* New York: Free Press.

Gans, H. J. (1967). *The Levittowners.* New York: Random House.

Geertz, C. (1973). *The interpretation of cultures.* New York: Basic Books.

Geertz, C. (1983). *Local knowledge.* New York: Basic Books.

Giddens, A. (1987). *Social theory and modern sociology.* Stanford, CA: Stanford University Press.

Goffman, E. (1959). *The presentation of self in everyday life.* New York: Doubleday/Anchor.

Hunter, A. (1974). *Symbolic communities: The persistence and change of Chicago's local communities.* Chicago: University of Chicago Press.

Hunter, A. (1984). Suburban autonomy/dependency: Elite perceptions. *Social Science Quarterly, 65,* 181-189.

Hunter, A. (1987). The symbolic ecology of suburbia. In I. Altman & A. Wandersman (Eds.), *Neighborhood and community environments.* New York: Plenum.

Hunter, A. (1990). *The rhetoric of social research: Understood and believed.* New Brunswick, NJ: Rutgers University Press.

Hunter, F. (1953). *Community power structure.* Chapel Hill: University of North Carolina Press.

Hunter, F. (1980). *Community power succession.* Chapel Hill: University of North Carolina Press.

Janowitz, M. (1967). *The community press in an urban setting.* Chicago: University of Chicago Press.

Lasswell, H. (1958). *Politics: Who gets what, when, how.* Cleveland, OH: World.

Logan, J. R., & Molotch, H. L. (1987). *Urban fortunes.* Berkeley: University of California Press.

Lynd, R. S. (1939). *Knowledge for what?* Princeton, NJ: Princeton University Press.

Lynd, R. S., & Lynd, H. M. (1929). *Middletown.* New York: Harcourt, Brace.

Merton, R. K. (1957). Patterns of influence: Local and cosmopolitan influentials. In *Social theory and social structure* (pp. 387-420). New York: Free Press.

Rakove, M. L. (1979). *We don't want nobody nobody sent: An oral history of the Daley years.* Bloomington: Indiana University Press.

Suttles, G. D. (1990). *The man-made city: The land-use confidence game in Chicago.* Chicago: University of Chicago Press.

Troustine, P. J., & Christensen, T. (1982). *Movers and shakers: The study of community power.* New York: St. Martin's.

Vidich, A., & Bensman, J. (1958). *Small town in mass society.* Princeton, NJ: Princeton University Press.

Walton, J. (1966). Discipline, method, and community power: A note on the sociology of knowledge. *American Sociological Review, 33,* 684-689.

Warner, W. L. (1963). *Yankee city.* New Haven, CT: Yale University Press.

*12*

# Research as a Communication Act

## A Study on Israeli Women in Local Politics

### HANNA HERZOG

My aim in this article is to share with the readers my experience in collecting data on women in local political elites in Israel. The subjects of my study were female politicians who were elected to town councils, held powerful elected offices, and became visible, at least, in the local political arena. My study of these local female elites tries to unveil their social world. As wielders of power and influence on the basis of their positions and control of political resources, they are elite among women.

Israel is a strong, centralistic state; its politics have been party politics, and party politics have been elite politics (Arian, 1985; Shapiro, 1977).[1] Political elites are central for the understanding of Israeli society. Even scholars who analyze Israeli society from a pluralist approach agree that at the crossroads of the "elite connection," from the pre-State period until today, stands the political elite, where the strings of connection begin and end (Etzioni-Halevy, 1993). The centralized structure of Israeli politics created a dependency of local politics on the national

AUTHOR'S NOTE: I wish to thank the editors and Dafna Izraeli for their helpful comments on an earlier draft of this paper.

one but at the same time endowed the mediators—the local politicians—with considerable local power (Weiss, 1973, p. 133).

As women are underrepresented in Israeli politics (Azmon, 1990; Weiss & Yishai, 1980)—currently, they are only 9% in the Knesset, the Israeli parliament, and 11% in local government—there is particular interest in those few who have nevertheless succeeded in paving their way into the political elite (Herzog, 1994). However, the aim of this article is to discuss my fieldwork.

A review of my experience suggests two major methodological themes which are interlocked. One pertains to flexibility in the research process, the other to the role of research and a researcher in the subject's world. Unlike the traditional approach, which requires that the researcher define the methodology before she/he enters the field, my experience teaches that it is more fruitful if the researcher chooses the appropriate methods while in the field. She/he should be attentive to subjects and ready to adapt new methods to uncover their social world as it emerges from interaction with them. Indeed, this is a story of introducing new, very often unplanned methods of data collection for an emerging study. As the study evolved and changed, additional methods were used and the problems and solutions were formulated and reformulated. The final outcome is a multi-method approach based on mail questionnaires, content analysis of written material, participant observation in group discussions, in-depth interviews, informal conversations, and analysis of private archives of local female politicians. Each method added new information and new dimensions to the understanding of female Israeli local politicians. On the surface, this represents the multi-method approach used in other studies of community elites in other countries (Brewer & Hunter, 1989; Hunter, 1993; Moyser & Wagstaffe, 1987). However, my central argument is that the decision regarding which method to adopt be largely dictated by the interaction in the field and not by a priori academic decision.

This brings me to the second theme: the role of research and a researcher in the subjects' world. Here I discuss how the very act of the research and I, as a researcher and a citizen, become a means for women's understanding of their being female politicians, and for me to gain new insights into their lives and my own as well. This is a story of how the research act and the findings serve as mediators for women to communicate, mainly among themselves, about their own experience. Becoming an integral part of the life of my subjects makes my study a part of a developing feminist critique.

## Trained Incapacity:
## First Steps Into the Study

The idea of studying women in local politics had been formulating in my mind since the eve of the local elections in Israel in 1983, when several female candidates reached local headlines as candidates for mayor. It seemed that a new trend in women's politics was about to occur, and I was curious to see if this indeed was the case.

As a trained political sociologist I turned to the literature, focusing my readings on two sorts of studies and theories: first, studies dealing with social and political structures of local politics, mainly in Israel, and then studies about women in politics. This resulted in formulating the preliminary research question and the population of this study: Is a new breed of female politician emerging in the local politics of Israel as a result of the decentralization of Israeli politics and the growing interest in and legitimation of local issues and welfare?[2] These changes began in the late 1960s. The key strategy in answering this question was to portray the social profile of the elected women, both before and after the process of changes had begun. A list of the entire population of women elected from 1950 (the first municipal election after the founding of the State of Israel) to 1989 was compiled. It included 382 women, for whom 331 addresses were traced in 104 different towns throughout the country. As most conventional studies on women in politics at that time were based on questionnaires, the same technique was chosen for this study (cf. Bristow, 1980; Constantini & Craik, 1972; Dye & Strickland, 1982; Hills, 1983; Karing & Walter, 1976; Means, 1972; Merritt, 1977; Weiss & Yishai, 1980).

Budget constraints required mailing the questionnaires instead of meeting personally with the women. The response rate reached 65%, a relatively high percentage, compared with other mail questionnaires (Nachmias & Nachmias, 1982, p. 105), and higher than the 51% response rate reached by Brichta and Levy (1985) in their study of mostly male council members. Thus, the shortcomings of this technique were hardly encountered. At a later stage of the study I found several more economical, and evidently more profound, alternatives for gaining access to many of these women.

Most of the items were closed questions, formulated so that the results could be easily compared with the major findings of the various studies on which they were based. A fundamental guide book used was Kirkpatrick's (1974) classic study *Political Woman.*

The results, however, were quite frustrating. In most of the variables examined, there was a conflict between the findings and my gut hypothesis. No indication of a new generation of female politicians emerged from the statistical analysis of the variables. The social profile of the Israeli female local politicians had not changed dramatically over the years and was very similar to that of their counterparts in other Western societies. Moreover, the political world of these women did not become clearer, although many of the questions attempted to reveal just that. For example, several questions were aimed at checking whether these women had become more feminist and had changed their attitudes toward the monopoly of men in politics in general and on certain spheres of activities within politics. The interviewees were asked if they agreed with widespread stereotypes on politics and women in politics. Most of the women agreed that politics is a male sphere, that politics is a "dirty job," and that women are not that prepared for it. The problem, I realized only later, was that most of these questions were closed, and thus they reflected the so-called dominant rhetoric. The interviewees did not get a real opportunity to express their own experiences and their own way of interpreting the world (Oakley, 1981). For example, one respondent corrected the questionnaire text and changed the words "politics" and "politicians," to "policy" and "policy maker" and "statesmen," suggesting that women attribute to politics different aims and qualities, which my closed question didn't give them an opportunity to express. The questionnaire framed them—and therefore my findings—in a given political culture. As put by Maines (1993): "The moment of data collection is thus not only confrontation with one who has already narrated him or herself, but has narrated society" (p. 24). "The closure of data at the moment of their collection," he continues, "limits possibilities for analysis and creates the necessity for speculation" (ibid.). The questionnaire I designed left too much room for speculation.

### Serendipitous: Qualitative Analysis of the Questionnaire

It was one of the open questions that led to a breakthrough. The interviewees were asked to describe the way they entered politics and how their position on the list was determined. Analysis of the content of these descriptions indicated that there is a new generation of women, characterized not by different social background or human capital, but by the way this background and capital is used in the political arena. A major expression of the decentralization of the political structure was direct personal elections for the mayor. Women bypass the party obstacles by direct bargaining with the candidates for mayoral positions. They rely on their local reputation in the community as users of services and volunteers. This finding confirmed the hypothesis that the structural changes that occurred in Israeli local politics might open new opportunities for women. Yet, the reasons were different from those assumed. Women who entered politics did it mostly because they changed their political tactics, using the structural change for their own advantage, and not as hypothesized, because of greater similarities between community needs and women's expertise and subjects of interest. It became evident that the focus of the study must be shifted to these women's daily experience in politics.

Moreover, the information learned from the answers to the above open-ended question indicated that there was a gap between the rhetoric women used to express their opinions and their "real" experience, mainly in their stories of how they entered politics. This gap was disturbing; therefore, an explanation was pursued. The large number of women who, although not asked to, added comments explaining their choices of the alternatives presented by the questionnaire, underlined the problem. The questionnaire imposed closures and denied the subjects from being biographical-embedded, self-narrating persons (cf. Maines, 1993, p. 24). Consequently, the research question was reformulated in order to focus on what being a female politician means for these women.

To unfold the meaning of women's experience in politics, the quantitative findings were reread, mostly searching for contradictions. For example, most women stated that they entered politics when their children grew up, arguing that role conflict was a major obstacle to entering politics earlier. Yet at the same time, most of them had worked at full-time jobs, were party members for an average of ten years, participated in various party activities, and had been very active in women's voluntary organizations. In other words, they were involved with public activity when their children were young but they didn't define it as being "politically active." Women did not perceive themselves as doing politics. They called it voluntary work or public service. There was a gap between what they did in reality and the way they presented themselves and interpreted their experiences. Following such findings, the focus of the study was changed, in search of appropriate methodology to deepen understanding of this phenomenon.

## Research as Information Agent

Usually the researcher is perceived as using the research subjects for her/his needs, as an information source for the study. In the course of this study, it became evident that the opposite is also true. Because substantial, additional qualitative information was needed, a search began for ways of going back to the women interviewed. The path was illuminated via an unexpected finding from the questionnaire, which was overlooked earlier. Although the interviewees were guaranteed anonymity, many of them identified themselves and requested the study's results. Part of the readiness to expose themselves was attributed to the fact that politicians want and need to be exposed and publicized.

Yet, there was something more to this readiness for self-disclosure. It seems that women also perceived the study as a means to communicate with other women, to share their experience with other female politicians. As one respondent put it:

The questionnaire is very complex, I suggest distributing it immediately among women, not only elected politicians, in order to prepare them for the future. This provides a good lesson for women before entering politics, so that they know what to strive and fight for. I wrote my name intentionally, in order to give an example to the rest of my friends.

Being isolated, I learned later, is rather characteristic for many women in politics, and for many of them this is one of the hardest issues to cope with in their political world. At that stage of the study, it also became apparent that the relationship with the subjects is not one-sided. The informants have interest in the information they provide, as does the researcher in gathering it.

Based on these women's willingness to expose themselves, contact was made, requesting them to send in all the newspaper articles featuring themselves. This data was going to be used as a source to explore their social world, because many politicians get full-color write-ups that include descriptions of their personal lifestyle. Another lens was used in the effort to scrutinize this women's world. The extensive media coverage on women in local politics made it possible to examine the candidates through the journalists' role as interviewer, on one hand, and at the same time to analyze how political women are perceived in the media.

There is no doubt that I would not have had access to this newspaper coverage without approaching the women directly. Many of these articles were published in local newspapers, which have no archives of their own. Traveling throughout the country to find these newspapers could be a very time-consuming project. Furthermore, the letters women wrote explaining why they were not covered by the media and how it made them feel were extremely enlightening. These letters, short as they were, served as another corpus from which I could draw on women's difficulties in local politics, on the way women prefer to present themselves, and on their alternative perceptions and definitions of politics. For the women who wrote the letters it was another opportunity to express their experience and share it.

It has become clearer to me that the research act is a two-way transfer of information for both researcher and research population. When the analysis of the quantitative data had reached a developed stage, I gave a talk at an academic conference. Consequently, a women's organization invited me to address women who considered presenting themselves as candidates for municipal elections. This was in 1988, a year before the local elections. The audience included women who were already city councillors. The fact that there are more political training seminars for women than men leads me to conclude that women, far more than men, prepare themselves for political activity before being elected, as well as during and throughout their terms in office. They attend seminars and workshops, and they read written materials. My study results became a part of their preparation for political activity.

Most of the female local politicians I met were highly educated and regarded my study data as a useful tool in building their own political education. It should be emphasized that I was not the only social scientist these women met. They exposed themselves to many professions on various issues related to their careers in politics. In my presentations I tried to present facts with minimum explanations and/or interpretations. I emphasized that I was recounting their own experiences as they emerged from the study. This was strikingly different from other professional talks that they attended, the aim of which was to teach them how to act as politicians or how to enhance their chances of success. My findings became a mirror, a measuring rod for them. Each woman weighed the data according to her own private experience.

The questions and comments following these presentations opened for me and, I believe, for them too new channels for understanding women's experiences in politics. From then on I was prepared, almost on a volunteer basis, to attend any meeting, seminar, or workshop organized for female local politicians. In some of these events I was invited to be the keynote speaker, in others a discussant, and in others merely an audience member. I became part of the natural ecology of these events. These occasions opened a new arena to gain access to the world of women in local politics.

### An Unplanned Method:
### "Natural" Discussion Groups

I was invited to join the political committee of the Israel Women's Network, a non-partisan feminist lobby, the members of which are political activists from various parties, including female Knesset members and several scholars who study women, mainly in politics. Most certainly my invitation was as an expert who studies women and teaches from a feminist perspective. The political committee of the Israel Women's Network was active during the 1989 and 1993 elections, initiating seminars and workshops for female local politicians. This forum presented me with the opportunity to be informed of activities that were held and to follow the discussions that preceded and followed those activities. It provided me with a better understanding of the ways women perceive and define the obstacles and needs of women in local politics, as well as the way they frame the political world in general, and themselves in this world. Several meetings of women in local politics were held in the Knesset (the Israeli parliament), hosted by the Prime Minister's Advisor on Women's Affairs. In addition to these, I was invited to some local meetings of female activists in their local communities, organized either by political parties, and more specifically by the women's divisions of the parties, or by the major women's voluntary organizations such as Na'amat (the Women's Labor Organization), WIZO (the World Zionist Women's Organization), and the

Women's Network. In many cases, the meetings were part of the political activity of these women, but there were also some for which women paid, as part of their preparation and training for political activity. Altogether, I participated in approximately 30 such meetings, lasting from two hours to half or a full day.

These meetings provided me with a new site for meeting many of the subjects and allowed me to overcome the geographical dispersion of the study population. It also provided me with an opportunity to interact with these women in various ways. The more formal interactions were through my presentations and the discussions that followed. Less formal were the conversations that took place later in these events between the women and myself, and among the women themselves, during coffee or meal breaks. Finally, in many of the seminars, there were discussion groups on various topics related to local political activity.

Thus data were collected from discussion groups organized not for the purpose of this study, many of them informal and spontaneous. This is a tremendous advantage for a researcher because no planned intervention is needed. The groups were not constructed for me or for my research goals, but rather for the women themselves. Note that I stress the term *planned* intervention, because I believe that any research act is in itself an act of intervention. The women in these meetings all knew that I studied women in local politics; in other words, they knew that they were being studied, but they never expressed any hesitation or reservations regarding my presence. On the contrary, they very often asked if my findings supported their feelings, or asked for my opinion. Some women even suggested study topics or ideas to think about.[3] Thus, unlike Hunter's report that his presence among the elite drew a veil on conversations (1993, p. 41), in my case women used my presence as a vehicle to discuss their experiences, their common difficulties and struggles.

For many women, these meetings served as a good opportunity to meet other women in similar situations, to share and compare their experiences and to learn from one another. The meetings were held in an ex-territorial, "safe" setting and were not part of the everyday political surroundings. Beyond the social control of their communities, the women did not feel threatened by political competitors. In most cases, these meetings were very supportive and a means for female empowerment. These settings enabled women to speak more openly with me and among themselves.

## Power and Empowerment:
## Being Part of a Group

According to Hunter (1993), "in the actual act of studying elites, the ethnographer cannot ignore the elite's power and must not ignore his or her own power in the relationship" (p. 3). Similarly, although I followed these group discussions as an observer, sometimes I was a participant observer. As the latter, I tried to be as "invisible" as possible in order not to become an advantageous, intervening social actor. I was fully aware that I was invited to these meetings as an expert who possesses relevant knowledge about the subjects. Although most of the female local politicians were highly educated, and many held university degrees, being a university professor could have placed me on unequal footing. It was very important for me to avoid such power relations. I generally opened my presentations by saying that I was always excited to be with them, to interact with them as real living women, and not only numbers or faceless interviewees. I always stressed that everything that I presented was what I had learned from them. This was not simply flattery; it was what I really felt. Nevertheless, it also helped me put myself on equal ground with them. Oakley (1981) argues that the best way to find out about people is through non-hierarchical relationships. I have no doubt that my being a woman, and a woman who studies women, was an advantage. My very presence in the research field gave the subjects a sense of importance. They were no longer a group of odd women striving to enter the "men's sphere," or a "bunch of frustrated women," but serious and important enough to serve as the focus of academic research. The participants of these meetings did not see me as an outsider, but as a partner for a common goal—equal opportunities for women. Relying on the findings, women in group discussions argued for "looking at the full half of the glass" or "stopping the yelling and complaining and adopting an assertive manner of self-presentation." The research act as it evolved became an act of empowerment for the women, and through them also for me as a female researcher.

### Confidence: Access to Private Archives

I developed particularly close relationships with a number of women who, more than others, provided a great deal of information regarding their political situation and shared their self-perceptions and experiences with me. Many of them shared their plans for future actions with me. I felt they trusted me. Two of these women, with what seemed to be similar political experiences, were chosen for further research. Both failed to be elected by their parties to head the party lists for the elections, and both left their respective parties. Consequently, both established and headed independent lists and ran as independent candidates for the position of mayor in their cities. Upon my request both agreed immediately and independently to open their archives for the study. One of them had no reservations at all, while the other attached a condition that her story not be published before she saw the material and granted her permission. We even signed an agreement. I spent several days in their homes, digging into their private archives. The two were very helpful. They opened all of their folders, explaining the background of some letters when it was not possible to understand the full meaning from the text alone.

Working in private archives, in private homes, created a very intimate interaction in terms of the research. Research of any kind is an invasion into the subject's world. This was real penetration. The social boundaries between me, the researcher, and them, the subjects, were blurred. The distinction between private and public disappeared as well. The material in both private archives and the close assistance of both politicians added a new angle to the study. The archival material unveiled the political game and exposed the world behind the scenes: the manipulation and the power relations among competitors and even political allies. Both these women shared a meaningful part of their lives with me. I felt trusted. Their confidence in me, and the belief that I would not publish anything that might harm them, presented me with a personal and professional dilemma which I had hoped to avoid. The intimacy also required me to be vigilant of the possibility of being used as well as being over-empathetic with the interviewees.

I handled the archive information as cautiously as I could. I was aware of the latent pressure presented in this situation, yet I decided to give a clear description as it emerged from the documents. When the section based on the private archives was completed, I offered both women the opportunity to read it. The one who had not put any precondition on publishing the findings did not even want to see it, arguing that "I am doing my job and you should do yours." The second woman read the text I had written about her, suggested I add some information, and had minor reservations about some of the interpretations but generally liked the piece and gave her permission to include it in the book.

My aim was to represent and analyze the complex world of women in politics, not to judge them or express personal views concerning their activities, their political decisions, and the paths they chose in the political forest. It was gratifying for me when a local journalist who interviewed me wrote: "With all her affection and appreciation, Herzog manages to retain a dry academic tone in the chapter that relates to Bar-Tal [one of the above two politicians]" (*Tzomet Hasharon,* June 3, 1994). I believe that the academic rhetoric combined with my desire not to judge my subjects helped me to preserve an adequate measure of detachment.

## Concluding Remarks:
## A Study by, for, and About Women

The above presentation should be treated as a methodological article in C. Wright Mills's terms. Therefore, it is not "codification of procedure" but rather "information about . . . actual ways of working" (Mills, 1970, p. 215). Reflecting on the various steps and strategies taken in constructing the research, I now have a better understanding of what he meant by "in actual practice, every working social scientist must be his own methodologist and his own theorist" (ibid: 135).

The study was a reciprocal action between myself, a female researcher, and the local female politicians who were studied. The mutuality in our relationship bred the exchange of information, enabling me to enhance the subject matter and intervene in their social world. Nevertheless, I believe it was not a one-sided relationship. It seems that the subjects also gained something from this act of research. They used me and my data as reliable sources of information and used me as a lecturer in their meetings, as a channel to publicize them, and as a mediator for mutual interaction among themselves. This mutuality put us in quite an equal situation. I suggest that the research situation be considered not as a one-dimensional power situation but as a multi-level interaction. There is no way to completely avoid power relations, but these power relations exist on various levels and operate in different directions. In some situations the studied subjects are more powerful, and in others, the researcher has an advantage. Reciprocity is thus mutual exploitation and not simple power relations. The researcher gets and gives back in return. Subjects are not mere subjects but also ends. The reciprocal interaction not only served to balance the power relations but also contributed to the empowerment of the female politicians and the researcher.

Several factors contributed to the emerging networking between me, the researcher, and the local female politicians. First, because Israel is a small country, the relationships among academia, policymakers, and politicians are closer, more direct, and more personal than in other countries. Because there are relatively very few studies on women in politics in Israel, there is a greater need to rely on the data collected by scientists. As there are relatively few studies on women in politics in Israel, I stood out for my uniqueness. Finally, there is a growing awareness among feminists in Israel about the importance of networking as a means of supporting and advancing women, obtaining information, and gaining easier access to power positions. Thus, women invest far more time and energy in creating social relationships with other women, and in developing extensive networks, including with academia. I became part of these networks through my study, if only by receiving and disseminating information. The very act of research made me part of the emerging networking of women who deal with local politics. These women regarded me as one of them, although in a different role.

I studied women in politics, a sphere of social activity that is regarded as public, but realized, as many feminists have claimed, that the boundaries between the public and private spheres are arbitrary social constructions (Pateman, 1988, 1989; Siltanen & Stanworth, 1984). The study shows how the social world of women is an interweaving of the private and the public. The study methods blurred these boundaries when the interviewees not only allowed me to intervene in their political life but also opened their private archives, which of course dealt with their public activities, for me.

Could my way of working be defined as feminist methodology? According to the Nebraska Sociological Feminist Collective (1983, cited in Ollenburger & Moore, 1992, pp. 65-67) it could. It is a research by, for, and about women. It enables women to speak about their own lives and in their own language. At the same time, it retains the perspective of the researcher. There is no doubt that I brought a feminist point of view into this research; at the same time, however, I used my sociological knowledge, which is an inseparable part of the research activity. Accordingly, I prefer to adopt Ring's (1987) position that feminist research is a dialectic process whereby former solutions become current problems, and to follow Reinharz's (1992) claims regarding feminist methods in social research. For her, feminist research is what feminist researchers define as such. It is not a uniform method, rather versatile numerous ways for obtaining knowledge. In my case the interaction with the subjects in the field dictated the methods I adopted. To paraphrase Reinharz (1992, p. 268), I hope that my study contributes in its own way to the feminist efforts in stretching the boundaries of what constitutes research in creative ways.

## Notes

1. Although there have been many changes in Israeli politics toward a more plural, decentralized, competitive, and open system, the basic patterns are likely to remain (Arian, 1985; Eisenstadt, 1985; Horowitz & Lissak, 1989).

2. Taking the traditional gender division of labor as given, local politics is perceived to be an easier political arena for women and a more suitable activity for them (Almond & Verba, 1965, pp. 324-335; Currell, 1974; Lovenduski & Hills, 1981; Nuss, 1980; Skard, 1981).

This question draws on a number of studies conducted on women in politics in other countries (Currell, 1974; Githens & Prestage, 1977; Kelly & Boutilier, 1978; Sapiro & Farah, 1980).

3. Oakley reports on similar reactions in her study on motherhood (Oakley, 1981, pp. 44-46).

## References

Almond, G. A., & Verba, S. (1965). *The civic culture.* Boston: Little, Brown and Company.

Arian, A. (1985). *Politics in Israel—The second generation.* Chatham, NJ: Chatham House.

Azmon, Y. (1990). Women and politics: The case of Israel. *Women and Politics, 10,* 43-57.

Brewer, J., & Hunter, A. (1989). *Multimethod research: A synthesis of styles.* Newbury Park, CA: Sage.

Brichta, A., & Levy, A. (1985). *Evaluation of the change in the elections system of mayors* (Research Report). Jerusalem: The Interior Office, Research Department. (in Hebrew)

Bristow, S. L. (1980). Women councilors—An explanation of under-representation of women in local government. *Local Governments Studies, 6*(3), 73-90.

Constantini, E., & Craik, K. H. (1972). Women as politicians: The social background, personality and political careers of female party leaders. *Journal of Social Issues, 28*(2), 217-235.

Currell, M. E. (1974). *Political women.* London: Croom Helm.

Dye, T. R., & Strickland, J. (1982). Women at the top: A note on institutional leadership. *Social Science Quarterly, 63*(2), 333-341.

Eisenstadt, S. N. (1985). *The transformation of Israeli society.* London: Weidenfeld & Nicolson.

Etzioni-Halevy, E. (1993). *The elite connection and democracy in Israel.* Tel Aviv: Sifrriat Poalim. (in Hebrew)

Githens, M., & Prestage, J. L. (1977). *A portrait of marginality: The political behavior of American women.* New York: Longman.

Herzog, H. (1994). *Realistic women—Women in local politics.* Jerusalem: The Jerusalem Institute for Israel Studies. (in Hebrew)

Hills, J. (1983). Life style constraints on formal political participation—Why so few women local councilors in Britain? *Electoral Studies, 2*(1), 39-52.

Horowitz, D., & Lissak, M. (1989). *Trouble in Utopia.* Albany: State University of New York Press.

Hunter, A. (1993). Local knowledge and local power: Notes on the ethnography of local community elites. *Journal of Contemporary Ethnography, 22*(1), 36-58.

Karing, A. K., & Walter, O. B. (1976). Election of women to city councils. *Social Science Quarterly, 56*(4), 605-613.

Kelly, R. M., & Boutilier, M. (1978). *The making of political women.* Chicago: Nelson-Hall.

Kirkpatrick, J. (1974). *Political woman.* New York: Basic Books.

Lovenduski, J., & Hills, J. (1981). *The politics of the second electorate—Women and public participation.* London: Routledge and Kegan Paul.

Maines, D. R. (1993). Narrative's moment and sociology's phenomena: Toward a narrative sociology. *The Sociological Quarterly, 34*(1), 17-38.

Means, I. N. (1972). Women in local politics: The Norwegian experience. *Canadian Journal of Political Science, 5*(3), 365-388.

Merritt, S. (1977). Winners and losers: Sex differences in municipal elections. *American Journal of Political Leaders, 21*(4), 731-741.

Mills, C. W. (1970). *The sociological imagination.* Middlesex, UK: Penguin.

Moyser, G., & Wagstaffe, M. (Eds.). (1987). *Research methods for elite studies.* London: Allen & Unwin.

Nachmias, D., & Nachmias, C. (1982). *Research methods in social sciences.* Tel Aviv: Am-Oved. (in Hebrew)

Nuss, S. (1980). The position of women in socialist and capitalist countries: A comparative study. *International Journal of Sociology of the Family, 10*(1), 1-13.

Oakley, A. (1981). Interviewing women: A contradiction in terms. In H. Roberts (Ed.), *Doing feminist research* (pp. 30-61). London: Routledge & Kegan Paul.

Ollenburger, J. C., & Moore, H. A. (1992). *A sociology of women.* Englewood Cliffs, NJ: Prentice-Hall.

Pateman, C. (1988). *The sexual contract.* Stanford, CA: Stanford University Press.

Pateman, C. (1989). *The disorder of women—Democracy, feminism and political theory.* Cambridge, UK: Polity Press.

Reinharz, S., with the assistance of L. Davidman (1992). *Feminist methods in social research.* New York: Oxford University Press.

Ring, J. (1987). Toward a feminist epistemology. *American Journal of Political Science, 31*, 735-772.

Sapiro, V., & Farah, B. G. (1980). New pride and old prejudice. *Women & Politics, 1,* 13-36.

Shapiro, Y. (1977). *The democracy in Israel.* Ramat Gan: Massada Publishing. (in Hebrew)

Siltanen, J., & Stanworth, M. (1984). The politics of private woman and public man. *Theory and Society, 13,* 91-118.

Skard, T., with the assistance of H. Herns (1981). Progress for women: Increased female representation in political elites in Norway. In C. Epstein & R. Coser (Eds.), *Access to power: Cross-national studies of women and elites* (pp. 76-89). London: George Allen & Unwin.

Weiss, S. (1973). *Politicians in Israel.* Tel Aviv: Achiasaf Publishing. (in Hebrew)

Weiss, S., & Yishai, Y. (1980). Women's representation in Israeli political elites. *Jewish Social Studies, 42,* 165-176.

## 13

# Exploding Anthropology's Canon in the World of the Bomb

## Ethnographic Writing on Militarism

### HUGH GUSTERSON

Anthropologists value studying what they like and liking what they study and, in general, we prefer the underdog.

—*Laura Nader* (1974, p. 303)

The truth of this statement struck me with full force when I began my doctoral dissertation fieldwork, studying a nuclear weapons laboratory,

AUTHOR'S NOTE: The research on which this article is based would not have been possible without the financial support of a Mellon New Directions Fellowship at Stanford University and an SSRC-MacArthur Fellowship in International Peace and Security. The article grew out of a paper presented at the annual meeting of the American Anthropology Association in Washington, DC, on November 19, 1989. As it has moved through successive drafts, the article has greatly benefited from the thoughtful comments of the following people: Carolyn Behrman, Donna Brasset, Carol Cohn, Paul Gelles, Stephanie Kane, Admiral Gene LaRocque, John Mack, Renato Rosaldo, Celeste Wallander, and the three anonymous reviewers for the *Journal of Contemporary Ethnography*.
NOTE: Reprinted from a special issue, "Fieldwork in Elite Settings," edited by Rosanna Hertz and Jonathan B. Imber for the *Journal of Contemporary Ethnography*, Vol. 22, No. 1, 1993, pp. 59-79. Copyright 1993 by Sage Publications, Inc.

the Lawrence Livermore National Laboratory, and a handful of antinuclear groups in the surrounding San Francisco Bay Area. I encountered
three other ethnographers while following the antinuclear groups. Two
of these groups had core memberships of less than 10 people, and on
bad days, when it was raining and the San Francisco 49ers were on
television, I used to dread finding as many ethnographers as informants
at meetings. I sometimes felt as if I was involved in an ethnographic
equivalent of the invasion of Grenada.

Meanwhile, I enjoyed uncontested ethnographic dominion over the
8,000 employees of the Lawrence Livermore National Laboratory.
There were five other social scientists investigating the employees at
this nuclear weapons laboratory, but none were ethnographers. All five
were psychologists, one of whom did his research by questionnaire
without actually meeting any weapons scientists.

My fieldwork situation was not unusual. Most ethnographers interested in American militarism have gravitated toward the oppositional
underdogs, leaving the elites to psychologists and political scientists.[1]
This skewed focus common to ethnographers interested in military
issues is, of course, symptomatic of a broader preference among American ethnographers for the margins rather than the centers of American
society. Just as ethnographers have given us more studies of antinuclear
groups than of the people whose work they contest, so they have given
us more studies of crack dealers, scientologists, Hare Krishnas, homo-
sexual communities, and juvenile gang members than of corporate
boardrooms, federal bureaucrats, or television network executives.[2]
Ethnography has, in America as much as abroad, been defined by what
Harding (1991) calls "a radically parochial imaginary of the margins"
(p. 376).

In this article, I use the particular case of nuclear militarism to explore
this skewed general focus in the ethnography of the United States and
to probe three interconnected questions that are of importance not only
to those ethnographers interested in war and peace issues but, by
extension, to all those concerned with the study of elites in contemporary Western society. First, I ask why anthropologists concerned about
nuclear weapons issues might legitimately have preferred to study
antinuclear groups rather than those who make and implement our
society's nuclear weapons policies. Second, I inquire into the unintended—and unfortunate—consequences of this collective bias. Third,
suggesting that contemporary ethnographers' aversion to studying military elites is symptomatic of a deeper dilemma at the heart of the

ethnographic project itself, I discuss the psychology and ethics of writing critically about those who have consented to be studied by us, and I ask whether, and how, it might be professionally legitimate for ethnographers to write critiques of their own society.

## Studying Down

There are many good reasons for studying antinuclear groups. It can be argued, for example, that studies of the ideology and culture of nuclear elites only focus more attention on a way of understanding the world that already has hegemonic status within our society and that it is more important for ethnographers interested in military issues to amplify and dignify what Foucault (1980) called "subjugated knowledges":

> a whole set of knowledges that have been disqualified as inadequate to their task or insufficiently elaborated: naive knowledges, located low down on the hierarchy, beneath the required level of cognition or scientificity. (p. 82)

Although it may appear a little odd to think of a white, middle-class movement often led by doctors and university professors as disadvantaged, antinuclear activists are at a distinct disadvantage compared to their opponents when it comes to communicating, or just sustaining, their understanding of the world. The Department of Defense, military contractors, and the weapons laboratories have vast material, human, and ideological resources at their disposal to develop their arguments about the need for new kinds of weapons. (For example, the Livermore Laboratory, seeking to persuade the public that its nuclear weapons work is both necessary and safe, is able to pay its head of public relations $115,500 a year ["Top salaries," 1991]—a sum greater than the annual budget of any of the antinuclear groups I studied. The laboratory also maintains a public relations staff bigger than the entire paid staff of any antinuclear group in the San Francisco Bay Area.) Antinuclear groups—underfunded, reliant on transient volunteer labor, and lacking the legitimacy of powerful institutions affiliated with the state—find it hard, despite the middle-class, well-educated status of most of their members, to overcome common suspicions that they are marginal idealists or maladapted troublemakers and to project their voices in the national debate on nuclear weapons.

If ethnographers, by writing about antinuclear activists, can legitimate and explicate their subjugated knowledges, then they enhance democratic politics and the richness of human knowledge while, however modestly, helping these somewhat marginal groups. There is ample precedent in the history of ethnography for this honorable role of the ethnographer as fraternal spokesperson or cultural translator for the disadvantaged. It began with Henry Morgan's (1851/1962) sympathetic explanations of Iroquois culture at a time when it was endangered by American expansion and continued with Benedict's (1946) defense of the cultural integrity of the defeated Japanese at the end of World War II and, more recently, with Stack's (1974) sympathetic portrait of Black ghetto culture—to give just three examples.

There are counterparts to the ethnographic impulses of Morgan, Benedict, and Stack in the recent ethnography of antinuclear groups. Ethnographers have uniformly portrayed these groups as deserving more sympathetic understanding on the part of the dominant culture. Parkin (1968), for example, in his study of the British antinuclear movement, gave a sympathetic account of people's reasons for joining the movement and argued against the common presumption, in the sociological literature at least, that people who join such movements are marginal and alienated. Similarly, Peattie (1986, 1988), Epstein (1985, 1988), and Sturgeon (1988) have done important work explaining the political theory and the subjective experience of those in the antinuclear movement, making the meaning of their work intelligible to a broader audience and presenting it in a new, more systematic light for the activists themselves. Finally, in a more immediately practical vein, Neale (1988), Mehan and Wills (1988), and Mehan, Skelly, and Nathanson (1990) painstakingly analyzed the successes and failures of various antinuclear rhetorical and organizational strategies, writing case studies that illuminate the means by which oppositional groups can conquer political terrain in their battle for position.

Besides the honorable goal of rescuing "subjugated knowledges," there are also good practical reasons for ethnographers to study antinuclear groups. For a start, they are easily accessible. They hold open meetings, they are organized to accept outsiders, and they welcome any ethnographer willing to lick envelopes and sort mailing labels. The Pentagon, large corporations, and nuclear weapons laboratories, on the other hand, do not readily welcome strangers with notebooks. These institutions consist of hierarchies of busy people with security clearances who are nervous that ethnographers may disrupt their relation-

ships with superiors or jeopardize the secrets, legitimate and illegiti-
mate, they are supposed to guard from outsiders. Even if the ethnographer manages to cross the bureaucratic tripwires that protect such
institutions, the world inside may be so complex and bureaucratically
parceled as to make conventional fieldwork by participant observation
a bewildering prospect.

In my own case, for example, I arrived in Livermore to find a
laboratory employing 8,000 people—far more than I could hope to talk
to—and so complex in its organization that no single employee, not
even senior managers, really understood it. More problematic, the
laboratory was segregated from the outside world by armed guards and
a barbed wire fence, and I was warned that because I lacked a security
clearance and there was no good reason why I might acquire one, any
attempt to enter the secret parts of the laboratory would get me turned
away or arrested. The laboratory's public relations personnel were
polite, friendly, and profoundly unhelpful in response to many of my
requests in studying their institution. I was only able to succeed in my
field research by arduously constructing my own network of weapons
scientists on the basis of personal contacts and by rethinking the notion
of fieldwork I had acquired as a graduate student so as to subordinate
participant observation, conventionally the bedrock of fieldwork, to
formal interviewing and to the reading of newspapers and official
documents.

The antinuclear groups I followed were, by contrast, profoundly open
to my presence, however much individual members might have quar-
reled with me about my research design or about my preference for
studying rather than denouncing nuclear weapons scientists. I often
thought that these antinuclear groups were designed for anthropologists. They tended to be organized more along the lines of Durkheim's
mechanical solidarity than around any complex role differentiation, and
their protests, which were full of elaborate symbolism on a par with the
Ndembus', often took the form of large Durkheimian rituals of collective effervescence. The only time I felt like a conventional anthropologist during my entire period of fieldwork was when I spent two weeks
living in a tent near the Nevada Nuclear Test Site, documenting the daily
protests and tribal-style council meetings of the hundreds of participants in the American Peace Test's Peace Camp.

Antinuclear groups, in other words, can look a little like so-called
"traditional" societies. For those unsure whether "real" anthropologists
study middle-class Americans, and even less sure how to study middle-

class Americans, the fact that antinuclear groups appear, at a stretch, to fit our accustomed conceptual tools may make them more attractive as objects of study than military or scientific bureaucracies.

## Consequences of Studying Down

In spite of all these good reasons for studying down, this asymmetric focus on antinuclear groups has two unintended consequences that should trouble us. First, however much it may be intended to redress the marginalization of antinuclear groups, the asymmetric focus on these groups ironically and backhandedly may help to perpetuate a twin marginalization of both antinuclear culture and anthropology. Given anthropology's history as an apologetic documentation of disappearing peoples being crushed or transformed by the imperial forebears of the people who now control nuclear weapons, there is a sense in which anthropologists implicitly place antinuclear activists at the end of a long genealogy of powerlessness and foredoomed otherness by singling them out for study. At the same time, we reinforce stereotypes of anthropology as the sentimental but largely inconsequential study of the periphery rather than the center.

This, in turn, contributes to what Rosaldo (1989) called the "cultural invisibility" and the "postcultural status" of the powerful in Western society. Rosaldo suggested that, by focusing their inquiring gaze only on certain kinds of cultures, ethnographers make these cultures appear particularly problematic: "Full citizenship and cultural visibility appear to be inversely related" (p. 198). He added—and perhaps this explains the convergence of all those psychologists on our weapons laboratory— that ethnographers, conflating "the notion of culture with the idea of difference . . . commonly speak as if 'we' have psychology and 'they' have culture" (pp. 201-202).

In other words, there is, ironically, a sense in which our studies run the risk of normalizing the culture of the weaponeers and "Orientalizing" the culture of the activists (see Said, 1979). As Rosaldo (1989) pointed out, the thrust of ethnography is not only to illuminate the internal logic of particular cultures but also, more deconstructively, to reveal their contingent and constructed nature: "If ideology often makes social facts appear natural, social analysis attempts to reverse the process. It dismantles the ideological in order to reveal the cultural" (p. 39). If there is any culture that deserves to be denaturalized and exoticized, hence opened up to a fresh and potentially critical perspective, it is surely that of America's generals, admirals, nuclear scientists, and defense contractors. Yet they have been largely exempted from the searching inquiries of the ethnographic gaze.

The second effect of contemporary antinuclear ethnography is that, even as it legitimates antinuclear activists as knowing subjects, it also turns them into known objects. Analyses of antinuclear rhetorical moves, recruitment strategies, and organizing methods may engender respect for antinuclear groups and even help them improve their performance. They may also help their opponents plan their defeat—as anthropological knowledge about Indo-Chinese peasants was used against those peasants during the Vietnam War (Wolf & Jorgenson, 1970). Sometimes, antinuclear activists asked me to assure them that my research would not harm their movement. In one case, trumping my invocations of Plato and Weber with Foucault, these disconcertingly informed informants quickly parried my arguments that knowledge is either neutral or intrinsically good. They forced me to acknowledge the irrevocable ambiguity built into any study of antinuclear culture. However noble and sincere our intentions to legitimate these voices of the periphery in the center, we also become, at least potentially, the eyes and ears of the center in the periphery. To be studied, my informants said, is to be vulnerable. Indeed, Western societies have traditionally used social scientists to collect data on the beliefs and behavior of those they wish to control—workers, peasants, welfare recipients, and so on. Hence, as ethnographers, we are presented with a dilemma: We may want to write about oppositional groups in order to cultivate broader sympathy for their goals and greater self-awareness among their members, but we cannot do this without rendering them potentially vulnerable to more effective social control on the part of the state and its allied apparatuses. We can better defend this imposition of vulnerability, in my view, if we simultaneously impose it on the nuclear elites. As Nader (1974) put it, "We cannot, as responsible scientists, educate 'managers' without at the same time educating those 'being managed' " (p. 294).

### Studying Up

So I want to reexamine our reluctance as ethnographers to study the weaponeers. I believe that, beyond the commonsense explanations that activists are easier to study and—like the Bushmen, say—need to be given more attention and respect, there is another reason why we avoid studying up. This has to do with a deeper, more subtle problem in the ethnographic project itself.

Every ethnographer I know who has written about nuclear culture is in some way critical of the nuclear status quo. They have been brought to this subject, often despite anxieties that such unconventional ethnographic research may compromise their academic careers, by a sense that nuclear weapons signify a hideous defect in our world. For the ethnographer studying activists, this creates an animating sympathy and dedication to fieldwork that is an asset. For the ethnographer studying the nuclear elite, however, this can lead to extraordinary problems of method, ethics, psychological stability, and writing.

As ethnographers, we are trained to attempt rigorous, objective studies of other cultures, using cultural relativism to bracket any moral disagreements we may have with informants. We try to see the world, as Geertz (1983) put it, "from the native point of view," to find and explain the sense in that point of view. Classic ethnographies, such as Evans-Pritchard's (1937) study of Azande witchcraft or Rosaldo's (1980) book on Philippine headhunters, are informed by this relativist liberalism. It is much easier, however, for the Western liberal to affect an attitude of cultural relativism toward shamans and polygamists, or even headhunters, in other societies than toward nuclear weapons designers at home. In the latter case, because they are engaged with a controversy within their own society, it is harder for anthropologists to affect an attitude of detachment, and they may be torn between their professional creed of relativism and the passionate concern that brought them to this project in the first place. The reformist and relativist impulses in liberalism grind against each other, and it may appear subjectively as if the price of doing ethnography is the destruction or mutilation of the self. As Ginsburg (1989), an American feminist who studied antiabortion activists in North Dakota, put it in the preface to her book,

Doing the research for this book often seemed schizophrenic: I was, at any given moment, both curious anthropologist and concerned native. Like internal tectonics, the layers of my own thought and unexamined beliefs began to shift and collide. (p. x)

As if this internal anguish were not enough, Ginsburg also discovered that there was a price to pay when she returned from the field and began presenting her conclusions to her liberal colleagues in the academy:

It is one thing, I learned quickly, for an anthropologist to offer the natives' point of view when the subjects are hidden in the highlands of New Guinea and have little impact on the lives of the assembled audience. It is quite another to describe the world view of people from the same culture whom some people in my audiences considered to be "the enemy." . . . Some explained to me their concern that I had "gone native" and become a right-to-life advocate. One skeptic suggested to me that my data were simply not true. (pp. 222-223)

In my own fieldwork—investigating why American nuclear weapons scientists felt their work was appropriate—I oscillated between a fear that I would lose my integrity as an anthropologist and a fear that I would simply lose my mind. Early entries in my field journal are full of paranoid fears that the weapons scientists would refuse to talk to me mixed with loathing of their point of view. After one of my first interviews, I wrote,

I interviewed Bill [pseudonym], who helped plant the test equipment at the Nevada Test Site, and I felt like an unclean sleaze sitting there in his living room getting him to trust me. . . . I felt throughout the interview that Bill was fragile and his views so rife with contradictions that I could smash him up if I wanted to press the pressure points.

At this point, I was having difficulty holding onto my relativism. As time passed, life around nuclear scientists forced me to reevaluate some of my own views about nuclear weapons and dislodged my sense of identity. Even my dream life, in which my own fear of nuclear weapons had formerly played a significant role, began to change. I had difficulty holding on to my critique. Again, my journal tells the story:

It's frightening to think that as their view becomes more natural to me, my own (former?) view becomes more unnatural, more something to be eyed critically and from a distance. . . . It can be partly refreshing, but partly lonely, scary, disorienting. You're set adrift. You are now just a point of view, an angle of perspective, which changes like the morning light.

The abrupt transformation of "me" into "you" in the middle of this passage catches my unexpected, disoriented experience of seeing myself too as an object.

How can the anthropologist and the political citizen learn to live together in the same person in such a situation? How, for example, should one write about an interview subject like Lester,[3] who told me that, although his university colleagues tried to talk him out of working at a nuclear weapons laboratory, their objections did not trouble him? He believes that it is more ethical to work on nuclear weapons than on less destructive conventional weapons because nuclear weapons are designed to deter wars rather than to fight them. He says that he could never work as a lawyer defending murderers or other criminals but feels morally comfortable with his work as a nuclear warhead designer and even wonders if it might be morally reprehensible not to work on nuclear weapons because, as he sees it, they make the world more stable. Lester is puzzled by those who cannot see that nuclear weapons make us safer by making war unthinkable. Like most of his colleagues, he is confident that nuclear weapons can be controlled by humans, that technological progress is unavoidable and beneficial, and that nuclear weapons are the embodiment of a transcendent rationality, which alone can discipline the dark impulses leading humans to make war. Everything in his life, where he sees the atom bent to the experimental will of human rationality on a daily basis, confirms those beliefs. Lester does not worry that the United States will misuse the hydrogen bombs he designs, bombs he describes as "no more strange than a vacuum cleaner. You don't feel a fear for them at all." In fact, he sees weapons technology as "beautiful." "How do I explain that?" he asked me. "To me, a spectrometer is a very pretty thing . . . and you feel badly that it's going to be destroyed [in a nuclear test]."

Should we write about Lester by bracketing our personal disagreements with him, as we might if he were an African polygamist, and simply report his statements, commenting on their internal logic and their relationship to his social environment? If we do, then we may achieve a disciplined form of ethnography but at the expense of the critical leverage we hoped our research would afford us. Should we, then, use our authority as ethnographers to dismiss Lester's views as inappropriate and naive rationalizations that misrepresent and endanger the world? If we do, then it is hard to see what, apart perhaps from our impenetrable jargon, makes us anthropologists rather than activists or partisan journalists. The condemnatory option also raises an important ethical question: Are we obligated to inform those we interview ahead of time that we disagree with them and expect to write a critique of their ideology? If we do, why should we expect them to talk to us? If we do not, are we behaving more like undercover journalists than anthropologists who, according to the American Anthropology Association ethics code, are supposed to obtain "informed consent" from those they study?

## Writing About Elites

In the rest of this article, answering these questions in a circuitous way, I want to explore three different strategies for writing about nuclear elites, examining their respective strengths and weaknesses with regard to the dilemma I have laid out here. I call these strategies the *objectivist* strategy and, adapting the terminology of Clifford (1983), the *dialogic* strategy and the *polyphonic* strategy. The objectivist strategy insists on the panoptical privilege of the writer to understand the world. The other two strategies reject this claim to privilege but in different ways.

Unfortunately, the monological objectivist strategy is the most common means of writing about such people as Lester. This involves criticizing weapons scientists' remarks as interesting but maladaptive rationalizations that, as the analyst if not the subject can see, misconstrue the world and enable the scientists to do a dirty job with a clean conscience. This strategy, organized around the concept of dysfunction rather than relativism, conserves the purity of the writer's politics but at the expense of an open encounter with a different political reality. It is an approach that comes easily to psychologists because it is based on the presumption that analysts understand actors' motives even if the actors themselves do not, and this surely accounts for the preponderance of psychologists among the social scientists who have studied the nuclear elite.

The work of the distinguished psychologist Robert Jay Lifton offers a good example of this way out.[4] In *Indefensible Weapons*, Lifton (1982) tells us that "nuclearism" is "an objective social madness" (p. ix). People like Lester who are content to work on nuclear weapons are victims of "denial," "psychic numbing," and "illusions" that can be understood by analogy with the citizens of Nazi Germany, who were also in denial about their participation in genocide. Those charged with making contingency plans should a nuclear conflict break out exhibit "something on the order of a psychotic fantasy" (Lifton & Falk, 1982, p. 18). Weapons scientists are infected with "a disease. . . . What is required is an examination of both symptoms and disease . . . which could lead to steps in the direction of a cure" (Lifton & Falk, 1982, pp. ix-x).

Lifton's strategy of analysis allows him to have his science without losing his politics. By medicalizing political disagreements, turning local knowledge into local neurosis, he is able to fuse scientific analysis and political critique. His opponents' bad politics become inseparable from their inadequate mental hygiene, and as a psychologist he has a special privilege to diagnose that.

There are three problems with this way of writing about weapons professionals. The first is that it confounds intrapsychic and social processes, encouraging readers to think of entire social groups as if they were giant personalities, and to reduce all members of social groups to a single psychological profile. In fact, although social and psychological processes are enmeshed with each other, neither can be reduced to the other, and any presumption to the contrary is likely to produce bad social analysis.[5] Understanding the psychology of, for example, Edward Teller, the "father of the hydrogen bomb" and the founder of the Lawrence Livermore Laboratory, may illuminate the arms race, but we would be badly mistaken if we thought it explained it and even more badly mistaken if we presumed that many other weapons scientists shared his rather unique psychological identity.[6]

The second problem with the objectivist writing strategy is its bad faith insofar as it dresses a partisan intervention in a political debate in the language of external, objective analysis. In the struggle over nuclear weapons policy, it is primarily political values that are at issue, not the mental health of the contenders. This gets obscured when experts trade on the symbolic capital of their expertise by presenting political interventions as authoritative statements of a collective, hence incontestable, knowledge. Physicists have been doing this for years, claiming that their understanding of nuclear physics somehow privileges their views on nuclear politics. The last thing we need is for social scientists to reinforce the spurious hegemony of the expert in modern society by doing the same. This is not to say that the expertises of physicists and social scientists are irrelevant to our society's decisions about nuclear weapons policy. Physicists and social scientists have information that is necessary but not sufficient for us to make decisions about nuclear weapons. These decisions are ultimately political, and we should be working to empower citizens by enlarging the space they recognize as political rather than playing what Haraway (1989), in an indictment of objectivist strategies of knowledge, calls "the god trick of seeing everything from nowhere" (p. 581).

The third problem with objectivist writing in the context of fiercely contested political debates is that it so easily short-circuits further dialogue. In holding tightly to one side's politics, it uses new kinds of analysis to reinforce entrenched political positions rather than to reorient the terms of the debate. Lester, who does not recognize himself in Lifton's work, complains that it forces him and his colleagues into "Procrustean beds." Instead of leading to enlarged understanding and debate, the objectivist strategy can lead to a zero-sum impasse: Either the scientists are victims of denial or else they have been squeezed into Procrustean beds. It can also lead to objectivist name calling: I have heard weapons scientists claim that they are in denial but that the antinuclear psychologists are guilty of "projection."

The dialogic strategy avoids these pitfalls by grounding its interpretive claims in what Haraway (1989) calls "situated knowledge." That is to say, practitioners of the dialogic strategy do not claim the omniperspectival privilege of defining what should finally be true about the world for all people; rather, they celebrate the particularity of their own perspective as a partial but hospitable vantage point from which to analyze other perspectives. This enables them to seek out the systematic sense in other ideologies but to retain a separate vantage point from which to mount a critique of those ideologies without having to don the white coat of the scientist. Thus social inquiry is redefined not as the conquest of other points of view by the privileged analyst but as a conversation between different situated knowledges (Haraway, 1989; Rosaldo, 1989, pp. 206-207).

In writings on nuclear culture, a good example of this approach is Cohn's (1987) widely read article on defense intellectuals.[7] Cohn frankly presents herself as a feminist both appalled and fascinated by the masculine world of defense intellectuals—those who analyze and develop strategies for using nuclear weapons. "I liked them," Cohn tells the reader. "The attempt to understand how such men could contribute to an endeavor that I see as so fundamentally destructive became a continuing obsession for me" (p. 690). She found the answer to her question largely by contrasting the language used by defense intellectuals with the language she herself used to construct the world. Giving her analysis an experiential base, she tracked the way her own internal attitude toward nuclear policy matters changed as she herself entered the linguistic world of defense intellectuals: "What I learned at the program is that talking about nuclear weapons is fun. . . . The words are fun to say; they are racy, sexy, snappy. . . . The more conversations I participated in using this language, the less frightened I was of nuclear war" (p. 704).

Unlike the objectivists, Cohn articulated her critique in terms of a positioned relationship with those she criticized. Although her analysis is nothing if not forceful, and of course we can object that the other side does not represent itself but is represented by her, her phrasing of the analysis in terms of an encounter between two points of view has a relativizing effect that keeps her own voice and those of the men she studied in tension and potentially enables the article to open up dialogue rather than closing it. This is particularly so because her own identity in the article is, in complex ways, in flux, moving at one moment toward and at another away from that of the defense intellectuals, alternating between sympathetic identification and critical distance. Thus her article offers one solution, and a more convincing one than the ojectivists', to the dilemma of how we might represent the views of political others with ethnographic rigor and with a degree of sympathy but without surrendering our own critical voice.

In the third strategy, polyphony, the critique comes not so much from the author as from characters within the cast of informants. Here the author does not lean so heavily on the device of the first person with its attendant temptations to slip into polemics. Polyphonic writing can still have the critical effect achieved by objectivist and dialogic writing, but it achieves this by juxtaposing different discursive surfaces, drawing more on the skills of the playwright than the psychologist. It places opposed discourses into conflict within its texts, rather than invoking the formal authority of the author to condemn or problematize particular points of view. The best example of this approach in regard to nuclear culture is, in fact, not an ethnography but a play: Kopit's (1984) *End of the World with Symposium to Follow*. In Kopit's play, military officers and defense intellectuals articulate their understanding of the world while the protagonist struggles both to understand them and to formulate a critique of their beliefs. Such an approach enabled Kopit, as the playwright-ethnographer, to enter into different realities and then to move away from them by presenting voices that undermine them. Ginsburg (1989) achieved a broadly similar effect in her model ethnography of a North Dakota abortion clinic by juxtaposing the voices of pro-choice and pro-life activists, allowing each to destabilize and flow into the other. This kind of polyphonic writing opens up spaces where different ideological perspectives can coexist and can be put into conflict in novel ways, while relativizing the position of the author. In other words, it begins within the text itself the kind of dialogue we might hope good ethnography would stimulate among its readers and subjects.

## *Conclusion*

The nuclear arms race has torn the discursive and political fabric of our society. Nuclearists and antinuclearists share a mutual hostility but lack a common account of the world. In this situation, any social scientist's attempt to write about nuclear or antinuclear institutions can only be contentious. Such contested terrain strains to the limit the social scientist's conventional pursuit of objectivity in his or her accounts of the world.

Anthropologists have dealt with this situation by indulging their traditional (and, one might add, honorable) predilection for studying and representing underdogs and, on the whole, avoiding a sustained encounter with the nuclear elite that might stretch their cultural relativism close to the breaking point. This predilection has, however, exempted nuclear elites from scrutiny, reinforcing the mystique that is part of their power, and it may even facilitate social control of oppositional groups.

Psychologists have found it easier to study nuclear decision makers but only by writing about them in terms that must make the anthropologist deeply uncomfortable, namely, as if their entire culture were a dysfunctional aberration. Where anthropologists have largely taken as given a romantic sympathy for the antinuclear underdogs, circumventing the question of why exactly we should feel this sympathy, psychologists have used their expertise in mental health to phrase a critique of nuclearism in the language of objectivist social science. This strategy enables them to maximize their critical leverage and to participate as partisans in the nuclear debate while appearing to be outside it—but at the expense of that openness to other cultural worlds that is usually the hallmark of good ethnography.

I argue here that ethnographers can best make peace with the dilemmas inherent in studying nuclear elites—and, by extension, any elite group whose exercise of power they may be inclined to oppose—if they seek to open up a space in their writing for the irreducible heterogeneity of human ideology and culture. This might be done, I suggest here, either by means of autobiographical narratives (dialogic writing) or by putting into dialogue opposed informant voices (polyphonic writing). Either way, ethnographers are able to map out bitterly contested cultural and political terrains without surrendering their own critical impetus but also without surrendering that impulse to understand and humanize the Other, which is the basis of our best ethnography.

## Notes

1. Various ethnographers have studied antinuclear groups: Krasniewicz (1992) on the women's peace movement at Seneca Falls, Mehan and Wills (1988) on Mothers Embracing Nuclear Disarmament in San Diego, Epstein (1985, 1988) and Sturgeon (1988) on the direct action movement, Peattie (1986, 1988) on the direct action movement and the economic conversion movement, Simich (1987) on the Italian antinuclear movement, and Wilson (1986, 1991) on women's antinuclear groups in the United Kingdom and on the Pacific island of Belau.

There are three notable exceptions to my generalization that ethnographers rarely study nuclear elites: Brasset (1988, 1989) studied high-level officers in the Pentagon, Cohn (1987) analyzed the culture of American defense intellectuals, and Eden is currently writing about the organizational culture of the Strategic Air Command (SAC) (for a preliminary account of her research, see Eden, 1989).

Psychologists who have published studies about the nuclear elite include Kull (1985, 1988), Lifton (1982, 1983), Lifton and Markusen (1990), and Mack (1985, 1986).

Political scientists interested in nuclear policy have almost exclusively focused on decision making among the nuclear elite and have often relied more on secondary sources than on direct study of the people in question. One exception is Rosenthal's (1990) study of the Los Alamos and Sandia nuclear weapons laboratories.

2. For a study of crack dealers by an anthropologist, see Bourgeois (1989). See Whitehead's (1974) ethnographic study of scientologists, Daner's (1976) writings about Hare Krishnas, Weston's (1991) ethnography of the gay community, and Keiser's (1969) classic study of gang members in the ghetto.

3. This is a fictitious name.

4. Other notable examples of antinuclear psychologists employing the objectivist strategy are Glendinning (1987), Holt (1984), Kull (1988), and Mack (1985, 1986).

5. To say this is, of course, to recapitulate the critique within the anthropology of the culture and personality school led by Abram Kardiner and Margaret Mead. For a good statement of this critique, see Wallace (1970).

6. I mention Teller in this context because Lifton repeatedly uses him as a prototypical exemplar of nuclearist psychology (even though many of his colleagues at the Livermore Laboratory strongly disagree with his political views and find his personality abrasive and obnoxious). See, for example, Lifton (1982, pp. 20-21, 91-92) and Lifton and Markusen (1990, pp. 42, 71-72, 81, 83-84, 92, 114, 124-125, 154).

7. Other possible examples are Powers (1982), Mojtabai (1986), and Nash (1981).

# References

Benedict, R. (1946). *The chrysanthemum and the sword: Patterns of Japanese culture.* Boston: Houghton Mifflin.

Bourgeois, P. (1989, November 12). Just another night on Crack Street. *New York Times Magazine.*

Brasset, D. (1988). Values and the exercise of power: Military elites. In R. Rubinstein & M. L. Foster (Eds.), *The social dynamics of peace and conflict: Culture in international security* (pp. 81-90). Boulder, CO: Westview.

Brasset, D. (1989). U.S. military elites: Perceptions and values. In P. Turner & D. Pitt (Eds.), *The anthropology of war and peace: Perspectives on the nuclear age* (pp. 32-48). Westport, CT: Bergin & Garvey/Greenwood.

Clifford, J. (1983). On ethnographic authority. *Representations, 1*(2), 118-144.

Cohn, C. (1987). Sex and death in the rational world of defense intellectuals. *Signs, 12*(4), 687-718.

Daner, F. (1976). *The American children of Krsna: A study of the Hare Krsna movement.* New York: Holt, Rinehart & Winston.

Eden, L. (1989, October 16). *Oblivion is not enough: How the U.S. Air Force thinks about nuclear war.* Paper presented to Program in Science, Technology, and Society, MIT.

Epstein, B. (1985). The culture of direct action. *Socialist Review, 82/83,* 31-61.

Epstein, B. (1988). The politics of prefigurative community: The non-violent direct action movement. In M. David & M. Spriker (Eds.), *Reshaping the U.S. left: Popular struggles in the 1980s* (pp. 63-92). New York: Verso.

Evans-Pritchard, E. E. (1937). *Witchcraft, oracles, and magic among the Azande.* Oxford: Oxford University Press.

Foucault, M. (1980). *Power/knowledge: Selected interviews and other writings 1972-1977.* New York: Pantheon.

Geertz, C. (1983). "From the native's point of view": On the nature of anthropological understanding. In C. Geertz (Ed.), *Local knowledge: Further essays in interpretive anthropology* (pp. 55-70). New York: Basic Books.

Ginsburg, F. (1989). *Contested lives: The abortion debate in an American community.* Berkeley: University of California Press.

Glendinning, C. (1987). *Waking up in the nuclear age.* Philadelphia: New Society Publishers.

Haraway, D. (1989). Situated knowledges: The science question in feminism and the privilege of partial perspective. *Feminist Studies, 14*(3), 575-599.

Harding, S. (1991). Representing fundamentalism: The problem of the repugnant cultural other. *Social Research, 58*(2), 373-393.

Holt, R. R. (1984). Can psychology meet Einstein's challenge? *Political Psychology, 7*(2), 199-225.

Keiser, L. (1969). *The vicelords: Warriors of the streets.* New York: Holt, Rinehart & Winston.

Kopit, A. (1984). *End of the world with symposium to follow.* New York: Samuel French.

Krasniewicz, L. (1992). *Nuclear summer: The clash of communities at the Seneca women's peace encampment.* Ithaca, NY: Cornell University Press.

Kull, S. (1985). Nuclear nonsense. *Foreign Policy, 58,* 28-52.

Kull, S. (1988). *Minds at war: Nuclear reality and the inner conflicts of defense policymakers.* New York: Basic Books.

Lifton, R. (1982). Imagining the real. In R. Lifton & R. Falk (Eds.), *Indefensible weapons: The political and psychological case against nuclearism* (pp. 3-125). New York: Basic Books.

Lifton, R. (1983). *The broken connection: On death and the continuity of life.* New York: Basic Books.

Lifton, R., & Falk, R. (1982). *Indefensible weapons: The political and psychological case against nuclearism.* New York: Basic Books.

Lifton, R., & Markusen, E. (1990). *The genocidal mentality: Nazi Holocaust and nuclear threat.* New York: Basic Books.

Mack, J. (1985). Toward a collective psychopathology of the nuclear arms competition. *Political Psychology, 6*(2), 291-321.

Mack, J. (1986). Nuclear weapons and the dark side of humankind. *Political Psychology, 7*(2), 223-233.

Mehan, H., Skelly, J., & Nathanson, C. (1990). Nuclear discourse in the 1980s: The unravelling conventions of the cold war. *Discourse and Society, 1*(2), 133-165.

Mehan, H., & Wills, J. (1988). MEND: A nurturing voice in the nuclear arms debate. *Social Problems, 35*(4), 363-383.

Mojtabai, A. G. (1986). *Blessed assurance: At home with the bomb in Amarillo, Texas.* Boston: Houghton Mifflin.

Morgan, H. L. (1962). *League of the Ho-de-no-sau-nee or Iroquois.* New York: Corinth. (Original work published 1851)

Nader, L. (1974). Up the anthropologist: Perspectives gained from studying up. In D. Hymes (Ed.), *Reinventing anthropology.* New York: Vintage.

Nash, H. (1981). The bureaucratization of homicide. In E. P. Thompson & D. Smith (Eds.), *Protest and survive* (pp. 284-311). New York: Monthly Review Press.

Neale, M. (1988). *Balancing passion and reason: The physicians movement against nuclear weapons.* Unpublished doctoral dissertation, University of California at San Francisco.

Parkin, F. (1968). *Middle class radicalism.* Manchester, UK: Manchester University Press.

Peattie, L. (1986). The defense of daily life. *IUAES Commission on the Study of Peace Newsletter, 4*(1), 3-12.

Peattie, L. (1988). Economic conversion as a set of organizing ideas. *Bulletin of Peace Proposals, 19*(1), 11-20.

Powers, T. (1982). *Thinking about the next war.* New York: Mentor Books.

Rosaldo, R. (1980). *Ilongot headhunting 1883-1974: A study in society and history.* Stanford, CA: Stanford University Press.

Rosaldo, R. (1989). *Culture and truth: The remaking of social analysis.* Boston: Beacon.

Rosenthal, D. (1990). *At the heart of the bomb: The deadly allure of weapons work.* Reading, MA: Addison-Wesley.

Said, E. (1979). *Orientalism.* New York: Vintage.

Simich, L. (1987). Comiso: The politics of peace in a Sicilian town. *IUAES Commission on the Study of Peace Newsletter, 5*(3), 5-9.

Stack, C. (1974). *All our kin: Strategies for survival in a black community.* New York: Harper & Row.

Sturgeon, N. (1988). *The direct action movement.* Paper presented at the annual meeting of the American Anthropology Association, Phoenix, AZ.

Top salaries at Lawrence Livermore Lab. (1991, February 22). *Tri-Valley Herald.*

Wallace, A.F.C. (1970). *Culture and personality.* New York: Random House.

Weston, K. (1991). *Families we choose: Lesbians, gays, kinship.* New York: Columbia University Press.

Whitehead, H. (1974). Reasonably fantastic: Some perspectives on scientology, science fiction, and occultism. In I. Zaretsky & M. Leone (Eds.), *Religious movements in contemporary America* (pp. 147-190). Princeton, NJ: Princeton University Press.

Wilson, L. (1986). Resistance to nuclear militarism: Greenham common. *IUAES Commission on the Study of Peace Newsletter, 4*(2), 2-10.

Wilson, L. (1991, November 21). *Rethinking resistance in Belau.* Paper presented at the annual meeting of the American Anthropology Association, Chicago, IL.

Wolf, E., & Jorgenson, J. (1970, November 19). Anthropology on the warpath in Thailand. *New York Review of Books,* pp. 26-35.

# About the Contributors

**Alan Aldridge** is Senior Lecturer in the School of Social Studies at the University of Nottingham, England. His recent research has focused on social change in the clerical profession. He has been particularly concerned with the professional careers of women and has acted as a consultant to the Church of England on the role of female deacons. In recent publications, he has analyzed the strategies of legitimation by which interested parties seek to construct "appropriate" career paths for women, arguing that discourse on women's careers involves a complex interplay between the sacred and the profane and between tradition, charisma, and legal-rationality as forms of legitimation. His current research is concerned with the ritualization of time and space in everyday life.

**Howard S. Becker** is Professor of Sociology at the University of Washington. He is author of *Outsiders*, *Art Worlds*, and *Writing for Social Scientists*, and co-author of *Boys in White*. His more recent books are *Symbolic Interaction and Cultural Studies* (co-edited with Michal M. McCall) and *What Is a Case?* (co-edited with Charles Ragin). He has just edited and translated a volume of essays by Antonio Candido (from Portuguese) called *On Literature and Society*. He is presently working on a hypertext volume on social theory and practice called

*Tricks of the Trade* and several papers in progress on various aspects of art worlds, including a piece on the world of hypertext fiction and one on the world of the American popular song.

**Joshua Gamson** is Assistant Professor of Sociology at Yale University, author of *Claims to Fame: Celebrity in Contemporary America*, and a contributing author of *Ethnography Unbound: Power and Resistance in the Modern Metropolis*. His writings on various aspects of contemporary culture, social movements, and sexuality have appeared in *Social Problems*, *Sociological Inquiry*, *Critical Studies in Mass Communications*, *Journal of the History of Sexuality*, *The American Prospect*, and *The Nation*. He is currently investigating internal disputes in lesbian and gay politics.

**Hugh Gusterson** is Assistant Professor of Anthropology and Science Studies at Massachusetts Institute of Technology. He received his Ph.D. in cultural anthropology from Stanford University in 1992. His book *Testing Times: A Nuclear Weapons Laboratory at the End of the Cold War* will be published in 1995. He is at work on a new project studying Russian and American nuclear scientists after the Cold War, funded by M.I.T. and the John D. and Catherine T. MacArthur Foundation. His articles have appeared in *Tikkun*, *The Sciences*, *New Scientist*, and *Journal of Urban and Cultural Studies*.

**Rosanna Hertz** is Associate Professor of Sociology at Wellesley College. She is editor of *Qualitative Sociology* and author of *More Equal Than Others: Women and Men in Dual-Career Marriages* and the forthcoming *Heartstrings and Pursestrings*.

**Hanna Herzog** is Senior Lecturer in the Department of Sociology at Tel-Aviv University. She is one of the founders of the Gender Studies program in the faculty of Social Science at Tel-Aviv University and is the current chair. She specializes in political sociology, political communication, and the sociology of gender. She has published articles on minor and ethnic parties, elections and political symbols, and women's organizations. Her book *Women in Local Politics in Israel* (in Hebrew) was recently published. Her current research is on involvement of Arab and Jewish women in peace organizations in Israel.

**Paul M. Hirsch** is Professor of Business and Sociology at Northwestern University's Kellogg Graduate School of Management. He has published articles on the production of culture, organization theory, and mass communication in a variety of journals, including *American Journal of Sociology*, *Theory and Society*, *Administrative Science Quarterly*, *Rationality and Society*, and *Communication Research*. He is also the author of chapters on consumption, in the *Handbook of Economic Sociology*, and the decline of internal labor markets, in *Explorations in Economic Sociology*; and is author of *Pack Your Own Parachute*, about managers in the 1980s. Most of his research is qualitative and/or theoretical, addressing ongoing issues in sociological theories about organizations and occupations. He is currently studying markets as social constructions, negotiated by interested parties and undergoing constant change. He is exploring the American savings and loan crisis from this perspective, as well as the effort of eastern European nations to create new capitalist infrastructures.

**Albert Hunter** is Professor of Sociology at Northwestern University. He has been Editor of *Urban Affairs Quarterly* and Chair of the Community and Urban Section of the American Sociological Association. He is author of *Symbolic Communities*, *Multimethod Research: A Synthesis of Styles* (with John Brewer) and, most recently, *The Rhetoric of Social Research: Understood and Believed*. He is currently at work on a comparative study of the politics in four suburbs of Chicago, a study of neighborhood responses to gangs, and a book (with Carl Milofsky) on the institutional and communal basis of the welfare state and civil society to be published as *Pragmatic Liberalism*.

**Jonathan B. Imber** is Professor of Sociology at Wellesley College. He is editor of *The American Sociologist* and author of *Abortion and the Private Practice of Medicine*, as well as the forthcoming *Trusting Doctors: The Rise and Fall of Cultural Authority in American Medicine*.

**Kathy E. Kram** is Associate Professor in the Department of Organizational Behavior at the Boston University School of Management. Her research interests are in the areas of adult development and career dynamics, values and ethics in corporate decision making, organizational change processes, gender dynamics in organizations, and workforce diversity. She is the author of *Mentoring at Work* and numerous articles in the management and social science literatures. She consults regularly with private and public sector organizations on a variety of human resource management issues.

**Susan A. Ostrander** is Associate Professor of Sociology at Tufts University. She is author of *Money for Change: Social Movement Philanthropy at Haymarket People's Fund*; senior editor of *Shifting the Debate: Public/Private Relations in the Modern Welfare State*; and author of *Women of the Upper Class*. She has also published a number of articles on nonprofit social welfare agencies and social change philanthropy. She speaks frequently on such topics as fund-raising and grantmaking for local organizing projects, especially women's projects; raising money from women; and community learning in the academy.

**Jennifer L. Pierce** is Assistant Professor in the Department of Sociology, and an affiliate with the Center for Advanced Feminist Studies, at the University of Minnesota. She is an associate editor of *Signs: Journal of Women in Culture and Society*. Her forthcoming book, *Gender Trials: Emotional Lives in Contemporary Law Firms*, is an ethnographic study of secretaries, paralegals, and lawyers.

**Robert J. Thomas** is Associate Director with Arthur D. Little, Inc., in Cambridge, Massachusetts, and Senior Lecturer in the Sloan School of Management of the Massachusetts Institute of Technology. His most recent book, *What Machines Can't Do: Politics and Technology in the Industrial Enterprise*, features detailed case studies of technological innovation and change in manufacturing firms. For this project, he conducted interviews with 300 corporate executives, managers, engineers, and workers in four major industrial companies. In earlier books, including *Citizenship, Gender and Work* and *Manufacturing Green Gold* (with William H. Friedland and Amy E. Barton), he reported on his work as a lettuce harvester and his interviews with farmers and ranch managers as part of investigation into the political economy of agribusiness.

**Michael Useem** is Professor of Sociology and Rose Term Professor in the School of Arts and Sciences at the University of Pennsylvania and Professor of Management in the Wharton School. He is the author of *Executive Defense: Shareholder Power and Corporate Restructuring*; *Liberal Education and the Corporation*; and *The Inner Circle: Large Corporations and the Rise of Business Political Activity in the U.S. and*

*U.K.*; co-author of *Turbulence in the American Workplace* and *Educating Managers*; and co-editor of *Transforming Organizations*. His study of institutional investors and large corporations, *The New Investor Capitalism*, is forthcoming.

**John P. Workman, Jr.,** is Assistant Professor of Marketing in the Kenan-Flagler Business School at the University of North Carolina at Chapel Hill. He has a B.S. in computer science from North Carolina State University, an M.B.A. from the University of Virginia, and a Ph.D. from M.I.T. His research focuses on the role of marketing within the firm and how this varies between high-tech and lower-tech firms. He uses a variety of research methods including field interviews, surveys, and secondary data analysis.

**Peter Cleary Yeager** is Associate Professor and Associate Chairman in the Department of Sociology at Boston University. His research focuses on questions regarding business compliance with law, constraints in government regulation of corporate business, and the role of organizational factors and professional socialization in corporate managers' perception and handling of ethical dilemmas. He is co-author of *Corporate Crime* and author of *The Limits of Law: The Public Regulation of Private Pollution*, and he spent the 1989-90 year as a research fellow in Harvard University's Program in Ethics and the Professions.